Times of Surrender

Times of Surrender

SELECTED ESSAYS

BY ROBERT COLES

UNIVERSITY OF IOWA PRESS

IOWA CITY

University of Iowa Press, Iowa City 52242

Copyright © 1988 by the University of Iowa

All rights reserved

Printed in the United States of America

First edition, 1988

Book and jacket design by Richard Hendel

Typesetting by G & S Typesetters, Inc., Austin, Texas

Printing and binding by Edwards Brothers, Ann Arbor, Michigan

Library of Congress Cataloging-in-Publication Data

Coles, Robert.

    Times of surrender: selected essays / by Robert Coles.—1st ed.

        p.   cm.

    ISBN 0-87745-188-5

    1. Psychiatry.   2. Psychology.   3. Literature.   4. Medicine.

5. Religion.   I. Title.

RC458.C553   1988

616.89—dc19   87-30221

                                                           CIP

To Shawn Maher and Phillip Pulaski

Contents

Introduction ix

Psychiatry, Psychology, and Literature

Unreflecting Egoism 3
Particular Memories 11
Man's Pride 18
Red Herring 24
Us Unmistakably 30
Commentary on Psychology and Literature 38

Medicine and Literature

Literature and Medicine 45
The Wry Dr. Chekhov 49
Why Novels and Poems in Our Medical Schools? 57
On Medicine and Literature: An Interview with Robert Coles 59
Medicine and the Humanities 77
Medical Ethics and Living a Life 88

Religion and Religious Writers

The New Being 99
The World and the Devil 107
Bringing Words out of Silence 113
Gravity and Grace in the Novel A Confederacy of Dunces 119
Bernanos: The Writer as Child 126
Bernanos's Diary: A Country Priest as Everyman 133
The Pilgrimage of Georges Bernanos 137

Minorities, Art, and Literature

Human Nature Is Finer 145
More Exiles 151
To Try Men's Souls 156
A Dream Deferred 160
Through Conrad's Eyes 162
James Baldwin Back Home 169
Behind the Beyond 175
Outsiders 181

Children and Literature

Lost Generation 187
The Holocaust and Today's Kids 194
Children's Stories: The Link to a Past 203
The Poetry of Childhood 209
The Vision of the Humanities for the Young 214

Politics, People, and Literature

Notes from Underground 225
An American Prophet 231
For Better or for Worse 237
"Are you now or have you ever been . . ." 244
Stories and Voices 247
Plain People 255
The Humanities and Human Dignity 263
Character and Intellect 268
Life's Big Ironies 274

Introduction

When I was a resident in child psychiatry at the Children's Hospital in Boston during the late 1950s, I was strenuously challenged and tested by a twelve-year-old boy who had all sorts of psychiatric labels attached to him—in the hospital chart and in my eagerly categorical mind. He was "impulsive." He had a "learning disability." Worse, he was "phobic" about school, reluctant to go and anxious while there. He had a "problem with authority." He had a "borderline personality"—a dire statement, indeed, with ominous implications for the future. All in all, this child, whom his parents called Junior for the usual, familial reason that he bore his father's name, seemed headed nowhere fast.

Junior was shy at first, and taciturn; but as we got to know each other better he became more forthcoming, and soon enough I began to realize how much sadness and disappointment and turmoil he had known already in the course of his brief life, as a consequence of the real events that had overtaken his family as well as his own mind's response to those events: his father's alcoholism and his mother's chronic and severe rheumatoid arthritis, with all the psychological as well as medical ramifications of both those diseases. The lad liked to play checkers a lot, and it was during those games, actually, that I learned the most about him. A sharp and careful player, he often trapped me, beat me—and as I would be stalled in some corner of the checkerboard, contemplating a seemingly inevitable disaster, he would talk about what had happened during the week or, for that matter, months or even years earlier. His remarks, of course, only distracted me further from the game at hand—and I began to realize that Junior had in his bright and observant way figured out my predicament: the earnest checkers player who was ever so anxious to hear more and more from a patient could be weakened by the patient's talking.

One day, as we were nearing the end of yet another game of checkers, Junior surveyed with tactful self-assurance my gloomy prospects. I was moving my black king back and forth in one of those corners of the board where losers are apt to take their last stand. "It's time to surrender," Junior announced. I can still remember the words, the look on his young face: eyes wide open and staring right at me rather than the board, the faintest of smiles, the front teeth showing, including the noticeable gap between two of his lower front ones. I didn't like the look, not that day. I said nothing. I kept moving back and forth, sending thereby my message: all right, fellow, come and get me. All right, he would. Rather as our navy gathers its boats from across the seas to one troubled spot, Junior marshaled his four crowned players. The closer he came to the coup de grace, the more annoyed I became—not only with him but myself: what was all this accomplishing? What would my supervisor, an experienced child psychoanalyst, think of these proceedings—of me as a novice, learning to work with children? Suddenly, Junior stopped short of finishing me off. He said he'd wait me out—and, of course, he put me on the spot: want to waste the entire "therapeutic hour"? I hesitated and made a gesture of continued resistance. He once more mentioned surrender as a suitable alternative, and I simply folded—whereupon he said, unforgettably: "Sometimes, if you surrender you're winning, because you're free of worrying about losing and you can find a better game for yourself!" There was a long pause—and then, as if to prove himself right, Junior for the first time mentioned some troubles he'd been having at home and asked for my sense of what they meant. Later, my supervisor would call that session "the start of therapy" for Junior.

Later that week, I found myself reading Freud's well-known essay "Dostoevski and Parricide," his effort to understand a great writer's personality and to indicate how a writer's fiction can be a response to his psychological difficulties. It is in this essay that Freud makes an interesting, edifying, and important renunciation of sorts: "*The Brothers Karamazov* is the most magnificent novel written; the episode of the Grand Inquisitor, one of the peaks in the literature of the world, can hardly be valued too highly. Before the problem of the creative artist, analysis must, alas, lay down its arms." In a sense, I began to realize, Junior had issued a similar warning to me. He had told me many times that I ought stop trying to "figure him out"—

and especially, he had been adamant about his checker-playing brilliance as a subject of my psychological inquiry: its purposes, its rationale in his overall emotional makeup. To be sure, he had his own "resistance" to a doctor's scrutiny, and it would not have been right for me to yield, in that respect, to his requests for an hour free of personal discussion. But he was, in his own manner, letting me know that my psychiatric and psychoanalytic intensity and eagerness ought to have limits—that at a certain point Freud's exemplary (though reluctant) modesty ought be remembered. I was all too full of youthful professional enthusiasm and no small measure, if not an excess, of ideological conviction—the heady faith of a mid-twentieth-century, agnostic upper bourgeois who was convinced that psychological analysis would provide answers to every one of life's problems, impasses, riddles. Such a naive Freudianism was, unfortunately, not only my particular idée fixe, as I think Junior knew when he cast his friendly, yet skeptical, glance at not only me but the clinic he entered once a week.

Gradually we got down to business, Junior and I; we worked at some of his troubles, and I learned to enjoy his capacity to play checkers and chess, too. This bright, sensitive, introspective boy helped me figure out not only some of *his* problems but some of mine, too—a lack of respect, at times, for the distinction between the intellect's realm, and yes, that of the spirit, too, as against the domain so often affected by our psychological burdens, if not demons. As Anna Freud once put it: "There are times when we can only be grateful for a child's mastery or talent—and at such times we ought not pause too long with our psychoanalytic questions." She knew so well how appropriate our questions are when connected to other times in a child's life. Her remarks, that is, were meant to be cautionary rather than an expression of fundamental skepticism or despair.

The foregoing is meant not to be discursive but rather to be a quite pointed prelude to the essays that follow. They form an account, really, of my struggle to find a point of view for myself that made sense, as I did my medical and psychiatric work but also tried to remember what Junior had taught me, not to mention the two Freuds and others in their tradition. Many of the essays that follow are witnesses of sorts to that struggle. All too often in recent decades, some of us in the social sciences have been unwilling to put suffi-

cient constraint upon ourselves, unwilling to accept times of surrender before life's thickness, its complexities, ironies, ambiguities,
and its chancy nature—meaning the ever-present possibilities (for
the good and bad, both) that arrive at our doorstep through luck,
fate, circumstance, or accident. One decides to make a turn, then—
a turn to our Dostoevskis, not with intrusive and all-encompassing
determinism but with respect and gratitude to our novelists and
poets and painters for their effort to understand the world, to do justice to its various aspects, to render it faithfully and suggestively and
compellingly. I think these essays, written during the past two decades or so, have that turn as a common theme—a turn to literature
as helpful, indeed, for one of my ilk.

I have let these essays stand as they were written. They address,
variously, my professional life, my work with children, my interest
in religion and politics. I have written books on those matters and
twice before collected essays on some of them—A *Farewell to the
South* (1972) and *The Mind's Fate* (1975). None of the essays that
appear here are to be found in those books, and many of the ones in
this book were written after those books appeared. In the past ten
years I have put a lot of energy into teaching medical students and
college students, and some of the writing that follows reflects that
commitment of time and effort. I have also tried to figure out how
to discuss moral questions with those students—in such a way that
they can connect what they learn to the way they live, no easy task
for any of us. In that regard, novels and short stories are a wonderful
resource, and some of the writing in the pages that follow has been
the result of my experience with such fiction in two ways, as the
solitary reader and as the teacher in a seminar or the lecturer before
a class.

Novelists such as Georges Bernanos or Dickens were no strangers
to their own kind of surrender. Like Freud, they respected the limits
a story demands, the requirements of plot and character portrayal.
Bernanos had no interest in using fiction to construct theology; nor
was Dickens taken with political science and psychology as disciplines—though, of course, both of those magicians of language
manage to convey experience wondrously: the nature of religious experience, or the nature of a kind of human experience we know all
too well today, the bureaucrat or political functionary or lawyer at
work. I rather suspect that it would not hurt some of us to become a

bit more intimate with writers such as Bernanos or Dickens, not only because they entertain us and keep us enthralled but because they have a very special way of instructing us—not through ambitious or pushy generalization and formulation but through relatively modest evocation of life in all its contrariness and with all its inconsistencies.

"Don't rush to clinical judgment," the psychoanalyst who supervised me as I worked with Junior repeatedly emphasized. That elderly and wise man worried about my nervous wish to tuck anything and everything under some broad theoretical rubric. Once, sensing those few words weren't enough, he went further and urged that I watch closely, listen hard, and "try to absorb the boy's story, as he lets you in on it." I was struck by his way of putting things—at such variance with the abstract, highly theoretical discussions I was having with any number of psychoanalytic teachers at that time in my life. I think I've held on to that bit of advice rather tenaciously over the years, and I think the essays in this book, in their various ways, reveal me still trying to do so. It would be a big boost for many of us if the world at large (America's late-twentieth-century culture) were more encouraging along those lines—less enamored of the conceits of theory. Still, there are plenty of encouragements around: the well-known writers of the past and present; or a wonderful gift that can be handed to us, out of nowhere, it seems—such as John Baskin's delightful and quite special *New Burlington*, a book that makes a whole library of sociology seem, somehow, not all that interesting.

I will not pursue the grinding of this particular ax any further here—only warn the reader of further attempts to come: a theme, a continuity, in the pages ahead. I conclude here with thanks to Paul Zimmer, Holly Carver, Brien Woods, and Wayne Arnold for their help with the emergence of this book, and especially to Shawn Maher and Phil Pulaski, who helped me in so many ways in that Harvard office during the past six years.

January 1988

*Psychiatry, Psychology,
and Literature*

Unreflecting Egoism

We are not doing well at all, the historian Christopher Lasch tells us in his latest book, *The Culture of Narcissism*. He links his psychological title to a sociological subtitle: *American Life in an Age of Diminishing Expectations*. He wants to show us how the latter is connected to the development of the former. He is a strong-minded cultural theorist, eager to reveal us to ourselves— an ironic effort, he must know, because if many of us have turned into the narcissists he describes, then it is narcissism itself, and not the desire for psychological insight, that will prompt an excited rush on our part to glimpse even this severely disapproving picture of our mental habits. His argument draws its ammunition from a growing psychoanalytic literature, which itself is a response to the everyday clinical work of psychiatrists, who have for years recognized the usefulness and importance of the concept of narcissism. As early as 1914, Freud observed that certain patients, much hurt in various ways at an early age, had essentially given up as far as love for others was concerned.

A child who is often rebuffed or who has to face constant irrational shifts in the emotional behavior of a mother or a father may learn to be exceedingly guarded toward people. The child also feels sorely aggrieved, hence resentful. Since the outside world is so untrustworthy, so unreliable (seductively there one moment, achingly absent the next), the child falls back on himself or herself with a certain vengeance. Rather than take emotional risks and quite possibly end up losing, the mind concludes that it would do best to stick with itself, so to speak. The result is what George Eliot called "unreflecting egoism"—a driven kind of self-centeredness that dominates a person's mental life. Today's psychiatrists refer to "the narcissistic character disorder"—the affliction of one whose central, controlling ways of getting on give evidence of a strong avoidance of lasting attachments to other people, accompanied often by a hunger for just such human bonds and, in the realm of feeling, by an anger (whose severity may not be recognized) at one's fate. There may be, too, a hard-to-shake sadness and a feeling of emptiness, of being lost, with no real hope of being found—by anyone.

Of course, we have all had our psychologically doubtful and threatening moments—in infancy, later childhood, youth, and beyond. Everyone has learned to fall back on his or her own resources, ideas, and daydreams. Few of us have failed to experience moments when just about no one seems worth counting on—except the self, as a body that needs care, a mind that needs its satisfactions. As is always the case in psychiatry, the issue is quantitative—the extent of a particular person's self-preoccupation and the effect it has on the way he or she lives. But Lasch insists that the issue today is also historical and cultural. He wants to make a connection between what he calls "the clinical aspects of the narcissistic syndrome" and "certain characteristic patterns of contemporary culture, such as the intense fear of old age and death, altered sense of time, fascination with celebrity, fear of competition, decline of the play spirit, deteriorating relations between men and women." His book is really a collection of essays meant to show that the so-called rugged individualism of the American past has given way to a collective narcissism, which suits the purposes of an economic system geared not simply to its own growth (as was the case in the past) but to a cultivated consumerism.

The first, and most devastating, critique is devoted to "the awareness movement." By now, we are rather accustomed to the dreary social stupidity generated by that movement, but the author is a historian, and he wants us to look back a little and be reminded of what went on recently in the name of "personal liberation." He goes directly to the sources—those who took part in the events of the last decade or so and decided to describe what they experienced. Here is Jerry Rubin talking about a stretch of twentieth-century time: "In five years, from 1971 to 1975, I directly experienced est, gestalt therapy, bioenergetics, rolfing, massage, jogging, health foods, tai chi, Esalen, hypnotism, modern dance, meditation, Silva Mind Control, Arica, acupuncture, sex therapy, Reichian therapy, and More House—a smorgasbord course in New Consciousness." I suppose such a list will make some laugh, and with good reason. But what kind of craziness, what kind of inner emptiness, what kind of blinded, rudderless personal condition has prompted many of us to join one, then another, then still another of these movements? They are, needless to say, quasi-religious in nature: an effort on the part of the lost to find something half-believable and at least a tiny bit transcendent. But the thrust of all those activities is eminently, if not obscenely, narcissistic—a glorification of the mind and body of the individual member or participant, for whom, most likely, God is dead and patriotism a joke. Once, most Americans committed themselves without qualification to religious passion; in some parts of the world people still do. In the early years of this century, the nation-state received the devotion formerly reserved for God. But in our time the flag, the military, and the political leadership of countries such as ours have excited the loyalty and enthusiasm of fewer and fewer citizens. What is left for them but themselves? Their narcissism, it can be argued, is a response to grim memories and terrible prospects. As Lasch puts it, "the Nazi holocaust, the threat of nuclear annihilation, the depletion of natural resources, well-founded predictions of ecological disaster have fulfilled poetic prophecy, giving concrete historical substance to the nightmare, or death wish, that avant-garde artists were the first to express."

Under such circumstances, why look back or think very far ahead? That is the question many men and women have asked; it represents a "waning of the sense of historical time," as the author calls this aspect of contemporary self-absorption. We want for the here and now "satisfying interpersonal relationships," "group skills." We want to own what is trendy to wear, to sit or sleep on; we aim to do what is chic or to go "where the action is." When a sense of the past or the future is either attenuated or lost, what is left but an endless series of fads? For every one of them, moreover, there seems to be a book that can command the dollars of thousands: *I'm OK—You're OK, Looking Out for #1, Your Erroneous Zones, Pulling Your Own Strings, Power!, Success!, How to Be Your Own Best Friend*, and many others. There are even some that are saturated with undisguised pornography or sadism. All are banal and are sold to the reader as an aid to his or her self-promotion and self-enhancement. The encouragement of greedy, combative self-assertion appeals, perhaps, to those who can no longer go to a frontier and explore it, conquer it, and plunder it, and who (after Vietnam and Watergate) can't work themselves up to nationalist truculence or self-righteousness. Why not learn how to win more limited victories over anyone who happens to come in sight or get in the way?

Psychoanalysts have wisely hesitated to make sweeping socio-logical statements on the basis of their direct observations in the doctor's office or in mental hospitals. But they do acknowledge that "changes in cultural patterns can affect family structure," and it is Lasch's chosen task to show how today's American culture does pre-cisely that—intrudes upon the manner in which we act as parents, thereby decisively influencing the way our children grow up. In chapters on our schools, our sports, our treatment of the elderly, and our various secular "experts," he argues that we have been taught the importance of conformity—hence the importance of "adjust-ment" and the acquiescence that characterizes much of our educa-tional and working lives. Once, there were families in which chil-dren saw their parents work and saw what that work meant—crops planted and harvested, or products made. But with industrialization, home life and work became separated, and the nature of the latter is such that few people get any real sense of achievement from it. As-sembly lines and vast bureaucratic offices are often places of con-finement, boredom, and despair—time clocked in. Meanwhile, children have to be taught that such is their future life. Parents who are not exactly sure what they dare to want for themselves or their children (besides the various objects incessantly paraded before them with wicked cleverness on the television screen or in newspapers and magazines) turn eagerly to psychologists and psychiatrists, members of the so-called helping professions, for advice; and they get it, in profusion. Even as parents have left the home to work in factories and offices, their children have had to come to quick terms with the outside world because of the significant surrender of parental au-thority over them.

The author refers at one point to "the evil of psychologizing," but he must be one of very few who have the detachment and moral self-assurance to use such a phrase. Millions of us are caught up in the pretentious jargon of child-rearing guides, manuals, and books. All that talk of "parenting." All those psychological explanations, not only naive and sometimes absurd but ephemeral as well—replaced by new guides or contradictory ones: psychology as an instance of consumerism. Is it the first five years that really count or the first three? And how you handle your child immediately after he or she is born? In one terse, sad quotation from a scholarly paper by Gilbert J. Rose, Lasch indicates what too many of us assume: "The naive idea that sickness accounts for badness and that badness necessarily results from being misunderstood is the prejudice of a therapeutic morality." We want to "analyze" everything, including our children's behavior, and at the same time we have convinced ourselves that we lack the authority to take a firm stand on much of anything—with respect to their lives or our own. A large crew of hustlers has gleefully moved into this moral vacuum talking "child development" and "human motivation." Why do parents rush toward these people, eager for their every pronouncement? What are the implicit promises made, if only one will obey all the rules handed down? As parents, we are obsessed with "techniques" in the home for the same reason that we turn to the counsel of industrial sociologists, practitioners of "personal management," and "guidance counselors." All these "experts" are disguised moralists who want to give us answers and more answers, to put us in our place: Do this, don't do that, lest you be judged "maladjusted," "sick," or "abnormal." The covert nature of their preaching (backed up by considerable political and economic authority) is a measure of how uncomfortable we have learned to be with an open acknowledgment of any moral—never mind spiritual—concerns we may yet have, despite the age and its culture.

A number of writers, Lasch points out, have referred to "the decline of the superego." But he wisely emphasizes that it is not enough to stop there or even to add, as he does, a cultural amplification—the obvious connection between psychological permissiveness and the hedonistic consumerism of advanced capitalist societies. To be sure, today's self-styled experts in "child care" don't encourage us to bring up thoroughly disciplined, proudly independent, morally concerned young men and women. ("Moral," for many, means "moralistic.") But Lasch goes on (backed, I would add, by plenty of evidence that has appeared in the literature of child psychiatry):

> The parents' failure to serve as models of disciplined self-restraint or to restrain the child does not mean that the child grows up without a superego. On the contrary, it encourages

the development of a harsh and punitive superego based largely on archaic images of the parents, fused with grandiose self-images.

Put differently, if children don't learn how to control themselves as they grow up they will forever be at the mercy of the worries, fears, angers, and desires that characterize early life. Hence the outbursts of wanton, senseless cruelty; the various binges of gratification (food, liquor, drugs, gadgets, travel); the spells of ferocious self-criticism that take the form of apathy, inertia, or the blues; a spurt of activity—motorcycles, cars—that is suicidal, and sometimes homicidal, in nature; the self-abasement that expresses itself not only in some of the cults we have recently had cause to notice but in the phenomenon of celebrity, which Lasch examines rather closely.

Who are these "stars" (not only, nowadays, entertainers but athletes, politicians, and even scholars, writers, and artists), and what does the adoring response of their followers tell us about ourselves? If the famous are caught up in the narcissism that this book analyzes, so are the various crowds that attend them with such abdication of personal responsibility and such apostolic fervor. Among those who regard religion as a joke, as inconsequential, or as a mere ritual, and who have come to view many institutions as corrupt or exploitative, there can be, ironically, a flight to individuals: a suspension of skepticism with regard to them, an outright worship of them. A mind deprived of one kind of discipline will somehow find another. We revert to a childlike narcissism; celebrities become the heroes that boys and girls dream of being, of knowing, of following in causes or cheering on various playing fields. We model ourselves desperately after other people because we haven't really been taught to accept the limitations of life—not when advertisers offer us the moon and one or two of us actually get there, whereupon we conclude that in no time at all the rest of us will be following suit. It is a grandiosity that serves the interests of those who have things to sell. But it is a grandiosity that finally becomes infectious and takes us all in— doctors who promise to "conquer" old age, engineers whose technology will supposedly subdue all of nature, and writers of futuristic stories, novels, screenplays, and essays who spin fantasies and more fantasies. Fantasies about what? About people sprung loose from themselves, on earth and in space—people who have become godlike. It is what Freud, in a paper ("On Narcissism"), once described with reference to the family:

> The child shall have a better time than his parents; he shall not be subject to the necessities which they have recognized as paramount in life. Illness, death, renunciation of enjoyment, restrictions on his own will, shall not touch him; the laws of nature and of society shall be abrogated in his favor; and he shall once more really be the centre and core of creation—"His Majesty the Baby," as we once fancied ourselves.

The trouble is, as this book convincingly demonstrates, such innocent and passing parental fantasies, as they once were, have become articles of faith for many of us. We possess no larger, compelling vision that is worth any commitment of energy and time. We are not inclined to settle for anything less than everything— all at once and at this very moment. What was once called "reality" has become for us a mere barrier, surely one day to be penetrated. We are good at getting things but unable to know where to start when it comes to facing the issues Freud referred to—the finite, complex nature of life itself. We shun the elderly, reminders of our own mortality. We worship superathletes, promoted by endless and sometimes corrupt schemes. We cultivate postures—ironic cynicism, skeptical distance—meant to keep us from the inevitable difficulties of human involvement. We play it cool, play it fast, and, in the clutch, place our faith in lotions and powders and soaps and dyes and surgical procedures so that we can stay—we hope, we pray—in the game as long as possible, playing at life, because from the outside (society) we have every encouragement to do so and from the inside (family life) we have also learned that such a way of getting along is desirable.

Christopher Lasch has given us a short jeremiad. Perhaps, in his urge to bring us to our senses, he has overstated his case and forgotten to mention some of the nonsense that *other* ages found congenial to their purposes. Certainly he has no answers for our situation. He distrusts many who have answers. His viewpoint is that of one who has looked back hard and looked around keenly. In a summary statement, he observes that "in its pathological form, narcissism originates as a defense against feelings of helpless dependency in early life, which it tries to counter with 'blind optimism' and grandiose illusions of personal self-sufficiency." He adds this:

> Since modern society prolongs the experience of dependence into adult life, it encourages milder forms of narcissism in people who might otherwise come to terms with the inescapable limits on their personal freedom and power—limits inherent in the human condition—by developing competence as workers and parents. But at the same time that our society makes it more and more difficult to find satisfaction in love and work, it surrounds the individual with manufactured fantasies of total gratification.

That is a serious bind to be caught in, and one wonders how we will ever get out of it—short of a drastic reshaping of our society and of ourselves as citizens of it. Meanwhile, our predicament would seem to resemble that of another civilization under extreme duress. When Aristophanes surveyed the Greek states caught up in the terrible destructiveness—personal, social, political—of the Peloponnesian War, he remarked, "Whirl is King, having driven out Zeus." It may give us some pleasure and yet be a blow to our narcissism as readers, writers, and social critics to know that in this "age of diminishing expectations" our doom is not as "different" as we like to think. The playwright's description still rings true, and the historical parallel is hardly reassuring. Even a widespread awareness of it would no doubt do nothing to lessen the narcissism among us.

New Yorker, August 27, 1979

Particular Memories

There are many dangers inherent in writing personal memoirs: inordinate self-display, self-flattery, a generally too narrow view of things. When these dangers are successfully skirted, however, the memoir can be a wonderfully educational and entertaining genre. It offers the writer a chance to share intimate moments with his readers, especially if he can put aside his egoism, or at least use it in the service of thoughtful detachment. Burrhus Frederic Skinner, the Harvard psychologist famous for his theories of behaviorism and his philosophical inclinations, has, in his seventy-third year, begun to look back upon his personal history; the result is the first installment of his memoirs, called *Particulars of My Life*. It is, on the whole, a successful job. Professor Skinner teaches us a lot about an earlier America, and about his family, his hometown, and his friends, neighbors, and teachers. He also speaks intently of the developing technology of the era—the telephone, the radio, the automobile, the airplane—whose imprint upon children, upon their assumptions and perceptions, has often been underestimated or overlooked by experts in child development.

In the first part of the book, Professor Skinner talks about his childhood. One might expect here the romanticized elaborations, the distortions, and the outright mystifications that adults often resort to when they talk about their early years, but Professor Skinner's astonishing power of recall takes him out of himself and helps him to avoid these pitfalls. "The first personal possession I remember was my Teddy Bear," he tells us early in the book. "Its imitation fur was light brown and it had a white knitted cap and jacket." This is obviously no vague recollection; Professor Skinner has a memory that penetrates decades of shadows with apparent ease. And he works into his detailed descriptions just enough social history and psychological comment to make his experience part of a past shared by many millions of his countrymen:

The Teddy Bear was a fairly recent innovation: a newspaper cartoon had shown Theodore Roosevelt sparing a bear cub during one of his big-game exploits, and copies of the cub came on the market as toys for children. It was the kind of doll a boy might respectably play with.

Professor Skinner summons up many other sights, sounds, smells, contours, and textures of the sort that most of us have long ago let slip into the darkness of the past. He recalls a jigsaw puzzle of a train, for example, that included advertising for the virtues of the Delaware, Lackawanna & Western Railroad; according to the puzzle, the company's trains used anthracite coal, not the bituminous variety, and were therefore said to be cleaner. The author tells us of "a beautiful girl named Phoebe Snow," who appeared in the puzzle clothed in white and standing at the rear of the train, and, miraculously, to this day he can picture "the polished brass railings" that enabled him to complete the puzzle. He remembers his toy trains in all their intricacy, and he can still call to mind a set of dominoes that he used over six decades ago; they were "made of thin slabs of ivory and ebony held together with brass pins turning green in the crevices."

This consuming attention to gadgets and other physical objects was not, apparently, a replacement for parental affection. Professor Skinner's mother was a kind and attentive person, and his father, an upright, conservative lawyer, treated him gently. Professor Skinner gives us, word for word, the "consoling" songs he heard as a child. He recounts the illnesses he suffered, the quarantines that accompanied them, and the earnest efforts of his parents to get him better. He recalls the old rituals of Christmas—the meals, the social arrangements and obligations, and, needless to say, the many rewards.

Professor Skinner's family was not rich, but it was comfortable, and the boy never lacked for material things. Just as important, he makes clear, was the assurance he came to feel as a result of his parents' reasonably secure social and economic position. Nevertheless, Skinner's childhood was not idyllic. There were tensions between his mother's family and his father's. His parents felt envies, rivalries, and apprehensions, and they were made nervous by anyone who was considerably better off than they were. His father never rose as high as he wished to, and his mother, who came from "better stock,"

sometimes adopted an aloof, condescending attitude toward him—
the author describes her as "apparently frigid." Yet he also emphasizes how kind and helpful she could be to her husband as well as to
his brother and himself.

Professor Skinner's memory for detail is also impressive when he
describes the natural world of his childhood. He was born in Susquehanna, Pennsylvania, which is on the Susquehanna River, and
his picture of the river—its twists and turns, its fierce struggle through
stubborn, hilly countryside toward the ocean—seems flawless. He
appears to have given an account of everything he saw growing
around his house—"Our backyard offered black cherries, red cherries (shared with the robins), purple plums, green plums, Concord
grapes, currants, raspberries, rhubarb, horseradish, and mustard"—
and of the trees, plants, flowers, and animals that flourished nearby.

But when he comes to human beings, Professor Skinner is often
guarded, tentative, and not nearly so thorough. After a long, touch
ing, and quite precisely rendered description of a turn-of-the-century
Pennsylvania landscape of meadows and forests, for instance, he observes that "there were people in that world, too, and some of them
were interesting," but when he tells us about these people, it is only
their work or their tools or their machines that seem to interest him.
He mentions the blacksmith, the carpenter, a woman who ran a
boarding house, and the owner of a candy store, and in each case he
moves directly from the person's occupation or name to a depiction
of something *done*: "The carpenter did cabinet work, and I was surprised to see how often he simply glued pieces of wood together, but
the glue was hot and hence presumably stronger than the kind
I used."

Even when Professor Skinner tries to be forthright about his parents and grandparents, he ends up giving more attention to their
social origins than to their personal hopes and fears, which we
are simply told were substantial. Concerning his relationship with
Edward, his only brother, Professor Skinner is still more reticent—
some might say naive. "Since my brother was two and a half years
younger than I, there was little competition between us," he tells us,
and we are also informed that there was "sibling affection" between
them. True, we are told at one point that the brother became un-
affectionate enough to write "Your a BOOB" on the flyleaf of the author's copy of *Alice in Wonderland*. But we might expect more from

someone who can remember the most minute details about forests, rivers, and towns, and who can describe down to the last button the winter clothes he wore as a young child, and the complicated, comic procedures involved in his learning to drive a car fifty years ago. One feels obliged to mention these emotional blind spots in an otherwise thorough and compelling narrative because they seem so closely related to Professor Skinner's psychological theories. He has strongly maintained that our mental development consists simply of responses to an assortment of stimuli, which "condition" us and thus account for our behavior; his critics have wondered whether this theoretical system does not ignore the spiritual side of our mental life, whether the stimulus-response idea does not account for human feeling rather casually.

It so happens that a central event in Professor Skinner's life was Edward's sudden, tragic death, at the age of sixteen. The family had moved to Scranton, and the author, then a student at Hamilton College, was home for his Easter vacation. Just after eating a sundae, Edward fell inexplicably and gravely ill. He died within an hour or two. Skinner was present the whole time, except for a brief interval when he went to get his parents, who were in church. The father would never again be the same. The mother's grief was strong and lasting and is movingly conveyed in Professor Skinner's book. The author seems to realize that his own reaction was, to say the least, idiosyncratic, and, if we can judge from the contents of this book, it continues to be so. He tells us that he was very helpful to the doctors; he gave a careful and instructive account of what he had seen happening to his brother, what complaints were made, what symptoms set in. The doctors, later on, were grateful: "They told my father that my objectivity was helpful," Skinner writes. "With the same objectivity I had watched my parents as they reacted to the discovery that my brother was dead." He goes on to say that despite his objectivity he was "far from unmoved."

Perhaps we would not be disturbed by any of this if Skinner had let the matter of his brother's death drop there. After all, we would not want to read a self-serving outpouring of sadness, and we cannot ask for a description of the intensity of mourning experienced by this sensitive and observant man if he does not want to give it to us. But he does not let the matter drop. Instead, he insists once again that his brother and he "had never competed for the same things." They had different hobbies, involvements, and aspirations. Edward was, we are told, "closer" to their parents, and his death put Skinner "in a position" he had never wished for—one that would "become increasingly troublesome in the years ahead." But we don't learn any more about those difficulties, and Skinner's response to this crucial part of his life remains elusive and troubling.

We do learn a good deal, however, about what Professor Skinner calls his "selfishness" as a college student—his ability to develop a rather large, "self-centered microcosm." He is quite able to give us at substantial length a description of that microcosm, vintage young adulthood. He writes shrewdly and sardonically of the world he created for himself. He wrote poetry, stories, essays, and, even as a youth, reflective autobiography. Not content with an exceptional memory, he has obviously held on to every scrap of paper that contains his words—old diaries, class papers and themes, pieces written as entries in writing competitions, pieces published or meant to be published in various school magazines and other periodicals. He is excellent at evoking the college literary scene, with its mixture of sensitivity, earnestness, snobbery, faddishness, and, alas, keen envy and outright malice. He indicates from his own experience the price paid by those young writers who have not only some talent but also misgivings about it: they can't know what chance of success they have, and, worst of all, they don't know what to do about the warnings against writing as a career that they get from parents or other relatives. Skinner's father wrote him a long, forceful, and affecting letter when the young man announced that he would spend a year writing a novel after graduating from college. The letter was kept, and its reproduction, which takes up three pages, stands as one of this book's most luminous moments—a clear statement of the bourgeois reaction against "art," one that most satirists would find extremely tempting. Parental love, and the sincere worry that a father has for his son's future social and financial situation, can be all too easily caricatured or misrepresented.

The book also contains a letter from Robert Frost, who saw substantial promise in Skinner as a storyteller. The letter is dated April 7, 1926, and it was sent from Ann Arbor, Michigan. In it, Frost tells Skinner that he possesses "the touch of art." He goes on to say that as a writer Skinner is "worth twice anyone else I have seen in prose this year." But, in a brief postscript, Frost adds a note of warning: "Belief, belief. You've got to augment my belief in life and people mightily or cross it uglily. I'm awfully sure of this tonight." The great poet had made a positive judgment but had qualified it enough to become a rather accurate prophet with respect to Skinner's lifework. Soon enough, the young man abandoned his short-lived career as a writer. He does so right before the reader's eyes, reenacting in the book his growing disenchantment with his writing and eventually, it seems, with literature as a whole. He presents one specimen of his work after another, and comments testily, acidly, on what he once set down on paper. "This was dredging up the past, not writing anything new, and what was new was sorry stuff," he says about a published poem of his. "The truth was, I had no reason to write anything," he says at another point. Skinner's reservations about writers and their craft are perhaps most strongly set forth in a passage taken from one of his old notebooks. He had headed the passage "Desire to Write," and in it he offered a psychological analysis of sorts—one that he tried to apply to other callings:

> I am convinced that an essentially false desire-to-write is necessary to any author. Whether it be the desire to make money, the desire to be known as a genius, the desire to get one's name in the paper, or some mystical desire to "express oneself," it does not bear analysis without resolving itself into a mean satisfaction of a mean instinct. By "false" and "mean" I do not intend to condemn exactly. I mean simply that the same desires quite as often prod a man into big business or eccentricity or acrobatics or driving automobiles at excessive speeds or marriage. . . .
>
> The facile liar has a great deal in common with the artist who is expert in embroidering detail.

Not long after writing those words, Skinner was on his way to Harvard's graduate school to begin his career in psychology. The book ends at that point; the author is twenty-four and is looking forward to a new and exciting life—one we will no doubt read of someday in another volume.

The bitterness of the young diarist, alas, has not yielded to time. The man who presented an all too unqualified theory about why people want to become writers is not very different from the man who, at the age of seventy-two, offers us these comments:

I had apparently failed as a writer but was it not possible that literature had failed me as a method? One might enjoy Proust's reminiscences and share the emotional torment of Dostoevski's characters, but did Proust or Dostoevski really *understand?*

A little farther on, he adds this conclusion: "Literature as an art form was dead; I would turn to science."

So he did, and partly because he has been so successful in his chosen career we must take notice of his earliest memories. We admire his precision, but we have the unfortunate experience (a "disedifying" one, his rather proper maternal grandparents might have said) of being witness to another part of him as well—a part that has always been, one gathers, arrogant and condescending. Each reader will have to decide for himself or herself whether Professor Skinner has added something to what Frost in his postscript called "belief in life." Perhaps in this book he has indeed contributed to that vision "mightily," but he has also at some points managed to "cross it uglily."

New Yorker, July 26, 1976

Man's Pride

E very day psychiatrists struggle with the staying power that all sorts of illusions have over the minds of patients—and of their doctors, too. The neurotic Viennese burghers Freud listened to at the turn of the century were not simply mixed up and at odds with relatives and friends; they were also tenacious and imaginative individuals who had come to grief because under no circumstances, it seemed, would they give up certain fixed notions and wishes. Most of them had been going from one doctor to another in the hope that someone, at last, would stop collaring them, stop telling them first piously, then threateningly, to shape up and look at the world *this* way, not some other way they found irresistible. Finally one doctor let them be; anxious to learn rather than preach, enough of a rebel to be open-minded and maybe a little contemptuous of prevailing orthodoxies, Freud listened and questioned his own assumptions as much as those of his patients. Eventually he saw what they were up to—how they regarded others, how their minds made sense of the various signals this world presents to us. He saw, too, his own blind spots. Reared in a particular way, trained to have certain expectations, preferences, and values, he had found himself for a long time as puzzled as his colleagues by the bizarre and apparently witless thoughts and deeds of the people who consulted him. Nor did he unravel "their" mysteries in a sudden burst of genius; in fact, for a long time he unraveled nothing—except, ironically, the sources of his own worldview. That done (the twentieth century was about to begin), he was helpless as a traditional psychiatrist. How could he wave his arms, fiddle with electricity, shake his finger, ply pills, call upon conventional morality, and throw around labels of one kind or another when he had come to realize how much he himself shared with "them," the outcasts he had come to know so well?

At such a moment one begins to ask who is the doctor and who is the patient—a question Freud knew enough to ask, as his correspondence with Wilhelm Fliess demonstrates, and a question, of course, patients and their doctors still pose for themselves. The answer is not clear-cut—and Freud was indeed in trouble with his colleagues once he insisted that the doctor had to shed a good deal of his socially sanctioned moral authority, his immunity from criticism, and instead find in himself the sources of unrest others seemed (and sometimes *only* seemed) to manage less well. Such an attitude does not have to be *stated* to a troubled patient; it comes across in dozens of silent but important ways—a nod, a gesture, a look—and the result for a patient can be nothing short of redemptive: at last someone will listen almost as a comrade, certainly not as a self-righteous judge. So doing, Freud could glimpse and begin to fathom what others knew nothing about. So doing, he also felt godlike; and again, Freud's correspondence with Fliess shows how naturally and unashamedly a bold investigator can acknowledge just such temptations. Unfortunately, history has a way of giving those temptations a kind of sticky institutional reality that for a while seems almost unshakable—hence the conversion of suggestive formulations into dogma.

Yet, other things also happen in due time. In the case of institutionalized psychoanalysis, a man like Allen Wheelis appears not to differ with or attempt to modify theories that are merely a bit overwrought but rather to take up once again Freud's kind of lonely vigil, in the course of which firmly held beliefs are shown to be no longer so compelling and new ideas about man's situation are mentioned and explored. As one goes through Wheelis's first and very important book, *The Quest for Identity* (1958), one feels that with respect to background, temperament, and sensibility he has what it takes to achieve what he has set out to do: an original mind; the ability to stand apart from prevailing orthodoxies without at the same time becoming destructively resentful; and not least, the capacity to bear a degree of loneliness. Freud often attributed his own qualifications along those lines to his Jewishness; born an outsider, he had less of the status quo to defend. Allen Wheelis was born in Louisiana, reared in Texas. Like other white Southerners he was drawn to the cosmopolitan intellectual world of New York, and like many of them, he both joined in and remained aloof. *The Quest for Identity* is an effort of a psychoanalyst (only recently finished with one of the longest apprenticeships our society demands) to lift his head from the clinics and consulting offices and find his professional bearing anew. The book offers an intelligent, lucid analysis of American society, both rural and urban, and implicitly but forcefully asks psychoanalysts to consider the reasons for their modern prominence. The book also offers the first example of Wheelis's distinctive method of presentation—the use of parables and short stories as a means of first making vivid and suggestive what is then written about analytically.

Wheelis next turned to a full-length novel (*The Seeker*, 1960) and a series of extended parables (*The Illusionless Man*, 1966) in hopes, perhaps, of making certain points quietly and without resort to the thinly disguised rhetoric and the discouraging jargon that plague the social sciences today. On almost every page of those two books, and throughout *The Desert* (1970), another blend of essays and fiction, the reader has to come to terms with Wheelis's ironic detachment. He misses none of the banality and occasional malevolence some psychiatrists foist upon us; but more important, he wryly takes note of our widespread gullibility and vulnerability as middle-class Americans who live in a thoroughly secular society. Blessed with money and comfort and (more or less) something called "success," heirs to the wisdom ("applied" all over the place) of Einstein and Freud, not to mention Darwin, Descartes, Newton, and Galileo—back, back into time one can go—we apparently have everything and know everything, and yet we are persistently naive in our endless search for new sources of satisfaction or fulfillment. The divorce rate climbs. Suicides are by no means rare. One fad gives way to another. Things are bought, kept around for a while, go increasingly unnoticed, and get thrown out. Our rivers are streams of acid; no matter, there is an island in the Caribbean for us, handily available in a jet-propelled cloud of smoke. In case anyone gets a little nervous, there is alcohol (and an estimated five million alcoholics) and drugstores full of millions of pills, all of them a collective promise of serenity to millions of citizens of the world's richest, most powerful nation; and for those who want to push things even more, there are a host of illegal substances now called "drugs"—as if the biggest and most respectable of American businesses don't already profit handsomely from the drugs they push quite legally on anxious, apprehensive men and women. Finally, of course, there are psychiatrists, so many of whose hours are reserved for those with money and a certain kind of social and intellectual background, as Redlich and Hollingshead indicated convincingly in *Social Class and Mental Illness* (1958). One prominent psychiatrist, Ralph Greenson of Los Angeles, has called attention to the shift in symptoms he and his colleagues have witnessed in recent decades. Freud saw patients who tended to have specific complaints tied to (he discovered) identifiable experiences or patterns of behavior. Now a more general kind of malaise, a sense of aimlessness and uncertainty tinged with vague moodiness, prompts many to see psychiatrists—and by no means is it likely that such difficulties can be traced back to some moment of psychological injury or sorrow in early childhood and then exorcised. Not that doctors don't keep on trying, even as their patients keep on coming. Where else are the patients to go? Whom can one really trust anyway? What is to be believed for any length of time—a year, say, never mind a span called by the superstitious "eternity"?

For Dr. Wheelis, those questions are not surprising; nor does he want to ignore them. In his latest book, *The End of the Modern Age*, he keeps putting forth such questions, and not in order to offer anyone some highly condensed and relatively inexpensive "help" or "guidance." Freud himself knew how to ask broad, contemplative questions, and after initially turning away from the excesses such questions can sometimes generate in favor of the clinician's realities, he was brought back to those questions, first by a terrible war and then in 1933 by the rise to power of the Nazi scum. In 1938, with scarcely a year of life left, the old psychoanalyst had to seek exile in England. No wonder a "death wish" became part of psychoanalytic metapsychology. No wonder Freud turned his attention more and more to religious and philosophical matters. Always one to correct his own mistakes first, he may have sensed that someone, someday, would have to give psychoanalysis a place in the larger tradition of the West's social and intellectual history. That is indeed what *The End of the Modern Age* manages to accomplish.

The book is short and possesses Wheelis's characteristic style— plain, understandable, strong prose harnessed to straightforward narrative presentation. The reader is meant to learn how many theories and pursuits are finally being seen for the illusions they have turned out to be, but the book is itself an illusion—so brief, unpretentious, deceptively easy to go through, yet in fact full of reflections about nothing less than the whole history of modern science. Though the title is dramatic, it is earned. The author goes back to the Middle Ages and shows how certain psychological assumptions began to be built up in the West as Copernicus and Kepler prepared the way for what, at last, became our age—in which humanity is known as an evolving part of the animal kingdom, the mind a deep mystery (but one that can be penetrated, if slowly and with difficulty), and the world made up of atoms (also now penetrated and somewhat under control). "The dream of mechanism," Wheelis says, is our conviction that everything in the universe, certainly including ourselves, "is nothing but a machine, and is thereby knowable as an object, as a machine can be known." Yes, we know now from theoretical physicists and cultural anthropologists how relative is the knowledge that for so long seemed to be fixed, simply waiting to be found. The mind boggles as "matter" is called "energy," as estimates are made about when and how the earth came into being, or about the number of light years that those stars we look at represent. Still, we hunger after certainty, and for many in the West certainty has to do with computers, statistics, and laboratories. Even among psychoanalysts, empathy and intuition can still be heard talked about as if one day they, too, will give way to an "objective," "value-free" study. (And, alas, there is the term *love-object*, which persists in the psychiatric literature.) In Wheelis's words: "So great has been the success of the scientific method that it has come to be identified with reason itself—as if there were no way of being reasonable with conjectures that lie beyond scientific reach. Such conjectures therefore are insidiously disparaged, ignored, as if to say, 'if it's not scientific, it's not important.'"

The point is not to mock the valuable things we have learned and continue to learn from natural and social scientists. Wheelis is no Luddite. Nor does he react against the excesses of this historical era by glorifying "natural man" or embracing a cult of craziness. He knows, out of his daily work he knows, how mean and brutish we can all be, and not *only* because a particular social or political system encourages such behavior. *The End of the Modern Age* was written simply to emphasize some of the distortions that have taken place in the course of the rise of the industrial West. There is, though, a passionate intensity that comes through in some sections of the book, no doubt a reflection of the author's sense of urgency as he looks back at what he, a man in his fifties, has already seen: the Nazi Holocaust; napalm bombs and atomic or hydrogen bombs; war efforts called "defoliation." So the book is many things: a sensitive and reflective essay on the West's intellectual history; an attempt to define the limits of words like "objective" and "subjective"; a look at what may be ahead of us as more and more people ask the kinds of questions Wheelis does: "What is important in life? What is worth struggling for, and how much? Should I love my neighbor, concern myself with his suffering? How far does neighborhood extend? To the coast? To North Vietnam?" Questions like those demand of us constant ethical concern. In Wheelis's words: "The computers are silent, the test tubes do not react to those queries, and he who concerns himself with them might do better in church than in a laboratory, and the church might better be a forest glade, if any such are left, than the temple of a tired sect."

I write this having just read that Werner Heisenberg believes "the ultimate has probably been reached in probing the innermost sanctum of matter." Indeed, as far back as the 1920s and 1930s Professor Heisenberg emphasized that there is a limit to what can be measured on the atomic scale because the process of measurement itself alters the situation. Our pride has brought us this far—for the good but also for the bad. Psychoanalysts, like physicists, can make the pursuit of knowledge a religion—and in so doing demonstrate how willfully blind even the best educated and most intelligent people can be. Allen Wheelis, in a sense, wants to help his colleagues come full circle around: Freud had a right to turn away from the temptations of moral philosophy and instead pursue the scientific imagery of his day, even if in so doing he fell prey at times to the pitfalls such imagery presents. But now, over seventy years since he made his great intellectual breakthrough, other challenges face us—challenges not unlike those that Schopenhauer and Nietzsche, the best of Germany's nineteenth-century philosophers, had the foresight to struggle with; and those challenges require from today's psychoanalysts the kind of ethical inquiry *The End of the Modern Age* at least begins to make.

New Republic, February 12, 1972

Red Herring

*I*f psychiatrists are anything, they are historians; their job requires skill at preparing a case history—the record that enables a doctor to study the past of a particular individual. Yet psychiatrists and psychoanalysts rarely think about the past of their own profession, and the history of psychiatry (or, indeed, of medicine) is not taught in many medical schools, so young psychiatrists often come to regard contemporary theories of mental illness as the revealed truths that our era has miraculously unearthed rather than as the latest in a long series of speculations, each of which has a substantial connection with its predecessors. But there *are* some good books on the topic; for psychiatrists, one thinks of, for instance, *The History of Psychiatry* by Franz Alexander and Sheldon Selesnick. And now there is *George III and the Mad Business*, the product of years of research by two English psychiatrists, Ida Macalpine and Richard Hunter. The book is an ideal one for medical students and young doctors, not to mention for the general reader: it is clearly written and utterly without dismaying jargon; furthermore, it is about a particular person, a particular set of "complaints"—and therefore full of concrete descriptions in place of abstractions and polemical theories. Finally, it is a historical study that asks the reader to think about all sorts of contemporary social and political issues—which is to say that the situation in which an English monarch and his subjects found themselves 150 years ago is not unique but is potentially the problem of any ruler and his people.

In June of 1788, King George III of England suffered what was called a "bilious fever." The attack (termed "smart" in those days rather than "acute" or "sharp") persisted for a fortnight, and the King went to Cheltenham to take the brackish waters of a spring believed to help gouty patients. During the summer, he became well again, but in the middle of October he once more took sick. His stomach hurt. He had trouble breathing and cramps in one leg. He was given purgatives, but a fever developed, as well as a slight yellowing around the eyes, and his power of concentration began to fail. His speech became rambling, his spirits were low, and his behavior was erratic. William Pitt, who was his Prime Minister, and the other men in the Cabinet began to wonder what they should do if the King's condition worsened, which it did.

The King of England was not then a mere symbol of continuity; he shared power with Parliament and his ministers. His "mental illness," which is what we would call it, precipitated a constitutional crisis, and the nation's leading physicians fought one another madly (one is tempted to say) over the King's diagnosis, prognosis, and treatment. Was George truly out of his mind? Would he ever recover? Ought the Prince of Wales to take over? Should the King, increasingly wild and incomprehensible, be restrained and coerced like any "ordinary" madman? These questions suggest only some of the issues. Pitt and Edmund Burke were battling one another for political power. Pitt had good reason to hope for the King's recovery and to insist that he be given the benefit of the doubt during his illness; for Burke and his fellow Whigs, the accession to the throne of the Prince of Wales, who favored their views, was desirable indeed. The King's wife and many children and aides and servants and helpers were also willing to scheme and take sides and reveal themselves to be less than totally loyal to him. At stake was power, in jeopardy was a nation's government, and at odds were those at the top—men whose devotion to King and Country was matched by their devotion to their own ambitions and purposes.

The fifty-year-old George waged a tumultuous and poignant battle for his sanity. He knew, even before his doctors did, that he was losing control of his mind. He felt driven to talk, to keep on the move, however frivolous or absurd the activity. He became confused—at times silent and sullen, at times talkative and expansive. He seemed incurable, and in November of that year it was rumored that he was dead. The Prince of Wales was already allotting ministries to his friends and associates, and the fights between George's doctors were as severe as his condition, as malicious as the political intrigue. Each doctor, it seemed, had his particular medical theory, his particular political cause. And the need to confine the King (and thereby acknowledge his mental state) intensified the arguments between the physicians. Let us cite the authors:

The situation in which the royal physicians found themselves was not an enviable one. They were frightened by their unmanageable sovereign and his unpredictable behavior. They had to account for his condition and their measures to the ministers of the crown. They had to consider the feelings of the Queen and her family and to bear in mind that the King himself was likely to see their reports in the papers—if not at the time then surely if he recovered. They were also apprehensive that the future of the Government hung on what they said. They were shadowed by the Prince of Wales and the Chancellor, harassed by public opinion, and had newsmongers breathing down their necks. They had to think of their professional reputation, and above all else loomed the remorseless fact that they did not, as indeed they could not, know what was the matter with their patient.

The doctors unquestionably helped the King feel weaker, more confused, more frustrated, more frightened. They bled him. They blistered his skin. They made him vomit. They gave him cathartics and little to eat. They talked about the "fever," the "disorder," the "indisposition," the "restlessness." They knew he had lost his mind (once he "talked for nineteen hours without scarce any intermission"), and so they hovered over him, cowering before him in his rages but nevertheless playing tricks on him, lying to him, restraining him by keeping him "swaddled in fine linen." Finally, despite his "oaths" and "indecencies," they got him to Kew, where he would be nearer his London doctors than in Windsor and not so easily observed by the public. There they tied him to his bed and called in a Dr. Willis, "the keeper of a madhouse in Lincolnshire," a man "of peculiar skill and practice in intellectual maladies." His presence embarrassed not only the King but many in the royal entourage; "the poor Queen had most painfully concurred in a measure which seemed to fix the nature of the King's attack in the face of the world."

Dr. Willis came with his physician son and three keepers, called "physical assistants." He talked about "breaking in" patients, rather as horses are tamed. The battle between the doctors and the poor, beleaguered, self-doubting, but assertive and courageous King intensified: "No account of the illness from this point on can disregard the King's treatment, and to what extent the turbulence he displayed was provoked by the repressive and punitive methods by which he was ruled."

The King took an intense dislike to his new doctors, and was declared to have a delusional hatred of them. They began applying not only force to his body but another label to his state of mind—"consequential madness." They boasted of their experience with madness. They tied George in a chair and lectured him for hours. (The elder Dr. Willis had been a clergyman.) When he objected, he was gagged. Nevertheless, he gradually improved. ("Not always can nature be trusted to triumph against such odds," the authors of this book dryly observe.) He became more composed. He slept better. His appetite improved. Eventually, he was once again able to speak and write coherently. At the end of February of 1789, he ordered an end to his physicians' public reports on his condition.

For the next twelve years, during which he was in good health, doctors all over England kept speculating on what had happened to their King and how he should have been treated. One ascribed the illness to "nervous fevers," and chastised his medical colleagues for the cruel treatment of the King. Rather than starve, purge, and bleed him, efforts should have been made "to invigorate, by all possible means, the body, and to afford every consolation to the mind of their royal patient." There was talk of his "species of mania." The speculations heightened in February of 1801, when he lapsed into a "hurry of spirits." The Drs. Willis returned. Again the patient was berated, intimidated, brutalized, and his relatives and friends helplessly obeyed the arrogant commands of the doctors, versed as they were in "the mad business." Yet the King recovered in a month or two, only to fall sick in 1804 and once more in 1810. He had by then held the throne for fifty years, and this last attack in effect brought an end to his rule. He was growing senile, and he was put in the care of the Queen, a group of advisers, and the Prince of Wales, now the Prince Regent. He died in 1820 at the age of eighty-two, still under constraint:

What had placed George III at such a disadvantage as a patient were the exigencies of being King. Now these had ceased, and yet—however sad to say, he was treated worse than many of his subjects might have been—he was still kept prisoner in close solitary and silent confinement.

In these words, Dr. Macalpine and Dr. Hunter declare their great sympathy for George III. They have written a lucid account of a perplexing royal illness, and they offer a diagnosis that contradicts the King's doctors and all the speculations of their confreres—that the King was afflicted with porphyria, a disease known only since the 1930s. In every cell of the body there are purple-red pigments, or porphyrins, that give blood its color. Patients suffering from porphyria secrete abnormal amounts of pigments, and this can damage the nervous system. The disease, which is hereditary, is transmitted as a Mendelian dominant, which means that half the offspring of an affected parent can be afflicted. The exact nature of the biochemical disorder is not known, and no specific treatment exists. One sign of porphyria is discolored urine. King George's physicians mentioned "dark" or "bilious" or "bloody" urine in their reports, but porphyria is not the only disease that can cause such a development.

This diagnosis of King George would not be convincing unless Dr. Macalpine and Dr. Hunter could prove that the reports of the royal physicians accord with present-day knowledge of how porphyria manifests itself in the few patients who suffer from it. The two authors had also to adduce evidence that George's disorder plagued his ancestors and his descendants. Porphyria is, as I have said, an inherited disease, but it resembles a wide variety of infections, neurological diseases, and psychiatric disorders. The history of the Houses of Stuart, Tudor, and Hanover had to be scrutinized for evidence of similar seizures. And are any living descendants of George susceptible to porphyria? One can carry the disease but lack any symptoms. The excess pigment shows up in laboratory tests, but without these an afflicted person will be unaware that anything unusual has happened to him.

Our first task was to ascertain whether porphyria actually occurred in the family. We therefore searched for living descendants in whom its existence could be established in the laboratory. Although this meant a bold intrusion into privacy for which we still feel apologetic, we were fortunate to obtain the necessary coöperation which made it possible to diagnose it in four living family members. This provided the material evidence of necessity lacking in posthumous diagnosis.

After intensive search, the authors feel that they can demonstrate strong evidence of porphyria in a number of England's kings, dukes, and duchesses. No one will ever be able to establish whether Mary Queen of Scots, say, or George IV, the eldest son of George III, had porphyria, but they certainly had symptoms not unlike those of George III, though not as severe. Even today, doctors can fail to spot porphyria or mistake it for something else; even today, the diagnosis is not always clear-cut. The authors do not say that certain people in the seventeenth and eighteenth centuries could have suffered only from that disease; the tone of *George III and the Mad Business* is quiet, thoughtful, and undogmatic. "Facts have their limits, but theories seemingly none," say the authors. They have not forgotten their words. And they have added an account of how psychiatrists and certain historians have considered King George—as a neurotic, a manic-depressive, a victim of a psychosomatic disturbance, and so on. Every whim and fancy, every habit and decision has been abstracted to fit the needs of this or that psychiatric or psychoanalytic ideologue. The authors of this book speak of the "moralising and patronizing attitude" and the "strange lack of sympathy" in accounts of the King's difficulties. Other historical figures, too, have been posthumously "analyzed" in such a way that they become cari catures of themselves—and, indeed, of any human being—and thousands of other patients are still described in a degrading, insulting manner and treated like King George; that is, stripped of their dignity, locked up, and kept locked up. The two psychiatrists who have written about King George deserve thanks from the people of their own country for helping set straight a period of English history, from readers lucky enough to come across this book, and from those of us who have daily cause to know the injustices that thrive even in the best clinics and hospitals.

Us Unmistakably

*P*sychiatrists are, of course, physicians whose everyday work confronts them with troubled people and turbulent emotions. In twentieth-century America, psychiatrists have unwittingly (and occasionally, I fear, by conscious design) become something more—heirs to the religious devotion that middle-class agnostics still have, yet make a point of denying. I have in mind the "progressive" or "liberal" parent who has no interest in the Bible or prayer and no comprehension of what a church service can mean to someone, can *do*—yes, to an intelligent and well-educated person who is not at all "superstitious" or hung-up by some neurosis or, as Freud put it, some "illusion." As a matter of fact, if anyone's name has inspired awe and faith in the twentieth century, it has been Freud's. Did Freud say this or that? Do his ideas suggest we do one thing or another thing? Is Dr. X a true follower of Freud's, or is he a deviant, a revisionist, a man who is not recognized by the orthodox? The orthodox, in this case, call themselves psychoanalysts, scientists, observers of human behavior; but a wry observer from another planet could as easily confuse them with any number of dogmatic, punitive, narrow-minded sectarians who have their own special world, their own exclusive liturgy, their own spelled-out idea of what life offers in the way of purposes, possibilities, and evils.

Actually, there are signs that the most austere, distant, and self-righteous of psychoanalysts are worried. Some of them still act like a small band of misunderstood, persecuted souls, whose every word will naturally, inevitably (and gratifyingly) be misunderstood by the "lay public"—as I hear *anyone* outside called, however literate and honorable. On the other hand, one prominent organization of psychoanalysts has taken its case to a public relations firm—and an important psychoanalytic journal recently published a letter from some distinguished analysts who reminded their colleagues that if the Roman Catholic Church would respond to John XXIII, then perhaps it was time for some analytic institutes and associations to "open the window a bit," to let in a little fresh air.

What *can* psychiatrists do—besides help the relative handful who can afford their private care? And what can they do theoretically— besides toy and tinker with whatever gospel they choose to call their own? There does come a time when nervous, self-conscious parents will realize that no advice, no acquaintance with the unconscious, however profound and endlessly sought (and, as well, bought) can offer children immunity from anger and envy and hurt and dis- appointment and sadness—yes, and passions that are inconsistent or inappropriate or ill-considered or whatever. There does come a time when even the blindest followers begin to question or stray; a time when bold, curious, intelligent, and sensitive people begin to go elsewhere, think differently, and in general do exactly what Freud did between 1890 and 1900, when he looked for his own vision and came to his own conclusions.

We can find one example of the "fresh air" so needed by the psy- chiatric community in the work of Robert Jay Lifton. His recent book, *Death in Life: Survivors of Hiroshima*, is extremely important and valuable in its own right. In addition, as a thinker and an inves- tigator the author offers us significant evidence that at least one young American psychiatrist can use psychoanalytic insight without worshiping psychoanalytic tenets; can observe the mind's life with- out turning all life into a subdivision of psychology; and, perhaps most important of all, can be both a doctor and a student of history and politics. Lifton's first book was *Thought Reform and the Psychol- ogy of Totalism*, published in 1961. The United States Air Force had taken him to Japan and Korea, and while there he became interested in Asia as well as in American military bases and the various tourist attractions that Westerners frequent. He also became interested in brainwashing, a particularly dramatic yet mysterious process that continues to puzzle and fascinate those of us in Europe and the United States.

What happened to those Western civilians who emerged from Mao's China in the 1950s full of praise for communism and full of criticism and scorn for themselves, their old ways and habits and beliefs? What happened to dozens of Chinese intellectuals who seemed to turn abruptly on their entire past, on all their ideals, for the sake of China's "new order"? How do revolutionary commissars go about indoctrinating a whole range of people, from Christian missionaries to Western intellectuals, from avowed anticommunists to vaguely sympathetic liberals?

Lifton tried to find the answers to questions like these by moving to Hong Kong and talking again and again with those who had gone through it all: the sequence of arrest, fearful interrogation, subtle and not so subtle intimidation, the trial, confession, "reeducation," and then, ironically, expulsion to countries like England, France, or America. Hong Kong was (and still is) the point of contact between two worlds, and there the youthful, curious, open-minded, hard-working psychiatrist could meet them one by one as they came from China—people who appeared tired, defeated, strangely exhilarated, confused, or anything but confused. What Lifton discovered cannot be easily summarized because he was, after all, a clinician. He saw all sorts of different people and in consequence wrote up a number of life stories, but he also extracted what he could from his observations and indicated how decisively we are all affected by political and historical events—particularly when men with power and cunning desire to *make* us be affected.

Nor did Lifton stop there. He was impressively willing to look at "totalism" as by no means a peculiarly Russian, Chinese, or "Oriental" phenomenon. In fact, he looked right here at home, at his own profession. We all learn to accept certain premises and values, to deny others as "wrong" or even "evil." Machines become gods, as do individuals and ideas. Particular theories are turned into catchall explanations for anything and everything. Tentative assumptions made by a man like Freud become for slavish followers the unassailable truth. Were Freud alive today he would be a different man struggling with different problems—but that makes no difference to dogmatic, partisan, arrogant psychoanalysts who claim his mantle, proclaim themselves his "heirs," build institutions around that kind of assertion, and proceed to demand of young aspirants compliance, devotion, and uncritical submission. Concepts like "resistance" or "transference" are used not only to explain what happens between a therapist and a patient but to stifle new ideas or disagreements with established doctrine. If I question the "libido theory" or something else that is "fundamental," I may be charged with "resisting," or with "acting-out" something in "the transference" that goes on in

my "training analysis." I can be called "borderline" or—in the
clutch—an "unsuitable candidate." In sum, Lifton did not shirk
pointing out the embarrassing parallels between psychoanalytic ide-
ologies and others.

What does such a psychiatrist do next? He can, of course, return
to the fold, return not only to America but to all the blandishments
and restraints that a somewhat nervous, uncertain, but eminently
trusted and even adored profession can offer the eager and uncritical
practitioner. He can join the groups, the organizations, the societies—and dismiss whatever doubts or misgivings he once had,
not to mention any inconveniently unpopular or unusual views or
attitudes. He can write out a check or two for a social cause here, a
charity there—and remind himself that he has his job, his compe
tence. Let the next guy do it—do whatever it is that *those people* do
when they get upset about wars, about atomic bombs, about forms
of violence that threaten to destroy the planet. And anyway, *those
people,* the ones who join demonstrations and protest against the
government—aren't they "neurotic" or "disturbed" or "sick" or
struggling with this or that "unconscious conflict" by "displacing" it,
by masking it with "nonpsychological" concerns, like the threat of
nuclear war, of our very extinction?

As a matter of fact, what about those two bombs we did choose to
let fall upon thousands and thousands of men, women, and children
back in 1945? What did the explosions do, not only to land and steel
and wood, not only to trees and water and fish and fowl, not only to
flesh and bones and blood, but to the minds of those who survived,
who were near but not fatally near, who barely escaped or were hurt
but not too much? Now how can *we* answer those questions? For
one thing, we are Americans, the ones whose deeds made the questions reasonable ones. We don't speak Japanese. We're here, not
there. And if we are psychiatrists, presumably interested in finding
out about such matters—oh, there are all too many barriers that face
us, like language, or "cross-cultural" differences, or the "limitations" of our professional competence.

Lifton somehow managed to overcome those barriers. Perhaps he
was "driven" to do so; and had he gone through that extra year of
analysis he might have become more "realistic," less involved with
the faraway, the morbid, the terrifying. Perhaps he is "rebellious":
while other American psychiatrists locate themselves by the hun-

dreds and hundreds near rich and disease-prone enclaves like Beverly Hills and Park Avenue, Lifton goes his own stubborn, defiant, unusual, original, and unsettling way. *Something* must be wrong; he *must* need "help."

In fact, Robert Lifton would probably be the first one to acknowledge that he and all the people he has observed in Hiroshima do indeed need our help. The survivors of the world's first atomic bombing need listeners, attentive listeners who will heed the grim and painful lessons that others have learned—and work to prevent the unlimited number of Hiroshimas now possible. Put differently, the survivors of Hiroshima need to be understood, not only as "others," as particularly wounded and unfortunate people, but very possibly, very easily, as *us*; indeed, at the push of a button, us unmistakably and us irremediably.

So, we can find out—those of us who want to know—what happened "back there" in 1945 when a plane, not an armada of planes, appeared over Hiroshima and dropped one small bomb, not a torrent of bombs. We can find out not so much what happened but what was set in motion and continues to exist: death in life. Lifton starts *Death in Life* by telling us honestly and directly about himself, his background, his interests, and his purposes. He wants to be a careful observer, but he knows that the cult of anonymity among psychiatrists can be as dangerous as the cult of personality is for a nation.

> In making arrangements for the interviews, I was aware of my delicate—even Kafkaesque—position as an American psychiatrist approaching people about their feelings concerning the bomb. From the beginning I relied heavily upon introductions—first from Tokyo and Hiroshima colleagues and friends to various individuals and groups (particularly at the University, the medical school, and the City Office), and then from the latter to actual research subjects. In the case of the randomly selected group, ordinary Japanese who would have been extremely dubious about a direct approach from a psychiatrist or an American, I first made a personal visit to the home together with a Japanese social worker from the Hiroshima University Research Institute for Nuclear Medicine and Biology. He and I, in fact, spent many exhausting hours that spring and summer

on the hot Hiroshima streets, tracking down these dwelling places.

He goes on to emphasize his "sense of the ethical as well as the scientific issues involved," and his hope that his work "might make some contribution to the mastery of these weapons and the avoidance of their use, as well as to our general knowledge of man." He also makes quite clear how flexible he wants to, indeed has to, keep his theoretical position. He was, after all, observing particular individuals, who nevertheless share a common social and cultural tradition. He was studying their responses to an overwhelming "moment"—a time in history. In a sense, then, he had to juggle all sorts of roles. He was delving into the minds of people; but he was also observing the way they respond as *Japanese* men and women; and in addition he was documenting certain universals—the way people respond to extremity, to the sight of widespread death, to the experience of lingering death, to the prospect of a deathlike life.

The heart of this book is its rich clinical material—pages and pages of words and feelings and ideas that give us a sense of what it was like when and after the Bomb fell on Hiroshima in the early morning of August 6, 1945. There had of course been the threat of bombings and, indeed, the likelihood that American planes would badly damage Hiroshima and many other Japanese cities. Yet no dread, no apprehension could prepare men and women for what happened:

> I was a little ill . . . so I stayed home that day   There had been an air-raid warning and then an all clear. I felt relieved and lay down on the bed with my younger brother . . . then it happened. It came very suddenly. . . . It felt something like an electric short—a bluish sparkling light. . . . There was a noise, and I felt great heat—even inside the house. When I came to, I was underneath the destroyed house. . . .

He was lucky. Thousands and thousands died instantly. A whole city was destroyed in a flash. A disaster not only occurred but persisted over time—with the deaths from "A-Bomb Disease," from the effects of radiation, from leukemia, occurring year after year.

Those who survived the immediate devastation became, for a while, dazed, broken in spirit, paralyzed, fearful, and "behaved like automatons." The world seemed at an end. Perhaps hell had finally arrived. But gradually the mind (so it seems) can deal with anything; and in chapter after chapter, Lifton shows us how various and particular men and women and children have done that—faced their unparalleled condition as *hibakusha*, "explosion-affected" people. The full play of human ingenuity was of course mobilized by such a disaster, and from year to year sick, anxious, desperately fearful people tried in all sorts of ways to keep their spirits up, to make do, to regain a sense of confidence and purpose.

Survival itself was a central issue for everyone who survived—and in much of this book we hear puzzled, grieving, lost souls wondering *why* and *when*: why it all happened, why they were still alive, when they would die. Lifton's portrayal of the scene makes one think of Dante's *Inferno*, with souls wandering about in terrible agony, guilt, remorse, pain, and terror. Everyone sought "trust, peace, mastery"—some sense that, after all and in spite of everything, the world was not beyond redemption. And everyone sought something else too: a conviction that life would somehow continue, no matter how imminent, inevitable, and specially triumphant death appeared to be.

I found it very hard to read this book. I found myself looking for diversions and distractions. If Hiroshima's *hibakusha* felt and continue to feel guilty even for being alive (as indeed do the relative few who survived the German concentration camps) then we, too, have every cause, every past and present cause, to shudder at what we did and continue to do as mighty, technological warriors who dominate the world yet also gravely threaten it (and ourselves). Lifton tells how the people of Hiroshima view America. We in America are perhaps less willing to think about Hiroshima—and, even more important, about what led up to it and what could yet again lead up to a total, annihilating war.

Still, toward the end of *Death in Life*, a certain measured but real and even inspiring sense of hope comes through to the reader. I do not speak of good cheer, or optimism, or a "cathartic" resolution of one or another "complex." I have in mind the kind of gloomy and severe and sharp but humorous sensibility that William Faulkner demonstrated again and again. The *world* is almost unbearably awful, but the *individual*, no matter how hard-pressed and death-bound, can endure and prevail *because* he or she is human—

vulnerable and sick and weary and abused and abusive; but also able to make, driven to make, the effort toward coherence, toward understanding. And so little Jewish children in the Terezin camp drew haunting pictures of the gas chambers, and little Japanese children wrote poems to celebrate, yes, celebrate, the "curse" their city suffered; yet this was also a celebration of their city's persistence, its lingering sadness, its protracted pain, its continuing rage. Death had a grip on Hiroshima, but at the same time its people could shake their fists at the world and try to live, live at whatever cost.

Despite the sensible and sensitive criticism that Lifton directs at rigid (and by now deathly boring) psychoanalytic doctrine, the formulation implied in the title *Death in Life* and developed throughout the book is essentially very similar to Freud's later view of humanity's central struggle—to stay alive and be nourishing in the face of the mind's destructive inclinations, the body's relentless decline, and the world's increasing threat to everyone and everything. In the latter part of the twentieth century, we have to pray not for a victory in that kind of struggle—by definition there can never be one—but for *time,* for the very time to continue to wage the daily struggle for life and against death.

Kenyon Review, Autumn 1968

Commentary on
Psychology and Literature

I don't think it is melodramatic to suggest that literary talent, in its inspired forms, has obsessed if not haunted psychoanalytic psychology. Freud's well-known remark on creativity, set down in an essay (1928) on Dostoevski ("Before the problem of the creative artist, analysis must, alas, lay down its arms"), indicates the frustrated combativeness of a man himself exceptionally talented. The psychoanalyst who thought of himself as a conquistador had a canny sense of when to abstain from a battle. Nevertheless, all of Freud's followers by no means followed his lead. In the 1930s Edmund Bergler, a New York City analyst, turned out a succession of books and articles meant to show how "sick," how "neurotic" writers are. (In that regard, the irony of his own writing campaign never seemed to strike him as odd or amusing.) When I got to know William Carlos Williams fairly well (I wrote my college "major paper" on his poetry), I was warned several times in letters about a trend he considered dangerous indeed: "I'm tired of seeing writers singled out for these blasts. If I read doctor Freud right, he's telling us that we're all full of conflicts—the way it goes for the human mind. So what's new! Oh, I pull back: what's new is that he's probed our mental affairs—whereas Sophocles or Shakespeare brought them to life. The probe is for doctors! When you leave the theatre and go to your office you need a probe! But some of these psychoanalytic literary critics have created a new medical specialty: the artist or writer as victim! You remember my dogs, 'sniffing' in *Paterson?* Some of the psychology I read, about writers and their writing, makes me think of 'sniffing'—that 'I smell shit look' people sometimes get."

In his paper on Heinz Kohut's interesting and important work, Dr. Ernest Wolf suggests early on that psychoanalysts have been wrongly charged with "besmirching and degrading" their various "betters," who have given us what gets called in the essay "sublime inspirations." Such a charge, we are told, is incorrect: "This distorted view of the psychoanalysis of literature surely does not fit Freud nor most psychoanalytic commentators." Yet later on the same author quotes Heinz Kohut himself as feeling it necessary to take issue with a good number of his colleagues: "He sharply criticizes the amateurishness and reductionism of some psychoanalytic critics." Needless to say, the issue is not percentages. Many, maybe most, psychoanalysts have all they can do to deal with the challenges of their everyday clinical work. But from those who have chosen to pursue "applied psychoanalysis," there have been plenty of logical lapses, not to mention abusive sprees, as Kohut seems to imply when he hesitates long and hard about the very point of using psychoanalytic ideas in a nonclinical intellectual setting.

Maybe Anna Freud had it right, so far as some psychoanalytic criticism of artists and writers goes, when she referred to "the universally envied gift of creative energy." Envy can take many forms, one of which is condescension—as in the astonishing acknowledgment in Marie-Louise von Franz's paper that "psychology . . . can even learn from it [literature]." Why the author felt it necessary to use the word "even" is, of course, her own business, but one is struck at the gratuitous presence of such an adverb. Nor is the following remark anything but a reminder of the kind of self-serving arrogance one not rarely encounters in supposedly "friendly" comments from analytic psychologists of the Jungian persuasion: "But more frequently the artist just simply has no idea himself of what has been said through him and is relieved and impressed if one can show it to him." A bit further on we are told that "all truly creative people know [this]: the woundedness of their soul through the creative impulse." No wonder Flannery O'Connor, in her letters (*The Habit of Being*, p. 491), observes that "to religion I think he [Freud] is much less dangerous than Jung." Maybe the same holds for literary criticism—because an apparent friendliness can mask a brutal hauteur. Nor do murky pieties about "archetypes" bring us all that closer to the contours of psychological reality, be it that of a patient or that offered us on a canvas or in the words of a poet, a novelist.

I refer to the above comments because I believe they indicate, yet again, some of the difficulties that plague a kind of psychological literary criticism. Nor is the issue only a matter of arrogance or single-minded (and self-serving) professional simplification of exceedingly complex issues. I wonder whether, finally, we are not confronted with a question of sensibility—that of the social scientist as against that of the humanist. "It is the business of fiction to embody mystery through manners," said Flannery O'Connor—and then she added this: "Mystery is a great embarrassment to the modern mind." For her, such mystery was not to be "resolved," that cool, slippery word that so many of us use today. If anything, stories and poems aim, unashamedly, to deepen mystery. To quote from another letter of Dr. Williams: "Some want to analyze the air—and tell us how much oxygen and hydrogen are around. Others want to enjoy the air, and mix things up—mist, fog, rain, blinding sun."

But even if we take social science logic on its own conceptual merits, we are in trouble when we come across a statement such as this: "An essay on Sylvia Plath by Weisblatt delineated the narcissistic elements in certain of her poems." Dr. Wolf admittedly has no time to tell us more about those "elements," but surely he ought to stop and remind us that there are "narcissistic elements" in *all* writing—all poems, all critiques of poems, and yes, all essays written on narcissism, or on other essays concerned with narcissism, not to mention comments such as these with respect to sentences that appear in that last-mentioned category. The issue is not narcissism—in Shakespeare's sonnets or the works of Yeats or Keats or, for that matter, in Heinz Kohut's writing. (The two leading theorists of narcissism, Kohut and Otto Kernberg, have proved their humanity by the way they have narcissistically argued with each other.) The issue is language—the uses to which it is put. There are "narcissistic elements" in all language, of course—that of the suicidally disturbed and that of the normal, that of smart critics and that of ordinary working people with no pretension to learned thinking, and not least, that of psychoanalysts and psychoanalysands, as well as that of men and women who write poems or who criticize the content of those poems and evaluate their words.

To tell us that Sylvia Plath shows to a reader "narcissistic elements in certain of her poems" is to tell us that Sylvia Plath was, finally, a human being. Sylvia Plath's narcissism was easily matched, if not exceeded, by the narcissism of thousands and thousands of other human beings. We remember her for her words and their arrangement. Her narcissism did not generate those words. What did? The mystery of the origins of language persists: neurophysiological and biochemical processes, speech centers in the brain—and on and on.

As for the cognitive gifts that enable a Sylvia Plath to see so much, understand so much—is biology to be denied a significant causative role? But geneticists and neurochemists or neuroanatomists or linguistic scholars or cognitive psychologists are not the ones who keep trying to "explain" talent or "delineate" this or that "element" in one or another poet's work.

Are we really helped to understand Shakespeare or Goethe, Tolstoy or Joyce (I disagree with, and resent, the characterization of *Ulysses* as a work flawed by "nihilistic bias" in the von Franz paper), by the statement of Freud's that "the creative writer does the same as the child at play"? The creative writer does quite something else. He doesn't "create a world of fantasy which he takes seriously." He creates a work of art. Sometimes, as we strain for resemblances (in pursuit of what—an explanation of someone else's enviable achievements?), we forget the most obvious distinctions in the world. Millions of children play; millions of adults create their worlds of fantasies and, God knows (as in mental hospital patients!), take their fantasies all too seriously. A few (James Joyce, for instance) come up with the astonishing subtleties and nuances of word and meaning, the triumph of scholarship and imagination, the bravura performance of a *Ulysses*.

What any number of us psychiatrists fail to perceive (and not only in connection with writers and artists) is that psychopathology and even normal emotional development are but one part of mental life. Language itself is, after all, what distinguishes us from all other creatures—the ability to gain distance on ourselves and our situation through words. We are the ones who ask why and how. We are the ones who come into consciousness through the strange phenomenon that still eludes us: the baby speaks—and thereafter, a new being, so to speak, has emerged. To paraphrase John of the New Testament: in the beginning, man's beginning, was the Word, and then "the Word became Flesh." For all Noam Chomsky's brilliance, or that of any other student of linguistics, semiotics, or whatever, we are yet left with cortical "areas," with inherited capacities, potentialities, and mechanisms. Granted, one day we'll know more about the mechanistic details of this most basic aspect of ourselves—but is there *any* reason why our emotional development need be so decisively and insistently brought into the matter? If both Chomsky and Piaget shrink from trying to explain to us the origins of literary accomplishment, if they refuse to tackle our Sylvia Plaths, whose cognitive and linguistic attainments are the reasons we attend them, then why are our experts in psychopathology so eager, on such scant evidence, to be so consistently interpretive, if not outright convinced of their speculative accuracy?

Why, moreover, these days, do literary critics, never mind historians, embrace so willingly these psychological ruminations? Is Jung doing religious thinking, not to mention ordinary, faithful worshipers of God Almighty, any favor when he tells us that we have a "religious need?" A noblesse oblige slap on the back, perhaps! A twentieth-century sanctioning nod to those who might otherwise worry all too much that they'll be considered naive, superstitious! Or a tautological banality: the observer who watches some of us praying quite hard, or struggling long and painfully to figure out the meaning of this life, and concludes thereafter that—we are doing, we are impelled to do, just that! Similarly with art and artists, literature and writers: they have graced us over and over again with their sketches and paintings, their statements, epic or epigrammatic, their chronicles, brief or ever so extended—and in this century some of us say yes, they are sick, this way or that, or yes, they would be sick, one way or another, if they weren't writing, or yes, it is a particular vulnerability, a certain reparative tendency, that accounts for *Middlemarch* and *War and Peace* and *Lear* and *Hamlet* and all the other plays, novels, stories, and poems. Maybe some of us are born (Nature's gift) with linguistic excellence. Maybe some of us have God-given visual or linguistic capacities—brains a touch more able to use words or to visualize and reproduce externally what is visualized. I don't know. No one does. Geneticists keep their silence and investigate. Neurobiologists do likewise. As do those psychologists who pursue the paths of our intellectual growth. I think that psychiatrists and psychoanalysts, some already struggling bravely to straighten out their own house, ought for a good while to stop poking into homes next door, if not those located on an entirely different street.

New Literary History, Autumn 1980

Medicine and Literature

Literature and Medicine

*I*n recent years an increasing number of medical schools have begun to offer medical students an opportunity to reflect upon the nature of their future work with the help of what I used to hear Dr. William Carlos Williams keep calling "the novelist's angle of vision." What did he mean when he used that phrase? He offered this explanation one day, in the last decade of his life, to a medical student who had crossed the Hudson river to visit him yet again:

> The abstract, categorical mind can be wonderful—the glory of the intellect at work, coming to its great big (and big-deal!) conclusions. But we've got to keep a close check on all that—the head running away with itself. The doctor treating a patient out there on the front line falls back on himself, his own manner of being with people—and he has to come to terms with not only a disease but a particular person: *this* patient, not patienthood, not lungs in general, or kidneys or hearts in general, but one guy, one gal, one kid who has some trouble and is handling it in a way that may be different than anyone else's way!

Vintage Williams, I'd learned by then—after years of hearing him whisper or quietly declare, but sometimes shout his head off. This was the writing doc who was always plain and unpretentious; who for years had been telling his readers "no ideas but in things"; who kept making the distinction between theory and conduct; who once exclaimed to his wife and a visitor that "smart ain't necessarily good." He was always doing that: slipping into the language of his working class and poor and immigrant patients of northern New Jersey—not to be affected, not to be a reverse snob, as I once thought, but to remind himself that language isn't important only to poets but to doctors who treat patients. He heard in the words of those he treated affirmations of strength, expressions of sadness, and not least, spells of great lyric power, no matter the grammar. "It's important," he once said, "to listen not only to the complaints of your patients but how they put them into words for you—how they choose to say (and regard!) what they want to tell you." Then he added this comment: "Of course, sometimes you're not only being told about your patients (by them) but told about yourself—even told off!"

I begin with those remembered moments because they address candidly and without affectation what the humanities have to offer us in medicine who want to pay them heed, whether teachers or students. Williams knew well the inherent affinity between medicine and the humanities—their shared interest in the concreteness of particular human experience. The poet sings of the seen, the heard, and puts in words, in images, what one mind has witnessed or imagined. The novelist spins yarns meant to evoke a specific situation or plot and specific characters. The doctor treats one person, then another, aware all the time (one hopes) that variation is a great constant of the work he or she does—those aspects of our individuality, those idiosyncrasies, those personal habits and beliefs and wishes and worries that distinguish each of us from the other, and that so often have a great bearing on the way a disease progresses (meaning how it affects a given life) and so, how a course of treatment will go.

Not that the humanities and (Lord knows) medicine are or ought to be unpreoccupied with principles, theories, and large-scale abstractions. The poet uses (or willfully chooses not to use) rhyme and meter; the novelist often has all sorts of ideas that get worked into stories; the doctor has that seeming infinity of factuality to tame, not to mention all sorts of formulations and rules. Yet, at a certain point there is, as Dr. Williams put it, "that awesome moment of application," when all the knowledge we have acquired, all the interpretations and theories, have to stand the test of—well, an *instance*: this poem or story, this patient here before me, who, yes, may have one disease, lupus, I have studied and know in general how to approach (which drugs, what "regimen") but who has a life and a mode of thinking and feeling and seeing and listening and responding that are no one else's and may well count for a lot in how that lupus proceeds. As Robert F. Loeb used to tell us medical students: "never say 'never,' and never say 'always'; and try to leave yourselves plenty of elbowroom when talking with a patient about what you've concluded and what you see ahead."

The linear mind and the categorical mind are an important part of ourselves. We all crave and need straight lines to connect the various points we envision, discover, or sometimes conjure up. We all rely upon generalizations, conceptualizations—abstract efforts meant to hold together "people, places, things." But life itself (so our poets and novelists remind us) and the practice of medicine (so we physicians discover after we've crammed all the data into our exhausted heads during the first year or two of medical school) have to do with the enormous range of possibilities our patients offer us. Life is not only cause and effect, not only "variables" with their inexorable and deterministic "symptomatology." Life is chance and circumstance and luck (good or bad). Life is surprises—irony, ambiguity, unpredictability, inconsistency. Life is strength coming out of weaknesses—even "diseases" prompting moral depth and intellectual growth, as Tolstoy knew when he gave us "The Death of Ivan Ilyich," in which a sick lawyer for the first time in his adult life (and at the very end of that life) recognizes the meaning of love. A medical or psychiatric "reductionism" does not quite explain how any given person comes to terms with his or her life, or illness, or final moments on this earth.

Novels and short stories or poems help us understand such matters: the patient confronting (and educating) the therapist or doctor in Tillie Olsen's "I Stand Here Ironing"; the decency and generosity of a particular alcoholic in her "Hey Sailor, What Ship?"—a contrast with the smug and self-serving "normal world"; the terrible irony of years and years of marriage, with no real knowledge of or trust for one another on the part of a husband and wife, as revealed by the onset of disease and the approach of death, evoked in her "Tell Me a Riddle." Also of obvious help are such old reliables of our literary tradition as George Eliot's *Middlemarch*, with its close examination of the moral and professional life of Dr. Lydgate; or Flannery O'Connor's stories—for instance, "The Lame Shall Enter First," with its hard look at a healer's pride and blindness, and yes, his need of a bit of the healing he offers others; and Dr. Walker Percy's serious yet comic "existential" analyses of our contemporary, late-twentieth-century American moral and spiritual lives (in his essays, collected as *The Message in the Bottle*, and his novels, such as *The Moviegoer* and *Love in the Ruins*).

All through Dr. Percy's writing, the reader is reminded of the spir-

itual "malaise" that afflicts so many of us, the boredom or mean-
inglessness of our lives, the hectic pace we maintain—an effective
deterrent to moral reflection. Like Tolstoy, Percy sees psychological
and physical pain as potentially redemptive—a means by which the
smugly self-sufficient are compelled to reach out, take note of others,
and think about this life's purpose.

I would like to end where I began, by mentioning the wonderful
storytelling and poetry of the physician William Carlos Williams.
His *Doctor Stories* brings to life the everyday hurdles we face in
medicine as we struggle not only with our diagnostic or therapeutic
challenges but with ourselves, our inevitably flawed humanity, our
times of bitterness or envy or frustration or greed, our passions and
dreams, our sometimes extravagant hopes and eager expectations,
and, of course (since our patients will one day die, and we as well),
our moments of disappointment and melancholy. Still, we persist,
as Dr. Williams did, through the efforts he made in his medical life
and, too, through the stories he produced during his writing life,
which render us and our patients in the round, so to speak: as whole,
complex, and many-sided as we all are.

Journal of the American Medical Association, October 17, 1986

The Wry Dr. Chekhov

Many of us who attended Columbia's College of Physicians and Surgeons in the 1950s admired the clinical teaching of Dr. Yale Kneeland—his everyday tact, his civility, his able and alert diagnostic mind, his ready wit, and not least, the breadth and depth of his knowledge. In that last respect he was outstanding and unforgettable—for the novels and poetry he had read and was constantly offering his medical students as a gift; for his touting the humanities as the best possible way to comprehend this life we live, with all its inevitable worries, surprises, hurdles, disappointments, and losses. I had the special good luck of getting to know Dr. Kneeland rather well; he was my tutor in medicine, and because we both loved to talk about Dickens and George Eliot, about Dostoevski and Tolstoy, about William Carlos Williams and T. S. Eliot, we became good friends. Many times I'd get discouraged, go to see Dr. Kneeland, tell him I was a sorry medical student, indeed, and utterly ill-suited for the profession I was pursuing (out of motives I couldn't at all figure out). He would have none of my self-pity (or the egoism behind it). He approached his patients with a directness and candor, with an utter lack of condescension or guile, which we student onlookers found to be magical, refreshing, compelling; and several times I had occasion to feel rather as those patients must have felt—grateful for a particular doctor's blunt realism (all the more affecting for the charm and courtesy that characterized its presentation).

I especially remember a day of despair that ended in a visit to Dr. Kneeland's Presbyterian Hospital office. A third-year medical student, I had witnessed a young woman's death. She had been sick for several years with a chronic leukemia, and her lively intelligence and apparent physical beauty had made her an object of great concern and interest in the course of her repeated admissions to the hospital. She had taught school for a while before getting sick, and she rejoiced in making the doctors who attended her a bit more literate, if not literary, during the course of her (by then) increasingly frequent hospitalizations. They hovered around her, I noticed, and sick as she was, healthy as they were, the energy seemed invariably to emanate from her, with her medical caretakers becoming more and more animated, even radiant, as they heeded her observations, interpretations, and *explications de texte*. Finally, she would have given out all she had, and she seemed suddenly to turn pale, become mute. She would, invariably, punctuate the end of her discourse by letting her head fall back on the two pillows that had propped her.

I remember, one day, she went further. She took one of the pillows in her right hand and held it over the floor beside her bed for what seemed like the longest time—to the point that the doctor at the foot of her bed, not to mention me, began to worry: was she becoming a bit "strange"? We were grateful when the hand released the pillow, but then to our alarm we noticed that immediately thereafter the patient's eyes closed. But our questions ("are you all right?") were promptly and sensibly answered: "Yes, of course." Knowing her interrogators to be unsatisfied, she added: "I am as tired of hearing myself talk as that friend of mine, that pillow, is of bearing my shoulders up!" We laughed nervously. Never before had I thought of a pillow that way; never would I forget the soft noise of the pillow hitting the floor—a quiet yet dramatic resolution to a given moment of sadness, of outright despair, provided by a remarkable, dying lady of twenty-eight.

Unfortunately, I was on duty (four months and two hospitalizations later) one evening when that lady suddenly took very ill. I was drawing blood from a nearby patient when I heard these words: "This is the last night of my life." There was no great urgency or alarm in the speaker's voice; rather, she seemed resigned, wistful. She was, yet again, the knowing teller—the narrator anxious for any nearby listener to be informed. I recall looking not only at her but at the space around her bed: surely someone was there to whom she was addressing her remarks. But no one was near except the other patient, whose blood I'd just taken, and I. Yet her head was not turned toward us. I wondered whether she'd become agitated or disturbed, whether she might not be hallucinating. I wondered whether she was newly sick and might not need some late-night medical scrutiny—even though I'd been assured a few hours earlier that she was OK and might even be sent home once more the next day. Then, another statement: "I wish the world well." The same tone—matter-of-fact rather than strenuously insistent. She had been given some new medication, I seemed to recall: perhaps it—in conjunction with the chloral-hydrate pill she took, sometimes, to induce sleep—had gone to her head, had prompted a "reaction." The patient I had been working on came to the same conclusion. He had a serious disease himself, lupus erythematosis, and he knew what medication (cortisone) could do to the mind. He suggested that I go talk with her. His reason: "At night it's worse here: everyone is closer to death around midnight."

Lord, I thought to myself: I have an exam tomorrow, and it *is* midnight. This visit to her, across the hall, would be a brief one. No lectures from her on Willa Cather and Eudora Welty, on Tolstoy and Chekhov, their different ways of seeing the world, of being! I entered the room. Right away she looked at me. She smiled. I was already sure that she was all right. She seemed comfortable and calm. Her face had a quiet steadiness to it. I asked her if there was anything I could do before I left the floor—a way of speaking I'd learned from Dr. Kneeland: the low-key, general question that gave the patient a chance to declare something, to stress a conviction, to make a request. She said this to me: "You can do—well, you can try to be a good doctor." She was still being rather soft-spoken and cool in her way of speaking, but I was again having psychiatric thoughts, if not misgivings. This phrase came to my mind, a phrase I'd decided to suggest (at our next morning's rounds) be written in the chart: Psych consult. I saw from the corner of my eye a nurse walk down the corridor: she might be the one to implement that order by making a phone call. Should I tell her what was on my mind—take credit for being the first one to realize that something else was now wrong with this lady who had been having such a terrible, terrible time for several years, and who seemed uncannily in control of herself, we'd often noted, to the point we'd as much as arraigned her on *that* score: an excessive normality, as it were, which masked a deep and abiding fearfulness?

Suddenly, as I stood there, silently ruminating, I was asked this: "I hope we're not on Ward 6." No, I said, this is the seventh floor. I thought I saw a look of uncertainty cross this dying woman's face. I was sure that she was becoming confused—an aspect of her deteriorating medical condition or, perhaps, her mind's response to the treatment she'd been receiving. In fact, I was later to realize, she was perplexed about me: how to tell this young man that she was making a literary reference, but not to show off, not to be frivolous or provocatively skeptical? But at the time all I knew was the sudden terror that soon enough seized both of us in that room. The patient began to sit up, as if (I thought for a second) she wanted to tell me something. Then she lurched back in her bed and appeared to be struggling hard for her every breath. I rushed to her side, saw how very sick she was, ran to the nurses' station to page the doctors on duty, rushed back to the room in a state of helpless alarm—to find the patient unconscious. As I tried to feel a pulse, all I knew to do, a nurse arrived, took one experienced look, and told me that the young lady had died.

When I told Dr. Kneeland about this melancholy, late-night incident, he shook his head. He'd known the patient, known the prognosis, and was not surprised. I remember him leaning back in his chair, asking me what I "made" of the "reference to Ward 6." I recited my aspiring doctor's hunches and interpretations—the disorientation of the very sick I'd already begun to recognize as familiar. Dr. Kneeland said nothing when I'd finished my nervously detailed explanation; he reached over to a bookcase near his desk, took in his right hand a book, opened it, scrutinized the table of contents, turned to a page, put a slip of paper from his desk in the book to mark that page, then handed the book to me. I opened it and there it was: "Ward 6." I remember reading quickly the first words of the story: "There is a small annex in the hospital yard. . . ." I remember closing the book, my right thumb still on the page marked for me by Dr. Kneeland, noticing (a bit ashamed, by now) who had authored this "Ward 6." Before I had a chance to say anything (and I didn't know what to say), I heard this: "Take it with you. Chekhov should be every doctor's lifelong companion."

I'd read Chekhov's plays in an undergraduate course but none of his stories. Soon enough I would read "Ward 6," and then, one by one, all in that collection. A week or so later I returned the book to Dr. Kneeland, and we talked about Chekhov the doctor, Chekhov the social observer and storyteller, and of course, about the suffering patient, near death, who'd asked me that question. I thought I'd understood "Ward 6," and so was all the more puzzled as I tried to figure out what possible reason a patient had found to compare, even by indirection, the good and earnest care she was receiving at the Columbia-Presbyterian Medical Center in New York during the middle 1950s with the care the patients of an obscure, provincial psychiatric ward received in late-nineteenth-century Czarist Russia. Dr. Kneeland didn't even have to ask me what was troubling me; he saw rather clearly my mind at work and responded this way: "She was very sick for a long time. Death was closing in. She felt trapped and cheated by life. You were the nearest person at hand, a representative of 'life'; and so she told you what she felt was happening to her—with the help of Dr. Chekhov." For me that moment was a critical one—the single most important experience during the years of medical training I'd had and would have. A writer had been urged upon me, suggested as a lifelong companion. A patient's agony had been translated—explained to my uncomprehending ears. The considerable risks of a doctor's self-important and self-serving isolation from his patients had also been set forth—by an astute clinician who had shrewdly comprehended why a Chekhov story meant so much to a lady for whom death was an imminent visitor.

Now I teach Chekhov to certain medical students. We read "Ward 6" and discuss the visionary Dr. Chekhov's apprehension of the topsy-turvy psychiatric world, where "normality" is often enough to be found in the eye of the beholder, and where medical judgments merge all too commonly with moral ones—so that those called "sick" are treated as bothersome if not evil. But Chekhov did not only anticipate R. D. Laing or Thomas Szasz (psychiatric critics of psychiatry) by almost a century. In "Ward 6" and in "An Attack of Nerves," he had spotted something larger amiss than a self-righteousness that defends itself at all costs. Dr. Ragin of "Ward 6" has not only put himself at a remove from his patients; he is also lost to himself. He drifts. He is easily distracted. He reads but does not live. He is resigned to this life's considerable injustices, its mean and nasty sides—and his attitude, we begin to see, adds to the sum total of the very evil he presumably wants to ignore, if not resist passively. His protagonist, Gramov, is a patient whose canniness and directness do indeed make the reader question the concept of "insanity," not to mention a politics that allows a Dr. Ragin the control over others he has. But Gramov is as wildly self-centered in his own way as Dr. Ragin certainly comes across as being, and clearly Chekhov is reminding all doctors and all patients of their common susceptibilities, flaws, and moral failings. When Dr. Ragin becomes aroused to injustice, becomes more concerned with at least one patient, and surrenders his protective aloofness, he is exposed and soon enough himself becomes a victim, a suffering and hurt person—and a much more honorable one, we are persuaded to conclude. Who is healing whom on this planet—in any hospital, clinic, office, home? Chekhov knew how to pose an ironic question.

Even now, a quarter of a century later, I think of that very sick young lady, her intelligence so textured and lively, wondering with Chekhov's help whether any doctor would willingly stop for long to talk with someone like her about more than a procedure, a test, a medical diagnosis or prognosis. Maybe many of us doctors, with good reason, lack the time to have the long talks some of our patients crave and need. We are overwhelmed with necessary burdens. Those procedures and tests, as a matter of fact, can be critically important for our patients, even lifesaving. Still, Chekhov was a philosophical writer, a doctor who was himself sick for years and who died of tuberculosis at forty-four. (As with William Carlos Williams, his medical work was not an incidental biographical fact but rather an important element in a particular literary and moral sensibility.) He wondered what this existence meant as a person destined to die relatively young often does: he felt life's fatefulness and arbitrariness, its paradoxes, as (in their sum) a continual, vexing pressure but also as a challenge. That young woman of my early medical career no doubt had been making Chekhov's kind of powerful if understated ethical inquiries all during her prolonged, painful illness, and like him, she had wondered whether the time we spend here is not absurd, a spell of being in a "ward" in which the blind lead the blind.

"I am tired of theorizing about life," Chekhov once wrote. He hardly need have said so. His gifts to us lack the arrogance of so much conceptual thinking—its conquering self-centeredness. His gifts are the concrete particulars of those stories and plays; and in them doctors constantly appear, usually wry observers and searchers, spiritual diagnosticians (as in Dr. Walker Percy's novels and essays) of man's earthly malaise: the creature of consciousness. Dr. Astroff in *Uncle Vanya* is a provincial doctor who is overworked and thoroughly cynical. ("There's nothing I want, nothing I need, nobody I love.") Still, he does "want" and "need"; and he can love—and the degree of his bitterness tells us that early on. The medical student in

"An Attack of Nerves" has learned, sadly, to be annoyed by his lawyer friend's horror at a brothel's degradation. This lawyer will eventually be declared sick and treated with quieting drugs—while his friend, a future doctor, consolidates even further an austere distance, a posture of iciness and smugness. At the other end of the age spectrum, "A Boring Story," a particular favorite of Thomas Mann's, offers a portrait of a distinguished medical scientist's old age—the isolation produced by years of self-preoccupation. (Ingmar Bergman's film *Wild Strawberries* uncannily pursues this same theme.) Chekhov also shrewdly evokes in this tale the loneliness of celebrity—the skepticism and suspicions generated by a person's fame or his achieved power. If patients languish, cut off sadly from others, so in their own way do big-deal doctors or others who have climbed to the top of one or another ladder.

It is a central assertion of all Chekhov's writing that few of us really escape one or another form of isolation—hence his constantly wry vision of the writer's distance as a true measure of everyone else's (if only they would know it) godforsaken apartness. Even those of us who claim to be "happy" (that is, reasonably content with this life) must rely upon the substantial reticence or tact or mute subservience of others—as if happiness for some requires that others be out of sight, out of hearing range. In "Gooseberries," a story recently brought to my attention by a friend, Chekhov is quintessentially his wry self: "I saw a happy man, one whose cherished dream had so obviously come true, who had obtained his goal in life, who had got what he wanted, who was satisfied with his lot and with himself. For some reason an element of sadness had always mingled with my thoughts of human happiness, and now at the sight of a happy man I was assailed by an oppressive feeling bordering on despair."

Such "despair," though, is never a final destination for Chekhov, it is rather an occasion for more wry probing, for philosophical (we today would say "existential") analysis:

> I said to myself: how many contented, happy people there really are! What an overwhelming force they are! Look at life: the insolence and idleness of the strong, the ignorance and brutishness of the weak, horrible poverty everywhere, overcrowding, degeneration, drunkenness, hypocrisy, lying—Yet in all the houses and on all the streets there is peace and quiet;

of the fifty thousand people who live in our town there is not one who would cry out, who would vent his indignation aloud. We see the people who go to market, eat by day, sleep by night, who babble nonsense, marry, grow old, good-naturedly drag their dead to the cemetery, but we do not see or hear those who suffer, and what is terrible in life goes on somewhere behind the scenes. Everything is peaceful and quiet and only mute statistics protest: so many people gone out of their minds, so many gallons of vodka drunk, so many children dead from malnutrition—And such a state of things is evidently necessary; obviously the happy man is at ease only because the unhappy ones bear their burdens in silence, and if there were not this silence, happiness would be impossible. It is a general hypnosis. Behind the door of every contented, happy man there ought to be someone standing with a little hammer and continually reminding him with a knock that there are unhappy people, that however happy he may be, life will sooner or later show him its claws, and trouble will come to him—illness, poverty, losses, and then no one will see or hear him, just as now he neither sees nor hears others. But there is no man with a hammer. The happy man lives at his ease, faintly fluttered by small daily cares, like an aspen in the wind—and all is well.

Chekhov has sometimes been described as *too* wry—as the detached stoic he parodies in "A Boring Story," or the distant, sardonic physician who appears in story after story. But in the above moment he is wry in quite another way: the poignantly humane social visionary who holds himself at arm's length from any number of polemical commitments not out of indifference but a precious wisdom—the kind, I believe, my old teacher, Dr. Yale Kneeland, offered us medical students when he remarked one day that "this life defies all who want to pin it down exactly." He too was a doctor wary of absolutes—as was Chekhov, for whom the mind's exertions were themselves a drama to be wryly rendered rather than embraced as God's answer to all eternity's riddles.

American Poetry Review, July/August 1984

Why Novels and Poems
in Our Medical Schools?

W hy novels and poems in our medical schools? I am hardly in a position to be objective about that question. I went into medicine, I think it fair to say, out of an enormous respect for and admiration of Dr. William Carlos Williams, poet, novelist, playwright, essayist, critic, and not least, physician. I wrote my college thesis on the first book of his long poem, *Paterson*, and thereby got to know him. Until then, I'd been a history and literature major, with a strong side interest in jazz. I went on house visits with Dr. Williams, came to know some of his patients, became utterly taken with the work he did, decided (quite belatedly) to take premedical courses—and had a devil of a time doing so. I managed the subject matter fairly well, but I had a lot of trouble with the fierce, relentless, truculent competitiveness that seemed inseparable from the study of biology, organic chemistry, and physics. And I regret to say that now, a quarter of a century later, I still see such an atmosphere at Harvard College—and no doubt other colleges have no immunity to the problem. Students come see me often, and their turmoil sends my head reeling with bad memories. How might we help intelligent, ambitious premedical students learn, yet reject the more unsavory aspects of premedical life? I do not think it an exaggeration to say that were it not for Dr. Williams' generous, personal support, I would not have lasted that first, college phase of scientific education, and maybe not the critical first two years of medical school—a continuation, then at least, of laboratory work, with virtually no chance to meet those ailing fellow human beings who get called patients.

What Dr. Williams did, over and over, was to suggest books I ought to read: Chekhov, Camus, Kafka, not to mention some of his own stories (collected as *Life along the Passaic*). He urged me to read *Arrowsmith* again—a book usually read in high school or early college, then forgotten by many of us who become physicians. He reminded me, repeatedly, how much Dostoevski and Tolstoy had to say about illness and its vicissitudes, and of course, Thomas Mann. As I responded, I found the pleasures a reader obtains from a good writer; but I was also prompted toward ethical reflection by novelists and poets who had a marvelous sense of life's continuing mystery, the ambiguities and ironies that never stop confronting us.

It is a privilege, therefore, to be able to urge some of those same books on others—on medical students who, of course, require a mastery of biological factuality but who also need (and in my experience, almost hungrily crave) a chance to ask those haunting moral and philosophical questions a George Eliot, for instance, in *Middlemarch*, keeps posing: what is the meaning of the life we doctors so constantly try to protect, and how ought that life to be lived—with what ideals and aspirations, with what accommodations, adjustments, and compromises in the face of this world's constantly pressing opportunities, frustrations, and obstacles?

Literature and Medicine, Autumn 1982

On Medicine and Literature
An Interview with Robert Coles

Interviewer: Much of the *Children of Crisis* volumes is made up of interviews. Do you generally use a tape recorder?

Coles: When I was in college, I got to know William Carlos Williams, and I used to follow him around and tape record his medical rounds in northern New Jersey. He was an old-fashioned, what we'd now call family practice, doctor—he was a pediatrician and an obstetrician, and basically a general practitioner. I'd visit him and he'd take me into the homes of his patients. He'd listen to them carefully, both as a writer and as a doctor, and then when he left each home, he'd sit in his car and write notes. I'd say, "What are you doing?" And he'd say he was writing down the wonderful expressions he heard from them. He would later use them in his poems. And some of the stories he heard from them he worked into those wonderful *Life along the Passaic* stories, which are doctor stories, really. He used to say, "The important thing is to *hear*." I've found that when I've used the tape recorder, at times it was because I thought I wasn't a scientist if I didn't have everything tape recorded. And then I'd remember what Dr. Williams said, and slowly I started weaning myself from it. But it's hard because you figure you get everything that way. And it has interfered at times, because I didn't listen as closely as when I didn't have it.

Interviewer: So when you didn't have it, you'd just write things down?

Coles: Afterwards. I'd write it all down. And I'd edit what I heard—you edit the tape anyway—I think I was editing in my mind as I was writing it down. You write down what you feel you really want to remember. It's a complicated thing, how you do this work.

Interviewer: I imagine you must have libraries full of tapes.

Coles: I do. I have a lot of tapes, and then more recently a lot of notes on my yellow pads. And often, even when I was using the tapes, I'd sit down in the evening and write an essay in which the important things that I heard were put together. Lately I've been working in Northern Ireland, in Belfast, with the Catholic and

Protestant children caught up in that struggle, and in South Africa with the black children in Soweto and Afrikaner children in Pretoria. I found myself not using the tape recorder.

Interviewer: Not at all?

Coles: Just occasionally. I'd use it so I could listen to the voices, for the use of language and dialect. I felt that I learned a lot just by listening and writing down afterwards what I had heard, rather than by trying to catch every word.

Interviewer: I carried several of your books home from the Cambridge library last week, a very thick stack of books—and I began to wonder how you are able to write so much. They had nearly twenty of your books: the *Children of Crisis* series, biographies, criticism, children's books, poetry. How do you manage to do all that?

Coles: I write on yellow lined legal pads. I write in the mornings, early, just after my children have gone to school. I think about what I'm going to write the night before. Then I sit down and by golly, I write. I write on a quota basis. I try to write three to four yellow pages a day, five days a week. And if you keep on doing that with some—almost a religious—dedication, the books mount up over the years. One of the reasons is some sort of a necessary feeling I have that I must do this fairly regularly. The only time I stop writing is when I'm out in the so-called field. That is, when I was in South Africa or Belfast I didn't write much, other than the notes I was taking. But when I'm at home either teaching or doing my work in this country, visiting families—usually I don't visit the families until the afternoons because the kids are in school all day—I will write in the mornings, and that writing mounts up. If you stop and think about it . . . also I have sort of a cramped hand, a cramped writing hand, so I would estimate that I probably write eight hundred to a thousand words a day.

Interviewer: Then do you revise a lot after that?

Coles: Yes. What I do is revise one time. All that is typed up. Then I approach the typed version with a whole new personality. I look at it as an editor—and I'm very tough with my own writing. Maybe some critics would say not tough enough. But there is a difference. If you saw the first draft, you'd see the difference. I cannot edit my own handwriting. It has to be typed. And then I just slash into it. As I say, maybe I should learn how to slash into it better.

There is that very important second stage of the writing, though—it's edited. And then it's done.

Interviewer: You mentioned your friendship with William Carlos Williams. How did you come to know him?

Coles: As an undergraduate at Harvard I majored in a combined English and history field, and I wrote my thesis on Dr. Williams and his poem *Paterson* and the novel *White Mule*, which enormously interested me. At that time, in 1950, Dr. Williams was not quite as celebrated as he later became in the sixties. He died in 1963, and when I was doing this writing he was a well-known poet but by no means well accepted in the academic circles, the university circles. The only reason I was able to work so well and congenially at Harvard on that subject, namely him, was because of Perry Miller, who was a professor of English and American literature at Harvard and was an enormous influence on me. He was an English professor, but I think it's also fair to call him a theologian. He was very much interested in the Puritan mind and in the moral issues the Puritans struggled with, and he was interested in the literature which that generated. And that was my major undergraduate preoccupation. But I had read Williams' poetry and wanted to write about him, and Miller encouraged me to do so and was my mentor. I envisioned myself going to graduate school and becoming a student of Miller's in American Literature. After I had written my paper on Williams, Miller encouraged me to send it to him. I got a reply from Dr. Williams, saying, "Any time you're here, come and say hello." And boy, I went down to New York fast. I then became a friend of his, a young friend of his. He was very, very helpful, as an older person. I talked a lot with him.

Interviewer: And he encouraged you to go into medicine?

Coles: Well, yes. I became so impressed with the dual life he lived as a physician and as a writer/social observer of sorts that I thought maybe I'd give it a try myself. So I started taking on premedical courses, and I applied to medical school. I was turned down by four or five of them, because they thought I was a little flaky, I think, although I did well in the premedical courses. They'd often ask me what kind of a doctor I'd want to be. I'd say that I wasn't sure but . . . and then I'd tell them what I'm telling you now. But at Physicians and Surgeons, at Columbia, I was interviewed by a man named Philip Miller—the same surname but obviously no relation to Perry Miller. He was a biochemist. He interviewed me, and I told him how I'd come to that point in my life. He said, "We ought to take someone like you, even if you're not sure you want to finish medical school." So they did take me. I had to struggle in medical school, because I wasn't really adequately prepared for the sciences, and I didn't do too well in them. But I managed to get by. I would visit Dr. Williams, and I was very much interested in religious matters through Perry Miller and through my own life. I would go to Union Theological Seminary, where I took a seminar which Reinhold Neibuhr gave before he had his first stroke, which was in '52, I think. I guess I was trying to combine my medical life as a student with these interests in religion and in literature. That I think has been the struggle that I've waged all my life.

When I finished medical school I interned at the University of Chicago. And even then I remember, as an intern, with my white uniform, dashing out of the hospital because Paul Tillich was giving some lectures at the University of Chicago. Also during that year, Dr. Williams came, even though he'd had a stroke and was partially paralyzed. He came and read in the Rockefeller Chapel there, read his poems. It was a very poignant meeting for those of us who knew him, because it was hard for him to talk. Yet there was something in him that wanted to take that poetry of his and share it with others. When I finished up that year I came back to Boston. The question came up: what was I going to do with my medical training and internship? I guess by this time I realized I couldn't go into pediatrics, which was my major interest, because I wasn't tough enough. The kids would undo me. They'd start crying and I'd almost want to join up—cry. And that's not good. So Bill Williams suggested, "Why don't you try going into psychiatry, child psychiatry, and get to the kids that way." So I did. I took a residency at the Massachusetts General Hospital, at McLean Hospital, and then at Children's Hospital for a couple of years in child psychiatry. And by this time I had become so immersed in child psychiatry that I tended to stop reading a lot of the books in theology and even in literature that I'd been reading. But then I was drafted into the Air Force under the doctors' draft, and I went down to Mississippi where they put me in charge of an Air

Force neuropsychiatric unit. That was where my life really changed a second time, because the whole Civil Rights movement was getting going, and children were being marched into desegregated schools in New Orleans in the face of all the violence that was going on. I've described what happened to me in the first chapter of the first volume of *Children of Crisis*. This was kind of . . . This changed my life. I stayed there and got involved with these children, involved with the Civil Rights movement.

Interviewer: Were you particularly vulnerable then to getting involved in that conflict? You described in your book *Walker Percy: An American Search* that it was "a critical time" and you were "somewhat lost, confused, vulnerable, and it seemed, drifting badly."

Coles: I *was* drifting, I think. I guess I was trying to figure out how to combine this medical life that I had with my interests in literature and a kind of complicated religious background that I have. My mother comes from the Midwest, actually from Iowa. She is an Episcopalian. And my father comes from a Jewish and Catholic background, from England; they've lost their religion for a few hundred years. Some were Sephardic Jews who came from Spain, originally, and had been in England for several hundred years. Some were Catholic. He's an agnostic scientist.

Interviewer: So you had a religious and a scientific background.

Coles: Exactly.

Interviewer: Were you a religious child then?

Coles: Oh yes! My mother took us . . . We were brought up in Boston, my brother and I, with a good deal of religious, Christian, faith, I think it's fair to say. I struggle with that. At times I guess I'm an agnostic, and at times I'm very much connected to the Old *and* New Testaments. I love to read Jeremiah and Isaiah and Amos, and I love to read Mark and Luke and Matthew and John and St. Paul. The Bible means a lot to me, and theology means a lot to me. Williams, by the way, had no interest in religion. He was a wonderfully agnostic, exuberant, here-and-now person. And in a strange way that was a problem. Because I was drawn to T. S. Eliot's poetry, from college days on. And you know, Eliot and Williams had a rough time with one another.

Interviewer: *In the American Grain* by Williams is full of that.

Coles: Yeah, they really were antagonists. I couldn't figure out how it was that at the same time I was both an admirer of Eliot's and an admirer of Williams'. Once I talked to Williams about this. He said, "Well, you're not me. You can have this kind of distance. I'm in the middle of a fight, you're an observer." But you know, Williams was partly Jewish, too. And later I got involved with Erik Erikson, who is also partly Jewish. So this continuity in my life is strange, this involvement with people who have juggled religious issues. Erikson had been an artist before he went into psychoanalysis, and I think I identified with this struggle to go back and forth between the world of science—in his case psychoanalysis, in my case medicine—and the world of literature. And religion too, because of Erikson's involvement with Luther and Gandhi. *Moral* literature as well as novelistic literature.

Interviewer: So if you had it over again, would you have gone to medical school?

Coles: Definitely. It was a very important part of my life. I got to know patients as individuals, and I still remember many of them I treated as an intern. I went back and did a year of pediatrics just before I went into the Air Force, so I guess I managed to get that pediatric side of me well built up, as well as the psychiatric side. I think a doctor has a marvelous opportunity to get to know people in ways that perhaps no one else can.

Interviewer: Did your medical training make you a better writer?

Coles: Well in my particular case it did. My wife knew Flannery O'Connor when she was sick, in the hospital and very ill. She was in Georgia, and we were living in Georgia for several years, when I was working in the Civil Rights movement and with school desegregation in Atlanta. She had a long talk with her in the Emory Hospital. Obviously writers use their imaginations and don't need to have access to anyone, other than the richness of their own minds, which is more than enough for them. But because she had been involved with doctors in the struggle she waged against lupus, she said that she thought it would be a marvelous opportunity for a writer to be in these situations. And of course some writers have been doctors. One thinks of Chekhov and again Dr. Williams and Walker Percy. But clearly many writers have had no need for medical training to become the great writers that they've been. And obviously many doctors are not interested in writing. I think one thing that medical training offers, which is worthy of consideration by people with other interests, is that it's a really helpful antidote to social science. A person who has gone through the empirical training of medical school, and who understands the uniqueness of the individual which medical training reveals, does have an opportunity to do social science work in a way that I happen to think is very important, that is, with a respect for the humanities, for their concentration on individuality, their emphasis on irony and paradox and inconsistency and contrariness rather than the emphasis that social science training tends to place on theory and on abstraction and on trying to generalize almost at all costs. Sometimes the costs are very high.

Interviewer: Have you become more suspicious of abstraction and theory, of categorization into types and stages? It seemed to me, in going through your books, that there was a certain progression.

Coles: And you probably noticed a certain increasing animus against my own profession. Well, you're right. I started out as a psychiatrist, and I started getting psychoanalytic training in New Orleans at the New Orleans Psychoanalytic Training Center, which later became a full-fledged institute. I was . . . I think maybe I still am a smug, self-centered person. But if I am, I was even more so then. Boy, it's embarrassing when I stop to think of the psychiatric arrogance I was a victim of. It took me a few years to comprehend. This was what going into the homes of ordinary black and white people in the South tended to confront me with—my own narrowness and blindness and smugness and narcissism. Here I met people who were facing a tremendous social and historical crisis, and who were acquitting themselves with dignity, or showing the fear and anxiety of people who are threatened in ways that I had never been threatened. My whole way of thinking about them, with all the psychiatric terms and all the quickness to judge people indirectly through psychiatric categorizations—all of that was of little use in understanding the lives of these people. I had to begin to think of a way of looking at them that was different from that of psychiatry. Of course, what one realizes is that there are always George Eliot and Charles Dickens and Dostoevski—and all the writers who have helped one over the years to understand human beings—who are waiting in the wings to help you to get to know the people you're talking with in these homes. So I think I became somewhat disenchanted with my profession, and I think I began to lose interest in its way of thinking—and in its language, which is rather prolix and self-important.

Interviewer: Do you feel just that the *psychiatric* categorizations are useless, or that no system of thought can explain the various ways in which people, both children and adults, respond to crisis?

Coles: Flannery O'Connor put it beautifully. She said, "The task of the novelist is not to 'resolve' mystery but to deepen it!" The danger with social science, the danger for that matter with any kind of intellectual process, is that we take ourselves too seriously, and that we forget the difference between products of our own thinking and the world itself. We impose our notion of reality on the world and see only our notion of reality rather than the defiant complexity of the world—and of course the mystery of the world. Now, I'm caught in the middle, as you point out. On the one hand, I want to clarify and observe and point out and understand, and in a sense simplify in the nonpejorative sense of the word "simplify." But on the other hand, I'm constantly impressed with mystery, and maybe even feel that there are certain things that cannot be understood or clarified through generalizations, that resolve themselves into matters of individuality, and again, are part of the mystery of the world that one celebrates as a writer, rather than tries to solve and undo as a social scientist.

Interviewer: If you had it to do again, would you have not trained in psychiatry?

Coles: I think I would have gone into pediatrics and maybe family medicine, if I had it over again. I'd probably do primary care medicine is my hunch. At that time they didn't have it. And the kind of public health they had when I was a medical student was a matter of memorizing the charts of the life cycles of some species of worm in distant Africa, while at the same time there we were, just a few blocks from Harlem. And we never went there.

Interviewer: In reading *Still Hungry in America*, I was struck by the passages in which you talked about the diseases you'd seen—the malnutrition, skin ulcers, the parasitic infestations, the untreated serious kidney and heart diseases. Do you feel a special obligation since you're both a doctor and a writer? How can you leave those people after you've seen the very treatable conditions that are making their lives miserable?

Coles: That's a very important ethical point, and the only way I could answer that is to say that in the instances I have seen them I have done something. That's been a part of my work, to get them medical care. It's hard for me to write about that because it seems rather self-serving to say, "Look, I treated these people," which is what every doctor does. But the fact is that's what I have done. In every region of the country that I've worked, I've gotten involved with the existing medical situation. The kids and their families, I've come to know them over the period of a year or two, and pretty well. Visiting them I've come to know their medical problems, as well as trying to understand their feelings and their attitudes toward the world. And I have indeed gotten them connected to medical facilities when that's been necessary. Now the other side of one's contribution, at least one *hopes* it's a contribution, is that after all as a writer you can call attention to the larger issues that these people are struggling with. And in the case of hunger, my involvement in testimony before the United States Senate, and that very book which came as a result of that, was a part of the effort to get the Food Stamp program going, and to get this seen as a national problem rather than a series of individual cases.

Interviewer: So do you think your work has had a substantial effect?

Coles: Well I don't know. To tell you the truth I wish it had a *more* substantial effect. I've testified again and again before various congressional committees on migrant children, on the problem of hunger and malnutrition, on the problems of ghetto kids, on problems of school desegregation—a whole range of issues that have affected families and children. Sometimes I think some of that testimony has had some value, but at other times one despairs. But one tries. The problems of black lung disease among miners—I've testified again and again about that. And we have made some progress there. Black lung disease is now recognized as a medical entity that is connected to the occupational hazards of mining, and the miners who get black lung disease in recent years have been compensated for the disease. When I started this work in Appalachia, that wasn't the case, and I think part of the victory was due to medical and social testimony from people like me. And there've been a number of us who have offered that testimony—doctors and social observers who were involved with mountain families who had miners in the family, miners we got to know. Some of the legislation concerning migrant children drew upon the observations that some of us have made about how migrant children live and what their educational and medical problems are. I wish that migrant families were living much better than they are today. And as far as the occupational health legislation that affects black lung disease, and very importantly, *brown* lung disease among the textile workers of North and South Carolina, I wish that there were more and better laws. So on the one hand one works with these issues, but one is also pretty . . . at times discouraged. Certainly discouraged during the Nixon years, but even now, one wishes that this country could do more for the marginal social groups that are getting a pretty raw deal.

Interviewer: In *Irony in the Mind's Life*, you quote from George Eliot's *Middlemarch*: "Who can quit young lives after being long in company with them and not desire to know what befell them in their after-years?" I was wondering about the kids in the first volume of *Children of Crisis*—whether you'd ever be going back to them?

Coles: I have been. I go back once a year to the South and visit some of those families. I suppose I could call it follow-up work, but it's really just visits to people who were so wonderful to us, who taught us so much, and offered us so much hospitality. That's a beautiful quote from *Middlemarch*. We have done that, my wife and I. And some of those kids of course we've followed so long they are obviously no longer children but are themselves in their twenties or thirties and parents.

Interviewer: Have you written about it?

Coles: A bit in *Farewell to the South*, a collection of essays. There's a long introduction in which I offer some follow-ups. But you know, when you've travelled as much as I have, and lived in so many different parts of the United States—I've been in every American state, including Alaska obviously, and Hawaii, all fifty states, and worked in every region of the country, North, South, East and West—there comes a point when you can't follow up all the people you've met, unless you're in a state of constant manic ascension, with no sleep and moving around endlessly from airport to airport. But there always have been one or two families with whom we've been especially involved, and those are the families we've kept up with, just making a visit every year or so to

say hello. I'm haunted though by that question of George Eliot . . .
oh well, I'm haunted by George Eliot.

Interviewer: So you have seen changes when you've gone back to
visit the people you first wrote about?

Coles: Some changes. I see some changes, and Lord knows, having
been involved with SNCC and the whole Civil Rights movement,
I've seen wonderful changes with respect to segregation and school
desegregation, to the point that school desegregation by and large
is more a reality in the South than in my own hometown of
Boston, and if that isn't an irony, what is? I've seen a lot of social
and racial changes in the South, and I've seen some changes for
the better among the people in Appalachia, but there are also
things that haven't changed much. For instance, we lived in New
Mexico for several years, and I worked on the reservations of the
Southwest, and the problems of the Indian people are very severe
and *not* getting better. I worked in Alaska with Eskimo families,
and the problems that Eskimos face are now getting *worse* rather
than better, due to the pipeline, the refineries, the influx suddenly
of a combination welfare economy and a one-time glut of cash.
They've suddenly been yanked out of a subsistence economy in
which, nevertheless, they have a certain amount of dignity and
personal sense of themselves as hunters and fishermen—and now
what are they? So you see alcoholism, and you see a kind of pas-
sivity and dependence on the visit of the airplane once a week to
the village with pizzas. You go into the villages and you hear
Linda Ronstadt blaring forth on hi-fi and you see skimobiles and
kids drinking Cokes and eating pizzas and potato chips, and you
say, here's modern America in these Eskimo villages. And though
there are advantages to this, there are also severe moral and psychological losses. It's a real problem, how the Eskimos are coming
to terms with the sudden presence of technology and money and
so-called Lower Forty-Eight civilization. The risk is that one gets
condescending. The Eskimos themselves, some of them, will say,
"Hey, listen, this is what we want, just like you people have
wanted it." But there's a good deal of evidence that, in addition to
what they have gotten out of this, that is in the way of cash,
they've experienced a substantial loss in morale and in their own
self-respect. They weren't prepared for contemporary American

life as most of us were, because it crept up on us gradually over a generation or two. Our ancestors came here and were part of building up whatever this country is—and Eskimos suddenly had it thrown at them. So it's a mixed answer I'd have to give you.

Interviewer: In the past twenty or thirty years, medicine has become more institutionalized and technically oriented; and relatively little interest is placed in the kinds of social issues you're so involved in. And very little interest in what one might call the medical humanities. Do you as a result feel estranged from the medical profession?

Coles: I don't know, I don't know. You'd have to ask other doctors. One student here was interviewed for medical schools and mentioned that he'd taken a course with me—this in conjunction with his own interest in writing. He was told by the people on the admissions committee that they didn't think he ought to go to medical school if he wanted to be a writer, and that if I happened to have pulled this off that was fine, but they didn't want people announcing before they even get to medical school that they were interested in going to medical school because of an interest in writing and the help this would give them as writers. And I can understand that; I mean, there's such a need for doctors, and I think they felt this was a little frivolous. Also, I didn't go to medical school to get a medical education from which I would then draw upon as a writer. I went to medical school out of a real desire to become a doctor and live the doctor's life that I'd seen Dr. Williams living, and also that I'd seen an uncle of mine living, my mother's brother. And somehow, later in life, I connected these interests.

I've written articles for the *New England Journal of Medicine*, for the *Journal of the American Medical Association*, on writers—I've written on Flannery O'Connor and Dr. Williams for the *JAMA*, and I've even written about *Middlemarch* for the *New England Journal of Medicine*. And I've written for the *American Journal of Psychiatry* and for psychoanalytic journals—and I've done book reviews for many of them. So somehow, again, it's a tightrope. I've balanced this life in some way. I love . . . I still read the *New England Journal of Medicine* and I read the medical articles in it, not just the social comment. And I do think of myself as a physician, very much so. One reviewer said I'm a writing doctor. And that was very well put. If I had more ability, I'd write novels like Walker Percy or I'd write poetry such as Dr. Williams did—but I don't have that ability, I just don't have the ability to do that. So I . . . if you don't have the ability you don't have the ability.

Interviewer: Haven't you published a book of poetry?

Coles: I have written poetry, and I've listened to children and pulled their words together in a form that I guess one would consider a kind of poetry. It's not the best kind, but . . . but I have written poetry and some of it has been published, and there is the book of poems drawing on the work with children.

Interviewer: Are you teaching now?

Coles: Yes. I teach a course in the medical humanities at Harvard Medical School, and I teach undergraduates two things. I teach an undergraduate course called "Moral and Social Inquiry." We start with James Agee's *Let Us Now Praise Famous Men*. We read George Orwell's *The Road to Wigan Pier*. We go on to read Flannery O'Connor and Walker Percy, Ralph Ellison, Tillie Olsen, Dorothy Day's autobiography called *The Long Loneliness*, about the Catholic Worker movement. And we end up with *Jude the Obscure* of Thomas Hardy, and *Middlemarch* of George Eliot. So it's a mixture of novels and social documentary writing and autobiography and moral essays. And we see some movies that connect with the reading we've done. We read *The Diary of a Country Priest* by Bernanos, and we see the movie that Bresson did. And then last fall I taught a seminar called "Religion and Twentieth-Century Intellectuals." So I teach on both sides. And at the Medical School what we read is William Carlos Williams' doctor stories, *Life along the Passaic River*, Walker Percy's novels *The Moviegoer* and *The Last Gentleman* and *Love in the Ruins*— all of which have a doctor in them. The first one is a future medical student, and in both *The Last Gentleman* and *Love in the Ruins* a physician is a central part of the narrative. We read *Middlemarch*, which has Dr. Lydgate, and we read *Arrowsmith*, the old favorite, that unfortunately is read by too many medical students when they've been in high school or college. Anyway, we use novels to approach medical issues.

Interviewer: Do you read different kinds of doctors' writing—Céline or William Burroughs?

Coles: Céline is especially important, and I haven't used him yet, but I'm going to next year. I think he's a very interesting physician—that's for sure. Obviously it would be hard for some medical students, as he has been hard for a lot of readers, to take. But I don't regard Céline's fascism as the central issue in his life. I think the issue in his life is that of his disgust for the hypocrisy of the world, a world that he saw from the point of view of a doctor as well as a political person. He's an interesting writer, a very gifted writer. He would be a valuable addition to that course, you're absolutely right.

Interviewer: And Burroughs?

Coles: Burroughs I have trouble with. The trouble I have with him is that while politically I'm fairly liberal—quite liberal, I guess—culturally I'm more conservative. I used to have discussions with Williams about this. I guess I can go as far as Williams, not too much further. There's obviously a stodgy part of me culturally. I tend to want to assign nineteenth-century writers like George Eliot and Dickens and Hardy to my students—because I think they were wonderful moral observers. Someday I would love to teach a course, maybe at a law school, on Dickens and the law, because the various kinds of lawyers that he portrayed and the way he looked at a profession are, I think, still of great interest today. The moral insights he offers us about professional life are very shrewd. You go from *Bleak House* to *Great Expectations* to the lawyer in *Tale of Two Cities*. And of course, George Eliot, with Dr. Lydgate—you can teach a whole course around *Middlemarch* to medical students or undergraduates. The issue of what makes for the moral decisions of professional life, centered around Lydgate and what happens to him . . .

Interviewer: Have you become more interested in moral issues in recent years?

Coles: No question. I am increasingly interested in moral issues, and the ways that writers, that is novelists and poets, have come to terms with these moral issues. And I'm interested in what these people have to say to people like me, doctors and psychiatrists and intellectuals, though I don't like that last word—to people who are psychologically trained.

Interviewer: You say in the introduction to the first volume of *Children of Crisis* that "there seems no end to crisis in this world." Is that the case?

Coles: (Laughs.) Or whether I've manufactured crises in order to . . .
to justify my writing . . .

Interviewer: Let me rephrase that. How many volumes of *Children
of Crisis* will there be?

Coles: Well, there have been five dealing with twenty years of work
in America. It is important to point out—I want to make an edi-
torial point here, maybe a self-justifying point—I didn't publish
my first book until 1967. And the work started in 1959. So for
eight years there were no books. I think if you were to talk with my
editor, Peter Davison, who is editor at the Atlantic Monthly Press,
he'd tell you that he really had a devil of a time getting me to write
that first book. Hard to believe it may be right now, but I was very
reluctant about writing at first, because I was so overwhelmed by
the complexity of what I'd seen, and the enormous difficulty I had
in doing justice to that complexity as a writer. Now maybe I was
overly ambitious in wanting to do justice to that complexity. I suppose I could have carved out some area of it and written psychiatric articles about that area. But I had and still have, over my
shoulder, the shadow of someone like George Eliot. Now I'll
never be able to do justice to that complexity, the way she did in
Middlemarch. But by golly, those are the models. She and Tolstoy
and Dostoevski and Henry James, and one at least remembers
them as writers. Finally I did write those portraits, and the first
volume went to press. Since then I've done those other volumes,
dealing with the various parts of the country where I've worked.
I've been working recently in Northern Ireland, where I think any
observer would feel there's "crisis" going on in the children's lives.
And I've been working in South Africa, also critically caught up
in a racial struggle. And I must say, though I've just turned fifty
and feel myself entitled to stop this fieldwork, I can't do it. I love
going into a new part of the world and getting to know children,
getting to know their parents and their teachers, and just *seeing*
that world, the way maybe Orwell did when he used to do the
kind of travelling he finally wrote up in *Down and Out in London
and Paris* or in the *Wigan Pier* book. I can't write, again, as well
as he; I don't have the gift for narrative presentation that he had.
But I do just love to look at the world and try to do justice to some
of its rhythms, especially through the eyes of its children. The
other thing I would mention is the considerable interest I have in
the art of children and in interpreting that art, which goes back to

my mother's interest in art. My brother is very much interested in art and teaches courses at the University of Michigan that connect literature and art. I think that if I've done nothing else in those volumes of *Children of Crisis* and in my other writing about children, I've tried to point out what children's drawings and paintings can teach us about their moral and psychological perceptions. This has been an interest now for over two decades. I've interpreted drawings and connected them to the lives of various children, whether they be black or white or Appalachian or Eskimo or Indian or Chicano children. I think some of that writing has been valuable both for my profession and for other interested persons. And I'd like to continue doing that in connection with children abroad, in Ireland and South Africa, because I think it teaches us something about the relationship between a political or historical crisis and the ways that children grow up; more abstractly, call it child development or human development.

Interviewer: We've talked about your mistrust of psychiatric categories and language. Yet with the children's drawings you do make interpretations; you do make generalizations in a psychiatric framework.

Coles: But you'll also notice that I'm always taking one step forward and at least a half a step backward, or at least sideways, by making the observations and trying to put them in other contexts, and maybe even qualifying them or maybe even pointing out that they apply to these children but might not apply to other children—and that in any case they may be overwrought. And that my own writings may be guilty—probably are guilty—of the various sins that I criticize in other writings. And I use the word sin because I think the issue is moral. How presumptuous is the observer becoming? How godlike does he feel himself to be? And the best people in my profession—people like Erik Erikson and Allen Wheelis, who are my two heroes, of sorts, within psychoanalysis—they pointed out again and again the limitations of this work, and the need we have for understanding the dangers we get into in connection with our own arrogance, and in connection with gullible or hurt people who want to elevate us into positions we have no right to be put in, or to allow ourselves to be put in. Allen Wheelis points this out in a marvelous essay, "On the Vocational Hazards of Psychoanalysis," which is part of his really fine book called *The Quest for Identity.* He points out that we are put in a godlike position and become intoxicated with our own self-importance.

Interviewer: After your work with children in South Africa and Northern Ireland is done, what next? Are you working on other biographies or criticism?

Coles: The work in Ireland and South Africa and one or two other countries will take a number of years. I have a book on Flannery O'Connor coming out this spring. And I'm working, in a more intellectual vein, on the life of Simone Weil. She's a source of great interest to me as a moral philosopher, and her life as well as her writing can offer a lot for us to think about. There are certain people whose moral and intellectual example has meant a lot to me. I suppose I'm hoping that I'm given the life to do it, and in one way or another I'll come to terms with their lives. Not necessarily with long biographies, because I'm not really very interested in doing that. But in either intellectual biographies or essays or whatever, Erikson was one, I've done a book on him. I wrote a long paper on Anna Freud because she's meant a lot to me, her work with children. I've written a book in conjunction with a photographer about the Catholic Worker movement and especially Dorothy Day. I've written some about James Agee, and I think I'll probably end up writing some more about him. Same goes for Orwell. Dr. Percy, I've written a book about him, and a book about Dr. Williams. And Georges Bernanos, the French Catholic novelist, has meant a lot to me. *The Diary of a Country Priest* is one of my favorite novels, and I'd be surprised if in some way I don't come to terms with that. And that just about exhausts the list. (Laughs.) And probably will exhaust my life.

Interviewer: What do all these people who are your heroes have in common?

Coles: What they have in common, I guess, is that they've struggled with moral and religious issues. They have had their literary sides, too—more than sides in some cases. And more than that, there is the issue of service. Orwell struggled with this in a certain way, and Agee, and hence the anguish in *Let Us Now Praise Famous Men,* the issue of how much do you exploit as a writer, and what do you offer in return to the people you're writing about? This comes up if, as a writer, you are dealing with external reality, if

your writing is not made up only of the internal, or fictional, subjective experiences which you mold into characters and narration.
And since I've been so involved with the world outside of me, this
issue comes up: what does one owe the world? You brought this
up very appropriately in connection with the hunger issue in the
late 1960s. The hope is, if you're caught up in the Civil Rights
movement or in the struggle migrants are waging for both personal dignity and a larger share of the economic world that they
manage to hold up through their labor, that the writing and the
testimony and some of the medical work at least pay back some of
the debts that you've rung up from going place to place and asking
people to tell you things which you then write up and tell to
the world at large. It's a haunting question, though: what does
one owe?

Interview by David Hellerstein, *North American Review,*
June 1980

Medicine and the Humanities

*I*n previous centuries, the humanities were concerned with grammar and rhetoric, with the classics, with moral and philosophical inquiry through the essay, casual or systematic, or through the writer's imagination: the novel, the short story, the drama. Such "polite learning," as the humanities were once described, all too readily became connected to notions of class, privilege, and social position. In *Jude the Obscure*, Thomas Hardy dared broach such matters with a late-nineteenth-century Victorian audience. His central character, a sensitive, intelligent, idealistic member of the working class, watches all too closely the privileged students of a university community, which is thinly disguised but apparent to everyone as an Oxford, a Cambridge. The earnest affection for the humanities felt by the relatively uneducated artisan is made to contrast with the smug self-importance, the arid pietism, the callous arrogance of a community of much-honored scholars— whom Hardy knew to be as vulnerable to meanness of spirit and even, ironically, downright prejudicial ignorance as any other group of successful mortals. Of course, Matthew Arnold had already stirred things up among nineteenth-century England's custodians of high culture with a sweeping insistence that the literary sensibility, the informed intelligence of novelists, poets, and critics, be brought to bear on vexing contemporary issues—rather than be held in all too lofty and disdainful reserve as the property of a self-selected few.

Yet those writers were not everywhere heeded; nor were Dickens and George Eliot in England, Balzac and Zola in France—all proponents of a vigorous examination, through the novel, of the nineteenth century's social problems. In our time, the kind of social and psychological analysis Matthew Arnold urged upon his Oxford colleagues (to their considerable protest), the kind done so literately and circumspectly during the 1840s in America by Alexis de Tocqueville, has become the property of the social sciences. As for the natural sciences, they have become an adversary culture, of sorts, to the hu-

77

manities—a characterization C. P. Snow chose for dramatic emphasis but not without appropriate recourse to the way many of us tend to think: the hard facts, as against the mushy, anecdotal, impressionistic forays of "art." As for the sociologists and psychologists, no one is going to find most of them anywhere but in the camp of explicit, insistent "science"—arguably, as in the expression "more Catholic than the Pope," making up for any still-pressing element of professional uncertainty or confusion with nervous avowals of faith.

Of course, C. P. Snow knew how sad and wrong-headed the split between the "two cultures" has ended up being for all of us. There is no inherent conflict between a chemist or physicist at work in a laboratory and a novelist busy constructing a plot and a number of characters. A biologist may go full speed ahead, developing ideas and doing experiments without in any way casting doubt upon the worth of an artist, a sculptor, or a scholar anxious to figure out poetic imagery or the nature of the connections that bind a particular school of painters. The issue is not the antagonisms generated by different intellectual initiatives; the issue is, at heart, religious and philosophical—the ideological uses to which various disciplines have been put. In the nineteenth century, as science was growing in leaps and bounds, the German philosopher Hegel decided to become a "scientific" philosopher; he would banish mystery, ambiguity, and uncertainty, replacing them with the precise formulations that men who worked in laboratories felt able to offer. The Danish theologian (and wonderfully astute psychologist) Soren Kierkegaard read Hegel's treatises carefully, appreciated their unquestionable ambitiousness, and acknowledged that they explained virtually everything (how history itself had worked, was working, would until the end of time work) except for one small matter: what it means to be a particular human being, living in the world and aware of oneself, one's situation, one's unavoidable future—death.

It is possible, the cranky hunchback from Copenhagen was insisting, to know an enormous amount, to do research and more research, and yet miss the essential point of things. One need not, for example, in any way take issue with the honorable efforts of behavioral psychologists to connect human actions to the conditioned responses of rats who have learned to negotiate their way through various mazes. But when one hears those same "hard" social scientists referring to our "superstitious" anthropomorphic tendencies—

the inclination some of us have to attribute human characteristics to the natural world—one is tempted to remind these colleagues of an inclination of their own, perhaps best described as "ratomorphic": a tendency to attribute without necessary qualification to one kind of life on this planet—humankind—the qualities of the rat.

We all have our reflexes, but it is men and women who use language, know what their fate is, and struggle with the pleasures and disappointments of awareness. One says that not in self-congratulation but in order to point out one of the hazards of a kind of quantitative or experimental work: an overall context is lost sight of; a rather obvious qualitative distinction is too strenuously minimized. My own field, psychiatry, has had its problems in that regard. I draw from a distinguished psychoanalyst, Leslie Farber: "For while the creatures described [in psychiatry] may bear some resemblance to animals, or to steam engines or robots or electronic brains, they do not sound like people. They are in fact constructs of theory, more humanoid than human; and whether they are based on the libido theory or on one of the new interpersonal theories of relationship, it is just those qualities most distinctively human which seem to have been omitted. It is a matter of some irony, if one turns from psychology to one of Dostoevski's novels, to find that no matter how wretched, how puerile, or how dilapidated his characters may be, they all possess more humanity than the ideal man who lives on the pages of psychiatry."[1]

Does medicine have all that much to learn from such a way of looking at people—the psychological reductionism, so banal and pompous, that Dr. Farber is at such pains to deplore because he knows how influential it has been in this century? More broadly, has medicine become involved in the cultural crisis C. P. Snow referred to a while back—yet another ally of "science" in the increasingly explicit contest for mastery of a century's mind? One historian of medicine, Stanley Reiser, who teaches at this medical school, has recently sounded an important warning:[2] all too many of us physicians have confused science with technology and, so doing, have indeed become caught up in a polemical, and at times farcical, position. We shower our patients with tests, run them through a gauntlet

1. Leslie Farber, "Martin Buber and Psychiatry," *Psychiatry* 19 (1957): 110.
2. Stanley Reiser, *Medicine and the Reign of Technology* (New York: Cambridge University Press, 1978).

of machines, talk to them less and less, and ask them fewer and fewer questions about how they as individual men, women, and children are getting on with their lives. We are "scientists," so it is insistently said, and our aim is to go after patients with instruments, gadgets, and procedures in pursuit of "findings," the more the better.

Who in his right mind would want to ridicule those modern modes of medical inquiry in and of themselves? As one who lived and worked in the South for years, I know the risks of nostalgia—the foolishness, the outright mischief it can come to. The agrarian tradition, in the hands of many, became a clever apologia for the good old days of segregation, extreme poverty, and rampant, murderous racism. On the other hand, writers such as Robert Penn Warren and Ralph Ellison have known that both black and white people lost a lot when they came North and exchanged one flawed way of life for another in its own ways seriously deficient. Similarly, the point is not that medical technology is, in itself, anything but valuable. Rather, one wonders, as Dr. Reiser does in his book, whether today's doctors haven't been first captivated and then captured by that technology; it becomes *the answer,* a central, controlling preoccupation. Meanwhile, we rely less and less on our eyes, our ears, our ability to have a reasonable and revealing conversation with our patients— one in which they tell us about their complaints, the story of their aches and pains, and thereby let us know a good deal about themselves: human beings who have come seeking help from doctors, who are presumably fellow human beings rather than conduits for laboratory centrifuges, X-ray machines, computers, and yes, the overwrought theoretical classifications of psychopathology.

In 1964, while working in the Mississippi Project, an effort of American youth, black and white, to challenge once and for all the heartland of segregationist power, I came across an extraordinary young black man who had just finished the eleventh grade at a consolidated high school that served his community of Midnight, Mississippi, a sleepy Delta hamlet that for generations had been part of the South's sharecropper-based cotton economy and recently has been suffering the pain generated by a rapidly collapsing rural life. Machines have replaced people, who have the alternative of staying put and living a wretched life of extreme poverty or trekking North to increasingly inhospitable and dreary ghettos. This black youth had caught the attention of several black teachers in the all-black school he attended, and after a talk with him I could easily see why. He was a wonderfully thoughtful person, open to speculation, honest as could be, deeply religious but with no accompanying, cloying sentimentality. He hadn't received the best education, of course, but he also hadn't learned to be glib, jaded, all too sure of himself—or conventional in his way of responding to the world. He had none of the liberal agnosticism so many of us wear proudly, if discreetly, on our sleeves. He was a hard-praying Baptist, yet he could read J. D. Salinger's *Catcher in the Rye* with exquisite respect and comprehension; and even if he misspelled a lot of words in his themes, they were full of what Tolstoy or Dostoevski, without the least condescension, knew to appreciate as "uncorrupted peasant wisdom," the latter's polemical phrase meant to be a slap at the arrogance of Russia's nineteenth-century intelligentsia, and maybe at all of us who become overly impressed with ourselves as intellectuals.

A number of teachers knew that the black youth deserved better, in the way of higher education, than he would get at the time in his home state, and no doubt in the entire South. They wanted him in the North, in a "good school." He wanted to be a physician, they kept telling me, and after a number of weeks their student confirmed that impression of theirs: "I've wanted to be a doctor for a long time, but I fear to mention it. Christ healed the sick; he worried about 'the lame, the halt, the blind,' and he tried to do something good for them. He worried about the poor. He worried about the 'rebuked and the scorned'—the folks all the uppity ones looked down on. You mustn't *decide* to be a doctor. It's a *calling,* our minister says. If you're hoping to walk down Christ's path and be a healer to your neighbors, then you've got to have his blessings. So, no sir, I can't say I *want* to be a doctor, or I'm *going* to be a doctor; I can only say that in my prayers to God Almighty I tell him that I'd like his blessings, and then I might try to be one."

At the same time this humble person could be assertively knowing; he thought that "the trouble with Holden Caulfield is this: he has everything but he doesn't know what the purpose of his life is, so he doesn't have everything, after all." As for Walker Percy's *The Moviegoer,* which I had strongly recommended, the young reader was not in the least daunted by the barriers of class and race that separated him from the novel's main character, Binx Bolling: "That guy in the story is trying to find out how you should live your life—

how *he* should live *his* life. He knows a lot. He's figured out that you can be real smart, but that's just the beginning. He's figured out that you can be on top but feel real low, because you're looking around and you're seeing how bad things are, instead of fooling yourself by painting a pretty picture of the world. A lot of people, they spend half their lives trying to kid themselves, and the other half they're sick, because they're in pain, their soul is, and they don't know how to cure themselves of the trouble. They've gotten themselves an illness, but they don't know it, and they don't know who to go see—for a diagnosis and some treatment."

Not a bad analysis of a notable American existentialist novel. In the youth's senior year, we all set to work on our errand, liberating from the Delta a bright and studious black person, the son of grievously poor tenant farmers who had precious little schooling to their name (we had not yet, in the middle 1960s, come upon all those fancy, self-important phrases—"culturally deprived," or "culturally disadvantaged"). For my part, I wrote to the then president of Amherst, a physician who had taught me medicine, and he was anxious to help. Eventually, this young, black Southerner came to Cambridge, Massachusetts, where he tried hard for four years to learn—to find a direction for his life. He told his freshman adviser of his *hope*, medicine—not his "goal," and not his "plans" for his "future career." The adviser wasn't quite able to comprehend the young man's tentativeness; one either wants to be a doctor, or one has doubts, or one doesn't have in mind medicine as an occupation. As for the "waiting" the student mentioned, the "waiting for God's judgment" on the matter—it has for a long time been the function of universities such as Harvard to replace naiveté and superstition with "enlightenment." Time, and four courses a semester, would work miracles (of a decidedly unreligious kind) on the student's way of thinking about himself and his possibilities—or so it was thought.

And so it seemed to happen. In his sophomore year the student, as a matter of course, and with no mental scrupulosity or religious anguish, became a "premed." He took biology and inorganic chemistry. He was, though, still a reader of novels, short stories and poems; so he chose to become an English major, and as such did not forget to heed Ralph Ellison's advice (and warning) that blacks ought to hold on, for dear life, to their regional roots. He studied Flannery O'Connor's short stories, Faulkner's novels, Eudora Welty's tales,

Walker Percy's fictional exercises in soul-searching, and Reynolds Price's efforts to harness the genre of family romance to the requirements of plot and character portrayal. By the time junior year came around, the student was heavily involved in organic chemistry and physics, while at the same time taking English and history courses.

He seemed on top of everything, an example of a broadly educated student on his way, soon enough, to being accepted at a first-rate medical school. But something happened in the middle of that fateful year, and I had best let the young man himself do the remembering: "I was doing fine, I guess, until one day in the lab, the organic chem lab, I saw a kid take out something from a bag, and wink to his partner at the next bench; and then seeing me looking at them, they turned their backs on me. Suddenly I woke up from a long sleep. This wasn't the first time I'd seen kids cheating, but I guess I hadn't wanted to notice, not *really* notice. Now I remembered other things—slips of paper I saw kids sneak in and use on the tests, and the yields made bigger with sugar or salt, or other stuff. I used to think the things I heard were funny; I used to think that no one *really* cheated on those tests or in the lab. But I had conned myself and I know the reason now; I didn't know what to think, what to do. Once I saw some bad cheating on a chem hour exam, and I was going to report the kid, but I couldn't bring myself to do it.

"After I saw the lab cheating, I went to see the minister in the church I attended, and talked to him. He said you can't always be your brother's keeper, you have to try to be good yourself, and leave the rest up to God. I told him it was fine to say that, but what if a lot of cheaters became doctors later on? He said that maybe I was exaggerating what was happening in school. I said that, to tell the truth, I was doing just the opposite. And besides, there were plenty of kids who were killing each other for grades. You can't get them to tell you anything, to share anything, to help you in lab. All they say is that it's dog-eat-dog, and we're all enemies, fighting for our place on the curve. Then you go back to the Houses, and you hear these people planning, all day long they're planning: what to do for 'activities,' and what kind of voluntary work to sign up for, so it'll look good on their records. It's 'murder,' that's what they all say, and that's what I began to realize—that I was becoming a lousy, mean, selfish 'murderer,' like the rest of them. And I didn't want that to happen."

In his senior year this young man was in anguish. He had obtained good marks in all subjects, including the sciences, mostly B's and some A's. Yet, he did not like the premed students he had spent so much time with, and he began to have second thoughts about a career in medicine. He told his adviser of his misgivings and was encouraged to think of other occupational choices. Still unsettled and increasingly apprehensive in the late autumn of that year, and now a member of this century's American intelligentsia, he sought psychiatric "help." After three "sessions," he had even more to worry over: "The doctor said I am afraid of competition. He said I'm letting other people—what they do, and how they act—determine my behavior. He kept on asking me how I get along with my brothers and my sisters. I told him fine, but I don't think he believed me. The more I told him about the premed people, the more he told me the 'problem' was mine. Then I got angry and asked him what he thought of people who bragged about cutting each other's throats. He said that was '*their* problem,' and we should look at '*my* problem.' He's just like the minister up here.

"No minister back home would talk like that. No one in my family would, either. Up here, the ministers (a lot of them) don't really believe in God, not like they do where I grew up. Up here the ministers try to talk like psychiatrists, and the psychiatrists talk to you like some of the ministers do back home—as if they have a direct line to Heaven! I guess I'll do without any of their 'help.' I guess I'll try to get a job teaching. I may go to the graduate school of education. I'd like to be able to go back to Mississippi and get a job in a school, somewhere near home, helping people—introduce good books to kids and get their minds going. The only thing that bothers me is this: some of the kids will end up in my boots—up here, wondering what's right to do, and what's wrong, and being told they're 'depressed' because they shouldn't wonder, shouldn't ask questions; they should just go ahead and get ahead, and if people get pushed to the left and to the right or in back, then that's *their* problem!"

He graduated *magna cum laude* in English, went on to get a master's degree in education, did indeed go back to Mississippi, to a job as a high school teacher in the town of Greenville. He still wonders whether he made a mistake, whether he ought to have gone to medical school. Sometimes, with undue bitterness perhaps, he turns on those of his classmates who did pursue his original dream and are now young physicians. At other times, he is more self-critical, more resigned, more humble, and, I think, more challenging: "I wasn't made to be a doctor. I wasn't determined enough, tough enough. There are so many people who really want to go to medical school. They've dreamed all their lives of going. They'd do anything to go. The medical schools haven't got any time to waste on people like me. I'm too shy; I get absorbed in a novel I'm reading, and it becomes my life for a while. If I can help some of the black kids I teach, through these novels, to think about what life is all about, and what's important, and what's not important, then I'll be glad. Doctors are too busy to worry about life the way a good novelist does. But I'll never forget *Middlemarch*—the doctor in it, Lydgate. I think of him a lot when I think of my years in college."

A young teacher, highly ethical and reflective, a decent and compassionate man, makes mention of George Eliot's great nineteenth-century novel, and in it, the doctor who as a young practitioner wanted to help change a sadly ignorant and corrupt profession. The idealistic doctor who comes to naught, to ruin, is hardly a stranger to literature. F. Scott Fitzgerald, in *Tender Is the Night*, has shown a twentieth-century audience what George Eliot offered the Victorians—a portrait of hopes and dreams badly undercut by the flaws of character that all too promising individuals manage to conceal from themselves, never mind others. Perhaps the young black man had seen not only his own severe limitations but a few warts, and more, in those of his classmates who were not afflicted with his fateful inclination toward a loss of nerve. In any event, we need not be haunted only by his example. Lord knows, there are others who stayed the course, who are right in this profession of ours, and who also wonder quite earnestly what is happening to it, given the fierce competition, the sometimes sleazy manipulations that are connected to undergraduate premed life and later to admissions procedures; given the unqualified emphasis, in some quarters, on grades or scores; given the obsession many of us have for technological procedures, tests, and routines; given the continuing coziness, in at least some parts of this country, between physicians and the quite well-to-do, whereas the poor, the socially or economically or culturally marginal, must often make do without us.

I recommend strongly the recent advice of one of this nation's wisest and most literate physicians, Lewis Thomas. In the *New En-*

gland Journal of Medicine of May 25, 1978, he strenuously criticizes the premedical curricula, as all too often given sanction by our medical schools. He is not calling, in remediation, for the nervously bloated, pseudoscientific language one finds in too many psychological, sociological and psychiatric conferences—the blah-blah that is part of the problem rather than an answer to it. He makes clear that he is calling for a recognition of the importance the humanities have for us—not as pieties to be conveniently summoned, then easily shoved aside, and not as a bit of slick polish to be worn with self-congratulation, but as a terribly important part of our lives when we are college students, medical students, and well beyond, too.

Perhaps the time has come for a careful look at the relationship of the humanities to undergraduate premedical training, medical school curricula, and our postgraduate education. I remember two of my favorite medical school teachers, Robert F. Loeb and Yale Kneeland, Jr., referring to the novels of Dostoevski, which they as busy, full-fledged professors were reading in a "study group." One day, as a matter of fact, Dr. Loeb reprimanded us for knowing a given patient's lab scores better than the details of her life: "You don't have to *be* a Dostoevski, but you ought to read him, because he had an eye and an ear for people, and that's what you'll need as much as knowledge of what the normal values are in the blood tests you're ordering."

No one would fault that great Russian novelist the "eye and ear" mentioned, but he had something else, as did George Eliot, as does an important, contemporary American novelist who also happens to be a physician, Walker Percy: an abiding interest in human complexity and a determination not to see it "resolved" (that cool, slippery word of our time) by any scheme of classification, by any inventory of traits or symptoms. What these storytellers have wanted to examine is the nature of human *character*, an old-fashioned word badly in need of revival—in our national life, and in connection with medical school admissions, medical school education. Character is not to be confused with "personality" or "mental health," or with an "attitude" or two. Psychiatrists talk a lot about "character disorders," but what do they tell us about character? The young black mentioned earlier would be the last one to push himself upon us with applause, but in fact he did have "character," a good deal of it—maybe too much for his own good, things being as they are.

Character is connected to a philosophical search—a person's struggle to understand what is right, what matters, what in eternity's scheme of things is worth pursuing in the second or two, relatively speaking, we have on this earth. We each engage in that pursuit in our own way. If there is one central conviction of the humanities, it is that of human variousness, individuality. As physicians we also know, or ought to know, that each person is different, each patient reacts in his or her special way to any illness, indeed to life itself. A sense of the complexity of human affairs, a respect for human particularity, an interest in the ethical, the just and unjust sides of the social order, an awareness of life's unremitting contingencies, an awe of the mystery that clings to us "world without end"—these are the stuff of the humanities at their best, and ought to be, too, of the doctor's education, the doctor's everyday, practicing life. The knowledge that one gets in college and in medical school may no doubt have its uses—but it is, finally, worth little if not part of a morally sensitive and reflecting tradition, one to which each generation of physicians has to add its particular contribution.

Graduation address to the Harvard Medical School Class of 1978,
Harvard Medical Alumni Bulletin, July/August 1978

Medical Ethics and
Living a Life

Ablack woman in Mississippi's Delta told me this in 1969, as I went from home to home with other doctors trying to understand how it went for extremely poor and hard-pressed people:

We don't have it good here. It's no good at all. I turn and ask the Lord, a lot of times, why it's so—the unfairness in this world. But I'll never get an answer. My daddy told me: "Don't expect answers to the really big questions—not from anyone. We're put here, and we don't know why, and we try to figure out why while we're here, and we fight to stay around as long as we can, and the next thing we know, it's slipping away from us, and we're wondering where we're going, if we're going any place." If I was a doctor, I guess I'd wonder every day what it's all about, this life. A lot of times my children ask me these questions, ask me why people behave so bad toward other people, and why there's so much greed in the world, and when will God get angry and stop all the people who don't care about anything but themselves. I have to say I don't have the answers. Does anyone? If you go to college, my oldest girl said, you learn the answers. She's twelve. She thinks that the more education you get, the more you know about how to be good and live a good life. But I'll tell you, I'm not so sure. I think you can have a lot of diplomas to your credit and not be the best person in the world. You can be a fool, actually, and have a lot of people calling you professor, lawyer, even doctor.

That "even"—a measure of hesitation, of lingering awe, of qualified respect. She had experienced her "rough times" with doctors—not only segregated facilities but poor care and more insults than she cared to remember. A self-described "uppity nigger," she had finally spoken up to a doctor, had an argument with him. She remembered the critical essence of their confrontation this way:

I heard him saying bad, bad words about my people on the phone, and then he came into the waiting room and he gave me the nod. He never is polite to us, the way he can be with his white patients, and the more money they have, the bigger the smile they get out of him, and he's as eager to please as he can be. But with us, it's different; we get one sour look after the other. That day he told me to "shake a leg." I guess I wasn't walking into his office fast enough. Then he started talking about all "the welfare people," and saying, "Why didn't they go get themselves work?" Then, as he poked my belly, he gave me a lecture on eating and my diabetes—how I should "shape up and eat better."

That's when I forgot myself. I told him he should look to himself sometimes and stop making cracks at others. I told him he wasn't being much of a credit to his people and his profession, the way he was making these wisecracks about us poor folks. I told him he should know better, that there wasn't the jobs, and only now are we getting the right to vote, and the schools we've had weren't like the ones he could go to. I told him I expected more of him. Isn't he a doctor? If he can lord it over people, being a doctor, then he ought to remember how our Lord, Jesus Christ, behaved. He was the Son of God, but did he go around showing how big and important he was, and calling people bad names, and making wisecracks, and sidling up to the rich and looking down his nose at the poor? Jesus was a doctor; he healed the sick, and he tended after the lame, the halt and the blind, like our minister says. I told our doctor he ought to read the Bible more. I told him that instead of saying bad things about the poor people and us colored people, he should take a hard look at himself and see if he's living the best life he can—the kind of life a doctor should live—if he's going to preach to the rest of us, and be looked up to as if he's the best of the best.

She didn't get very far with such words, although, to his credit, the doctor not only heard her out but smiled and thanked her for the obvious courage (in the year 1967) that she had displayed. And it may be all too easy now, as it has surely been in past years, to call upon such an incident, the South being once again a convenient scapegoat for the rest of us. In fact, there aren't too many places in America, one suspects, where such a candid encounter could take place. How many of us in medicine have been asked by anyone— patient, friend, relative, student, or colleague—to connect our professional position with the kind of life we live, the way we get on with those we attend in an office, clinic, or ward? That woman, who today would be categorized as "culturally deprived" or "culturally disadvantaged" (the dreary banality of such language!), had managed to put her finger on an important issue, indeed—one that philosophers, theologians, and novelists have struggled for a long time to comprehend: How does one live a decent and honorable life, and is it right to separate, in that regard, a person's private life from his or her working life?

In a sense, too, that woman was struggling with the issue of medical ethics: How broad and deep ought such a subject cut—to the bone of the doctor's life? Without question, we need to examine the ethical matters that press on us every day in the course of our work. Recently, such matters have gained increasing attention and have been worked into the curricula of our medical schools. The traditions and resources of analytic philosophy have been extremely helpful, as we wonder when life ends or contemplate priorities so far as scarce (or experimental) technology and medicine go. It is utterly necessary for us to confront our values (or lack of them) as, for example, we work with patients too young or too old or too sick to be able to speak for themselves. And the dying patient has, of course, by and large benefited from the recent attention given that final stretch of earthly time, though one hastens to wonder whether a certain kind of psychological self-consciousness has not had its own dangers: all those "stages" and the prescriptive arrogance that can accompany "reform." Aren't there some people who have a right to "denial," not to mention to a belief in the Good News? When does psychological analysis become a kind of normative judgment, if not smug self-righteousness? Sometimes, as I read the literature on "death and dying," I get the feeling that agnostic psychological moralists have the complete run of the field, with all too many ministers worrying all too much about something called "pastoral counseling," when a few old-fashioned prayers might be in order for the sake of the patient, the attending clergyman, and the rest of us as well.

Be that as it may, the woman just quoted from the outer precincts of Clarksdale, Mississippi, was aware in her own way that there have been, all along, two philosophical traditions—the analytic and the existential. The former allows us to ponder a host of variables and to make a specific (for the doctor, a medical) decision. But the latter tradition urges us to go along with Kierkegaard, who surveyed Hegel's analytic abstractions with a certain awe but managed to remind himself and his readers that a man who had scrutinized all history and come up with a comprehensive theoretical explanation of anything and everything that had happened or would take place nevertheless had not much to tell us about how we ought to live our lives—we, that is, who ask such a question and know that we have only so much time to find an answer. The existentialists (I don't like the glib, trendy use of the word, but what can one do these days with any word?) have stressed the particulars of everyday life—hence their interest (Buber, Marcel, Camus, Sartre, and the father of them all, that at once high-spirited and gloomy Dane, Kierkegaard) in short stories, novels, plays, and essays concerned with specific, concrete matters, as opposed to large-scale theoretical formulations meant to explain whatever comes in sight and then some.

It is the everyday life that clinicians also contend with—the unique nature of each human being. Since no patient is quite like any other, the doctor has to step from well-learned abstractions to the individual person at hand—an important move, indeed. Novelists as well are wedded to the specific, the everyday; their job is to conjure up details for us, examples for us—the magic of art. And, as our black woman friend pointed out, everyday life has its own ethical conflicts. No wonder novelists do so well examining the trials and temptations that intervene, say, in a doctor's life. The point of a medical humanities course devoted to literature is ethical reflection, not a bit of culture polish here, a touch of story enjoyment there. There is an utter methodologic precision to the aim taken by George Eliot in *Middlemarch*, F. Scott Fitzgerald in *Tender Is the Night*, Sinclair Lewis in *Arrowsmith*, and Walker Percy in *Love in the Ruins*. They are interested in exploring a kind of medical ethics that has to do with the quality of a lived life.

In *Middlemarch*, Dr. Lydgate, a young doctor with high ideals, gradually must contend with a world of money and power. His marriage, his friendships, and his everyday attitudes and commitments are revealed to weigh heavily, in the end, on the nature of his work. When he leaves Middlemarch for his excellent practice "between London and a Continental bathing place," he is not only abandoning a promising research career; he has changed so imperceptibly that he has no notion of real change. The ethical implications of his change of career are rendered with great subtlety. This greatest of English novelists knew better than to indulge in melodrama—the high-minded doctor come to naught through bad luck or a bad marriage or the bad faith of a particular banker. She makes it clear that to the outer world Lydgate is never a failure; he becomes, rather, more and more successful, as judged by the (corrupt and ignorant, we now know) standards of his time and place. The measure of his failure is his own early and well-muscled ethical resolve. He had wanted to combat typhus and cholera—aware of the social as well as personal devastation those diseases wrought. He had wanted to take issue with the "principalities and powers" in his own profession. He ends up writing a treatise on gout. No doubt, gout, too, imposes suffering on people. And who is to decide what each of us ought to do—in any profession? But Lydgate had, indeed, made a series of decisions for himself and had hoped to see certain hopes and ambitions realized. *Middlemarch* provides a chronicle of disenchantment. A steady series of minor accommodations, rationalizations, and mistakes of judgment contribute to a change of purpose, if not of heart. A doctor's character is proved wanting, and the result is his professional success by the standards of the time. Such a devastating irony leaves the reader in hopes, no doubt, that a bit of contemplation will take place: a person's work is part of a person's life, and the two combined as lifework must be seen as constantly responsive to the moral decisions that we never stop making, day in and day out. What George Eliot probed was character, a quality of mind and heart sadly ignored in today's all too numerous psychological analyses.

Similarly in *Arrowsmith*, a novel that many of us, arguably, read and take seriously at the wrong time in our lives—as high-schoolers, rather than during medical school and the years of hospital training. Sinclair Lewis was no George Eliot; he had a ruder, more polemical nature as a writer, and he lacked her gifts of narration. But he knew how professional lives become threatened, cheapened, and betrayed. And he knew that such developments take place gradually, almost innocently—the small moments in the long haul, or the seemingly irrelevant big moments, such as a decision to live with one or another person and in this or that setting. His novel offered a powerful indictment of the larger society (always Lewis's intent) that exerts its sway on medicine, even research medicine, which is supposedly insulated from the vulgar world of cash and politics. But, of course, nothing is completely removed from that world—not doctors and not writers and not church people either. *Arrowsmith* is a novel that confronts the reader with a doctor's repeated ethical choices, a novel that makes it clear that such choices not only have to do with procedures (to do or not to do) or plugs (to pull or not to pull) but with the fateful decisions of everyday life that we are constantly making.

Such decisions are the stuff of each person's life. Once made, such decisions shadow us to the last breath. That is why Dick Diver haunts us in *Tender Is the Night*, and that is why Thomas More of Walker Percy's sad, funny, and compelling novel, *Love in the Ruins*, makes us so uneasy with his shrewd, satirical observations about himself and his fellow human beings. Those two physicians, the reader knows, have asked important questions about life—how to live it honorably, decently. They have also stumbled badly, and their "fall" troubles us. We want to know why. But the reasons, the explanations, are not the categorical ones of modern psychology—some emotional hang-up. Those two principal characters speak for novelists who know how seamless a web life is, how significantly each physician's career connects with his or her moral values. It is a truism that one takes a risk by isolating the various moments of one's time on earth; yet we commonly strain to do so, and we are even allowed, if not taught, to do so in our colleges and graduate schools and postgraduate training.

Every day, for instance, I see undergraduates not only working fiercely in courses such as organic chemistry but showing evidence of malevolent, destructive competitiveness. I have talked with some of those who teach such courses—heard the horror stories, the accounts of spite and meanness and outright dishonesty. Yet, again and again one listens to the same question: What can we do? And the students tell themselves and we tell ourselves—we, who have gone through the maze ourselves—that it is something inevitable and, once over, forgotten. But these bothersome novelists tell us that we don't forget, and Lord knows Freud managed to make that point rather tellingly during his lifetime. We may appear to forget; we may convince ourselves that we do, but the small compromises, evasions, and surrenderings of principle have their place in the unconscious, an element of geography yet to be done justice to by psychological theorists—the way we repress our moral sensibility, accommodate to various situations, and die in the way George Eliot indicates.

Each year I receive respectful letters from ministers, bishops, and church officials of one kind or another; I am asked to pass judgment psychologically on candidates for the ministry. Once my wife, in a moment of mischief and perhaps common sense, wondered what would have happened to all of us, historically, had Rorschach tests, Thematic Apperception Tests, or, yes, psychiatric interviews, been given to St. Francis of Assisi, St. Teresa of Avila, Martin Luther, or Gandhi, not to mention the Old Testament prophets or Jesus Christ. Would they have "passed" those psychiatric interviews—they with their anger at the injustices of this world and their extraordinary willingness to suffer on behalf of all of us? One shudders at the psychiatric words that might have been sent their way. For that matter, she also wondered: Would Freud be given a grant from the National Institute of Mental Health today, and would he even be willing to fill out those idiotic forms, one after the other? But setting that detour of my wife's aside, one is still left with the "spectacle" (to use a word that St. Paul favored at a critical moment in the affirmation of his faith) of religious authorities relying rather eagerly on the judgment of my ilk regarding the selection of candidates—as if psychiatrists were especially successful in finding for themselves, never mind others, how it is possible to live a principled life.

In psychiatry and medicine, as in other walks of life, we might ask for a few letters ourselves—not only appraisals of mental function but judgments about the ethical qualities of our various candidates. Do we often enough ask for such judgments? Do we ask ourselves and our students the kind of questions that George Eliot had in mind when she gave us (forever, one hopes) Dr. Lydgate, who would soon enough realize that there are prices to be paid for not asking certain questions? Dr. Lydgate forgot to inquire about what it would mean to him to become financially dependent on the philanthropist Bulstrode. Dr. Arrowsmith saw again and again the way doctors, like others, fall in line, knuckle under to various authorities who curb and confine independent thinking, never mind research. What those novelists move us to pursue is moral inquiry of a wide-ranging kind, in the tradition of Socrates or the Augustinian *Confessions* or Pascal's *Pensées,* or again, the best of our novelists: intense scrutiny of one's assumptions, one's expectations, one's values, and one's life as it is being lived or as one hopes to live it. The pivotal questions are, of course, obvious. How much money is too much money? Who commands one's time, and who does not? What balance is there to one's commitment of energy? And, from another standpoint, when do reformers start succumbing to the very arrogance or cruelty that they claim to fight? How ought we to resist various intrusions on our freedom, on our privacy as persons and as doctors—the bureaucratic statism that no one, however anxious for various governmental programs, should dismiss as being of little consequence, not after this century's testimony? And so on. Is there room to teach that kind of medical ethics, that kind of program of medical humanities in our medical schools? Is there any better way to do so than through the important stories and character portrayals of novelists who have moved close to the heart of the matter—the continuing tension between idealism and so-called practicality in all our lives?

New England Journal of Medicine, August 23, 1979

Religion and Religious Writers

The New Being

F or years, Paul Tillich struggled to bring the Protestant theology he knew so well into a forthright and necessarily unsettling encounter with modern scientific thinking. A restless man with a powerful and hungry mind, he allowed himself again and again to be brought up short by what physicists and anthropologists have discovered in recent times, or by what psychologists and sociologists have claimed to be important. He also did not shirk looking skeptically at his own training as a minister and theologian. Will traditional Protestantism, however numerous and influential its avowed adherents, ever recognize its crusty, dogmatic, self-centered side? Will the rich and powerful nations of the West, so proudly "advanced" politically and economically, ever realize how enslaved they are by outworn traditions, senseless antagonisms, and constricting loyalties? Tillich was not sure how those questions would be answered in the immediate future, but because he was a hopeful man he did envision an eventual, decisively changed set of historical circumstances—perhaps akin to St. Paul's "the new creation." For Tillich, the Christian message is the message of "the New Being," a phrase he uses repeatedly in volume 1 of his *Systematic Theology* to describe a "reality" this beleaguered planet will (one can only pray) finally witness—a reality whose power will overcome "the demonic cleavages of the 'old reality' in soul, society, and universe."

Tillich never expected to see "the New Being" become a fully realized "fact" of life. He was writing about matters insubstantial and spiritual—matters no one can record on a chart or measure with a ruler or experiment with in a laboratory. Yet he may have been onto something that future social historians will record—something that others also sense and are moved to write about. Recently, for example, three short books have appeared whose titles Tillich would find engrossing. And it can be said that "soul, society, and universe" describes accurately what these books concern themselves with as they examine "the demonic cleavages" in our contemporary world.

Ivan D. Illich is a Roman Catholic priest and theologian, and his *Celebration of Awareness* takes up issues of the soul; Robert Jay Lifton is a psychiatrist, whose *Boundaries* is concerned with the way our society is changing, thus making us in certain respects different human beings; Loren Eiseley is an anthropologist, archeologist, and naturalist, whose *The Invisible Pyramid* tries to comprehend the universe, from the bewildering vastness of the skies to the equally puzzling more immediate world we call the "mind" or the "self." It is not an accident that the titles of these books contain words or implied concepts Tillich came back to constantly during his long and productive life. Awareness haunted him—awareness, which can be so fickle and which churches ought to encourage but often stifle. Boundaries were to him a paradox—at once a stimulating challenge and an outright enemy if they are not questioned or transcended. ("The man who stands on many boundaries experiences the unrest, insecurity, and inner limitation of existence in many forms.") As for the invisible, a theologian of Tillich's stature could not for long whistle in the dark to the tune of religious pieties, not when there is so much for humanity to find out about our own mysterious origins, not when we will either learn the secret of self-mastery or perhaps disappear—one more dead end of inscrutable nature.

I think the religious and social activist in Tillich would especially respond to Illich's book, which is just what its subtitle says: *A call for institutional revolution*. To Illich, Christ was a passionate and uncompromising rebel who preferred to die rather than modify his positions so that they threatened no one and could appeal to everyone. But even Christ would not be spared the second death, so to speak, that institutions visit upon the ideas of those lonely people who inspire and arouse (and thus frighten) others. Tillich could never forget how blasphemous some of today's ministers have become as they mouth chauvinistic platitudes and self-aggrandizing slogans in the name of a man who challenged with every word the religious and political and economic power of his day. Now, in the early 1970s, Illich, who once served in one of New York's Puerto Rican parishes and later became vice-rector of Puerto Rico's Catholic University, proclaims openly and forcefully his disgust at the way his own Church and others offer us "pharisaic legalism" and endless justifications of unjust (un-Christian, one can say) social and economic institutions.

Illich is now in Mexico. He has for years observed the way his Church gets along in Latin America. He has tried upon more than one occasion to keep quiet when he felt there was reason to speak out. Indeed, he stayed within the Church's conventional structure long enough to become a monsignor, and an intelligent, eloquent, charming, even charismatic one at that. But enough was enough; eventually he spoke out, and this collection of short articles and speeches of his recent years shows how dismayed and aroused he is, and how unequivocally he condemns the Church's present jeopardy: "A large proportion of Latin American Church personnel are presently employed in private institutions that serve the middle and upper classes and frequently produce highly respectable profits; this on a continent where there is a desperate need for teachers, nurses, and social workers in public institutions that serve the poor. A large part of the clergy are engaged in bureaucratic functions, usually related to peddling sacraments, sacramentals, and superstitious 'blessings.' . . . Theology is used to justify this system, canon law to administer it, and foreign clergy to create a worldwide consensus on the necessity of its continuation."

He describes the manner in which this country has extracted oil, metals, bananas, and coffee from its poor and vulnerable neighbors to the south while aligning itself with military dictators who use American guns and tanks and planes to defend the interests of a handful of families. He wonders why a nation that fights dictatorships in Europe and Asia supports them in Central America. He wonders why the Vatican ignores the role of its missions in Brazil and Costa Rica and Paraguay and Colombia. "We must acknowledge that missioners can be pawns in a world ideological struggle, and that it is blasphemous to use the Gospel to prop up any social or political system." He struggles with the dilemma St. Paul posed to the Corinthians: "Do we begin again to commend ourselves? Or need we, as some others, epistles of commendation to you, or letters of commendation from you?" No, said Paul, with an emphasis only a tempted man could summon. The point is to seek a living truth rather than "tables of stone." The point is that "the letter killeth but the Spirit giveth life." Illich knows that it is hard to follow Paul's advice. Powerful institutions protect men from the uncertainties of life, give them their niche, and take away a million worries and fears. Still, if we are to grow, we have to realize that pain and suffering and doubt and nightmare are ahead. It is this kind of uneasy and troublesome growth that Illich celebrates. He seems to be saying that not only the Catholic Church but many of our schools, universities, corporations, and legislatures are losing their moral authority over us because they are now out of touch with their own purposes and values or because they are no longer interested in the rock-bottom psychological and spiritual needs of human beings. We may submit to the power of those institutions, but they do not inspire us, and the stage is set for unrest, skepticism, and social violence.

Such a social and religious crisis is also described by a scholarly Yale psychiatrist who has extended the boundaries of his profession and in so doing learned things about those "inner" boundaries that both help us clarify life and at times constrict our vision and possibilities. Dr. Lifton, in his *Boundaries*, never forgets how complicated the mind is and how hard it is to free ourselves not only from the tug of earlier experiences but from the powerful pull of the times in which we live. It is his thesis that today's world places on us severe demands of a very special sort: we can for the first time destroy all life in an instant; we are at the mercy of machines and industrial "processes" we hardly can fathom, let alone control; we are multiplying too rapidly—on an earth with diminishing resources. But we continue to display an ability to be mean and thoughtless and hateful to one another, not just as individuals but as collections of people who set ourselves off by class, race, neighborhood, region, nation, religion, and then—from those vantage points—feel self-righteous or distinctive in a way that requires the humiliation or weakness or vulnerability of others. To a psychiatrist like Lifton or a theologian like Illich, the existence of sinful and destructive qualities (one takes one's choice with the descriptive words) in human beings is not surprising. What makes our waywardness so urgent a matter is the world's economic and technological situation: never before has it been so important that our leaders get along rather than go after each other with those followers who always do the dying in the name of jingoist or ideological slogans.

In response to such a state of affairs, we as individuals are going through private changes, says Dr. Lifton. Some of us are pulling the shades down and cursing anything new or controversial; others (and not just the young, who can produce their share of submissive, conformist, and narrow people) are in the best sense unnerved, puzzled, questioning. We see how blind we have been to the needs and aspirations of others. We recognize that something is not only wrong but mad about an industrial empire whose rivers are foul, whose air is dirty, whose land is ravaged, whose wildlife is being killed off, whose machines are dangerous, and whose food is contaminated. And because we trouble ourselves about such things we become broader, more alert, more responsive, less complacent and self-satisfied. In Lifton's terms, we are on the way to becoming "Protean man"—not free of flaws and limitations but alive to the disasters that threaten us: "The Protean style of self-process . . . is characterized by an interminable series of experiments and explorations, some shallow, some profound, each of which can readily be abandoned in favor of still new psychological quests." And if the quests fail or become dangerously single-minded or bizarre, that is not cause to deplore the efforts. "I want," Lifton adds, "to stress that this Protean style is by no means pathological as such, and in fact may be one of the functional patterns necessary to life in our times. I would emphasize that it extends to all areas of human experience—to political as well as to sexual behavior, to the holding and promulgating of ideas, and to the general organization of lives. To grasp this style, then, we must alter our judgments concerning what is psychologically disturbed or pathological, as opposed to adaptive or even innovative."

It is no accident that both Illich and Lifton use "revolution" in the subtitles of their books. Illich is making "a call for institutional revolution" and Lifton is attempting to assess "psychological man in revolution." Illich finds arrogance and thoughtlessness in various religious organizations (among others), and Lifton scolds his psychiatric colleagues for being self-aggrandizing, limited in vision, and moralistic in a way that helps out those who uphold the status quo; men and women, he says, who question our various norms too closely and take action to show their disapproval are called "psychologically disturbed" or "pathological."

In contrast, Loren Eiseley seems untroubled by such problems, though he does not conceal his judgment that there is a great deal wrong with our institutions and how we get on with each other. What distinguishes him from Illich and Lifton is not his profession but his philosophical viewpoint and the way he conveys it. He is not concerned solely with the last half of the twentieth century, nor does he write with any special program or appeal or critique in mind. For him, our contemporary ailments have origins we will never know in full and a destiny that is beyond any era's (let alone generation's) comprehension. His range of reflections makes the broadest of our historians seem a trifle parochial. He has been looking at the stars farthest away from us as well as at the earth, which still holds on to a large number of apparently inaccessible secrets. He feels a lonely awe at the hugeness of the universe. In a touching beginning to his speculative journey, he brings us back to his childhood and to the childhood of the human race, whose ancestors must have had the same sense of doubt and mystery and passionate curiosity the author had when he was a boy, and still has. He assembles thoughts and speculations he has struggled with over the decades. They are questions, really, that perhaps can be asked only as Gauguin did when in 1897 he wrote on one of his canvases, "From where do we come? What are we? Where are we going?," or as Richard Strauss did when he tried to make music respond to Nietzsche's philosophy in the tone poem *Also Sprach Zarathustra*. The mysteries that command Eiseley's attention defy any particular art form, and he himself harnesses lyric metaphors and allegories to the task of scientific exposition.

Who, indeed, can possibly fathom the riddles of the universe in phrases alone—even the rich and suggestive ones a good poet constructs? As Eiseley cannot stop reminding himself and us, we are here for a fraction of a second, and all our vanities and conceits and proud achievements and noble dreams amount to little—once the archeologist and the astronomer in us stop us in our tracks and get us to think a little. Not that an active, energetic, effective man like Loren Eiseley wants us to become paralyzed by useless ruminations. He realizes that we are entitled to a certain amount of self-centeredness. He recognizes how significantly modern technological civilization has confronted at least some of the universe's inscrutability. We will never know what we are blessed and cursed with the desire to know, but we do have the ability to find out so very much, and we are on our way to places in the sky as well as deep within ourselves.

For Eiseley, those inner, essentially ethical explorations (and they are explorations people like Illich and Lifton continually make) may be more important and decisive than any landing on a distant planet. Eiseley is a moral philosopher and a passionate naturalist. He is

worried: "In the endless pursuit of the future we have ended by engaging to destroy the present. We are the greatest producers of non-
degradable garbage on the planet. In the cities a winter snowfall
quickly turns black from the pollutants we have loosed in the atmosphere. This is not to denigrate the many achievements and benefits
of modern science. On a huge industrial scale, however, we have
unconsciously introduced a mechanism which threatens to run out
of control. We are tracking ourselves into the future—a future
whose 'progress' is as dubious as that which we experience today.
Once the juggernaut is set in motion, to slow it down or divert its
course is extremely difficult because it involves the livelihood and
social prestige of millions of workers. The future becomes a shib-
boleth which chokes our lungs, threatens our ears with sonic booms,
and sets up a population mobility which is destructive in its impact
on social institutions."

So it goes in America, a great and confident world power whose
well-to-do people (never mind our poor) feel uncertain, frightened,
and at the mercy of forces hard to understand, let alone control.
Eiseley is a scientist, but he fears that we are beguiled by our scientists (and engineers and doctors and planners), whom we turn into
prophets and magicians, and upon whom we project "questions in-
volving the destiny of man over prospective millions of years." He is
also a blunt and uncompromising essayist. Like Tillich, he feels that
we are driven from within by demonic forces one can call greed,
selfishness, or arrogance. (The list is a long one.) Eiseley has little
hope we will ever be rid of this inheritance. In a sense, tragedy is our
birthright: "Suppose, my thought persisted, there is still another answer to the ruins in the rain forests of Yucatán, or to the incised
brick tablets baking under the Mesopotamian sun. Suppose that
greater than all these, vaster and more impressive, an invisible pyramid lies at the heart of every civilization man has created, that for
every visible brick or corbelled vault or upthrust skyscraper or giant
rocket we bear a burden in the mind to excess, that we have a biological urge to complete what is actually uncompletable."

And yet we have to go on, lucky to have among us the sensibilities
a person like Eiseley demonstrates. Driven, wild, thoughtless, and
hurtful we are—and maybe doomed—but because we are human
we have a chance to show the tact and intelligence and decency

Eiseley has achieved. If his words that evoke images and suggest a universe of their very own make the reader more thoughtful and considerate, more a part of "the New Being," that is enough for any explorer before he ends the journey all of us make and try to comprehend and struggle to shape and know must end but hope in some small way to make significant.

New Yorker, November 6, 1971

The World and the Devil

Theologians can easily acquire lack of interest in the world's condition. They seek after knowledge of God and formulate the nature of religious belief. Since the supernatural offers ample leeway for the theoretical mind, as well as enough problems to keep it busy, a sensible division of labor seems in order: let other scholars try to make sense of "the things which are Caesar's." Even if Christ himself made a distinction between political authority and God's realm (though not with any intention of telling theologians what are or are not their proper objectives), he more than once became immersed in secular matters. While promising those who would follow him another world, he took after moneylenders, rebuked the rich and powerful, and linked God's grace to a social ethic he not only preached but tried to practice. By the time he was on the cross, he had managed to alarm all sorts of influential people, and the representatives of a powerful empire felt they had to do away with him. No wonder some of the best philosophers and theologians (from Augustine, Aquinas, John Calvin, and Martin Luther to Paul Tillich, Karl Barth, and Reinhold Niebuhr) have not been able to keep their minds from concerns that sociologists, historians, and political scientists (not to mention politicians) might well consider theirs and no one else's. No wonder kings and emperors were told by Christian students of the Bible not only what they should do to save their souls but how they should rule: by which avowed authority and set of principles, which hierarchical and administrative apparatus. No wonder, in our time, Reinhold Niebuhr found himself writing *The Structure of Nations and Empires*, becoming a founding member of Americans for Democratic Action, serving as an adviser to George Kennan's policy planning staff in the State Department, and, toward the end of his life, receiving visits and letters from the scholar Ronald Stone (he teaches social ethics at Pittsburgh Theological Seminary), who was working on the book now published by Abingdon as *Reinhold Niebuhr: Prophet to Politicians*.

Professor Stone has concentrated on Niebuhr's political attitudes and activities and on his enormous influence on a significant number of this nation's policymakers and politically active intellectuals. To deal more comprehensively with his wide-ranging social and historical essays (even without an analysis of his more conventionally theological writing) would require a much longer book, perhaps a biography. Niebuhr has made it clear, in *The Nature and Destiny of Man*, that he regards irony and ambiguity as the essence of what all people must understand and live with, and as one goes through his work the ironies and ambiguities mount to a point at which, for the sake of comprehension, they are best fitted into an account of a vigorously productive life of seventy-nine years or organized around a specific theme. An avowed pessimist and skeptic, Niebuhr worked tirelessly to bring about social and political change, no matter how gloomy he felt about the prospects of the human race, at least on earth. A thinker called upon for counsel by architects of this nation's Cold War posture, he revealed a strong if qualified Marxist streak. A contemporary intellectual who insisted upon the usefulness of a concept like original sin (as a metaphor that suggests the limits and problems every mind has, however cultivated and probed), he was widely read in psychoanalysis and drew upon that discipline with intelligence, discrimination, and restraint—no easy achievement in the 1930s. A man of deep feeling, a powerful and unashamedly emotional preacher, an activist far too responsive (for his health's sake) to the demands upon him, he could be severely logical, given to precise abstractions, and detached to the point of resignation, of *che sarà sarà*.

Such qualities will give Dr. Niebuhr's eventual biographer a deal of work; meanwhile, Professor Stone shows how a gifted, unconventional, and energetic Christian theologian could immerse himself in the political struggles of his time, occasionally feel hopeless about their outcome, hesitate one moment and plunge ahead the next, remain consistent here but contradict himself there, sign dozens of statements, urge many kinds of programs, stand up for a succession of causes and candidates, and, despite all that commitment of time and effort, develop a carefully reasoned and persuasively argued political philosophy set down in scholarly and by no means out-of-date books—as opposed to his incessant political journalism, much of which was casually written in response to one crisis after another.

Professor Stone wrestles briefly with biographical enigmas. Why did a man of German Lutheran ancestry, born in Wright City, Missouri, brought up with the values of the American heartland (optimism, patriotism, the virtues of hard work and good works), a graduate of a theological seminary, become in his forties the deliverer, at the University of Edinburgh, of the Gifford Lectures, in which so many of the West's pieties, to say nothing of those of his native American Midwest, are challenged or, as in his treatment of the doctrine of original sin, given a new and startling meaning? As the author indicates, young Niebuhr was brilliant, strong-willed, and possessed of a creative mind. The book starts where his childhood and youth ended—with the developing thought of a grown man who in 1915 became a pastor at Detroit's Bethel Evangelical Church and soon showed himself willing to take risks (in the way he thought as well as acted) others found unacceptable.

Even in the early years of this century, Detroit meant automobiles, and the city Niebuhr lived in for thirteen years was the germ plasm of America's highly developed industrial society: a plasm to be found first in the factories and stores and homes Niebuhr came to know so well and wrote about in *Leaves from the Notebook of a Tamed Cynic*. The title is misleading, because one is asked to believe that a young cynic was brought under control. The fact is that Dr. Niebuhr came to his parish a somewhat naive but resourceful man who only in time sensed how effectively he and his kind were used; the high rhetoric of Protestant idealism, he finally realized, concealed the ugliness and exploitation of an expanding but morally regressive economic system. In the author's words, "Ford became a symbol to Niebuhr of America's technical genius and social ineptitude." He began to think about questions many of us don't want to. Who owns what, who works for whom, and at what wage, in contrast to what level of profit? In the 1920s, there was no United Auto Workers union, and few ministers were advocating one, let alone advocating, as Reinhold Niebuhr did, a guaranteed annual wage. Thus, a somewhat innocent and well-intentioned person became familiar with the seamier aspects of this country's social order, began to speak out against injustice (on account of which efforts were made to strip him of his position) and to change the way he thought about his responsibilities as a Christian. Christ said that whoever wants to change the world must have the qualities of a serpent as well as those of a dove, and such a balance, as Niebuhr spent a lifetime learning, is not easily obtained.

From the late twenties until the early sixties, when, under the threat of a long and exhausting struggle with illness, he gave up everything except writing, Niebuhr taught at Union Theological Seminary. However developed and intricate his philosophical ideas, he never could forget the experience in Detroit, and in essence Professor Stone's book shows how a man grandly preoccupied with nothing less than "creation as revelation" (to draw upon the title of one section of *The Nature and Destiny of Man*) could also be obsessed by the everyday dilemmas that confront us as liberals or conservatives, Americans or Russians, workers or owners. Perhaps that obsession became a distraction; perhaps Niebuhr never fully realized himself as a theologian and philosopher because he spent so much time struggling on behalf of the poor, trying (in the thirties) to alert this nation to the menace of fascism, wrestling with the problems Stalin's Russia presented to the Western democracies, agonizing over the domestic and international crises we have lived through in these recent decades. Yet Niebuhr's "Christian interpretation" of humanity's role, as offered in the Gifford Lectures, called for the kind of life he lived, and a man who railed against hypocrisy and the arrogant self-righteousness of the intellectuals could not stand aloof, sending down from his academic study a few prescriptions and ex post facto reprimands. He preferred to test the validity of his ideas by fighting for them—and was self-critical enough, when he found himself wrong, to admit publicly his errors and use them to encourage his readers to ponder whether they, too, have blind spots, whether they justify in the name of God or a moral code something that is flagrantly self-serving.

Niebuhr's career as (in Professor Stone's words) a "prophet to politicians" took a series of dramatic turns, each of which involved a renunciation of held positions. In the 1930s, he renounced his liberal views and insisted that men never can be assumed to be without greed and self-serving ambitiousness, despite their generosity and kindness to others; liberals, he felt, emphasize too strongly these last two qualities while ignoring the first two or attributing them to "environmental factors"—poverty, for example, or the effect that an economic system or educational philosophy has on a growing child's character. It was in this context that Niebuhr began to formulate his bold ideas about human "nature"; the best of us are sinners, he told his secular, optimistic, liberal friends, and no matter how much money we are guaranteed by the state, or how satisfying our work, or what dignity we achieve, or how well we know ourselves or express ourselves, we will still covet, be envious and smug, self-pitying, and so on and on. He told them that no mixture of Marx and Freud would turn men and women into angels. If all that seems not especially original, one need only recall, in our recent history, how many utopian promises have been offered to us under many auspices, and how many messianic creeds persist today, *if only* we enact this law, live this way, or get rid of those ideas (or people). Niebuhr was aware of the fallacy of such reasoning and, too, the pride involved, though there were sins that, in his particular hierarchy of them, were much more serious: a skepticism that leads to indifference; an awareness that leads to a paralytic self-consciousness, a faith in the next world that numbs any sense of outrage (and any political activity) that might be mobilized in this world.

In the middle 1930s, Niebuhr added some Marxist thinking to his Christian philosophy and—essay by essay and book by book—tried to find a position both radical and solidly grounded in the realities of life. It is possible to become so wildly hopeful that one whistles in the dark as a Stalin crops up out of nowhere. It is also possible to be so realistic that one unwittingly speaks for those who plan to seize whatever social and political power they can. Niebuhr came to admire certain British Socialists, envied their political closeness to a powerful trade-union movement, and wondered why American liberals and progressives of the middle class have such a hard time getting along with the working people whose cause seems to be at the heart of our reform movements. Professor Stone shows how the activist theologian tried to make sense of that irony, and finally managed it, in the interpretation of our society he called "the irony of American history." Indeed, Niebuhr spent much of his later life insisting that irony, ambiguity, paradox, and mystery are inescapable in the life we lead, no matter what the achievements of the natural sciences and the social sciences; thus there is need for what Professor Stone names "Christian realism." He quotes from Niebuhr:

> Yet the Christian faith tends to make the ironic view of human evil in history the normative one. Its conception of redemption

from evil carries it beyond the limits of irony, but its interpretation of the nature of evil in human history is consistently
ironic. This consistency is achieved on the basis of the belief
that the whole drama of human history is under the scrutiny of
a divine judge who laughs at human pretensions without being
hostile to human aspirations. . . .

The Biblical interpretation of the human situation is ironic,
rather than tragic or pathetic, because of its unique formulation
of the problem of human freedom.

An honest man, Niebuhr acknowledged his inclination toward
the kind of sin this passage obliquely refers to; he could be grim and
scornful, haunted by the abundant tragedies of this century, sure
that nothing really would work out well. He could become preoccupied with involvements and issues that were petty and passing.
Professor Stone's book reveals how a farseeing philosopher could be
trapped by the confines of his era, especially when he moved close to
those "powers and principalities, those political leaders and government agencies," that his Biblical self should have told him to avoid.
Still, a kind of grace came upon him toward the end, or perhaps was
always at his side. If, in middle age, he dared unmask the pretensions of his own liberalism, at the end of his life he was issuing
Isaiahlike denunciations of the folly of those who adhered so literally
to the political realism he had advocated and even, at times, thrown
in the teeth of his idealistic friends who talked of "One World" and
"man's basic goodness." Early on, he saw what we were doing in
Vietnam under cover of that "realism," and at home he saw "realism" called upon to defend vested interests, to keep black people in
their place, to deny the working people a larger share of the wealth
they produce. Ailing and old, he spoke out, sparing nobody, including himself. So the end was like the beginning and the middle; a
social thinker's agile mind, able to shift from theme to theme, and to
weave criticism and self-criticism into a coherent, Christian view
of life, remained steadfast, whatever the challenges. One is left
with that final irony of a career: none of the historical discontinuities
the theologian Reinhold Niebuhr sought to understand could break
up the continuity of his own life.

New Yorker, October 7, 1972

Bringing Words out
of Silence

*I*n early October, 1948, the firm of Harcourt, Brace in New
York published the autobiography of a man who was then only
thirty-three years old and living in rural Kentucky at a Trappist
monastery. The book's title was *The Seven Storey Mountain* (in
Dante's *Divine Comedy* Mount Purgatory has seven stories), and the
original printing order was for 5,000 copies. But a young editor,
Robert Giroux, a contemporary of the book's author at Columbia
University during the late 1930s, had sent galleys to Evelyn Waugh,
Graham Greene, and Clare Boothe Luce, and soon enough their
enthusiastic praise would alert those who worked in the publishing
house that, with luck, they might have a modest success on their
hands. Instead, they had the enviable task of keeping up with an apparently insatiable (and continuing, and international) demand for a
book whose cover, today, announces "over one million copies sold."

Not that *The Seven Storey Mountain* was the only book the young
Cistercian monk Thomas Merton (known in his monastery as Father
Louis) would publish in 1948. The purely religious books, *A Guide
to Cistercian Life* and *Cistercian Contemplatives*, were published
without his name. A good and caring friend, James Laughlin of
New Directions, published a collection of Merton's poems. A Catholic publishing house issued *Exile Ends in Glory: The Life of a Trap-
pestine, Mother M. Berchmans*, and a Catholic college (St. Mary's,
Notre Dame) brought out *What Is Contemplation?* All this—and so
much more to come in the years that followed, forty books, hundreds of articles, and thousands of letters addressed to men and
women the world over—from someone who had chosen to live a
cloistered, predominantly silent life.

In retrospect, it is not hard to figure out why *The Seven Storey
Mountain* caught on so astonishingly well that year, the same one in
which readers were offered Orwell's *1984*. For the second time in
less than half a century, the so-called civilized nations of the world
had resorted to prolonged war, with millions of soldiers and civilians

killed. All the faiths, religious and secular, had not prevented those wars. The nation of Goethe and Beethoven, and of Luther and a strong Catholic tradition as well, had built genocidal crematoriums. Science had enabled nuclear bombs to be built. A poet of Ezra Pound's vast knowledge and powerful literary gifts had ended up mouthing fascist doggerel for Mussolini. High communist and socialist ideals had become Stalin's monumental perversities; they were comprehended quickly for what they were in the 1930s by Orwell, Ignazio Silone, and Simone Weil, and in the late 1940s they were being seen by more and more people as, in their sum, one of the worst tragedies in recent centuries. Meanwhile, millions of men who had fought in obscure Pacific islands or yet again in France's bloody northern territory, had returned home, all too familiar with pain and suffering and death, with the workings of fate and chance and luck, good or bad—the old familiars of storytelling.

No wonder that, at such a time, a young man's struggle to find meaning and purpose in this often cruel and always unpredictable life attracted the attention of so many readers. Still, as Waugh realized instantly (and before the book was even published), the compelling power of *The Seven Storey Mountain* had to do with more than its poignant personal and spiritual story: a boy of relatively good fortune, both social and economic, loses his mother at the age of four, his father at fifteen, watches the world go murderously crazy as he grows into manhood, becomes a bit of a rake, drinks a lot, flirts with Freud and Marx, turns relentlessly to Catholicism, and chooses to be a priest, one willing to accept the stern discipline and the demanding isolation of the Trappist order. Waugh spotted the emergent lyric writer in Merton; he understood that a poet of some considerable skill had found in the personal memoir a congenial means of gaining the attention of others and eventually captivating them. Skeptical of the all too numerous sentimental or melodramatic conversion stories he'd heard or read, he yielded nevertheless to Merton's charm, passion, and adroitness as a writer.

This still haunting and influential autobiography (marred only occasionally by moments of religious triumphalism) would not be the last of Merton's self-presentations. He had started a journal of sorts when he was eight and kept one all during his adult life, persisting even as a Trappist monk. He shaped his ideas and worries, the thoughts that came to him as he lived his life, into one book after another. He also dispatched a stream of letters to friends near and far; and those letters, too, were instruments of spiritual discussion— with himself, often enough, as much as with his particular correspondent. In the end there were 1,800 separate folders, many containing scores of exchanges with the famous and distinguished (Boris Pasternak, Czeslaw Milosz, Walker Percy, and Dorothy Day). On the other hand, Merton responded warmly to certain unknown individuals who occasionally more than held their own with him—such as the sixteen-year-old California girl who posed this startling question to a monk she had taken to calling "Tom" in her letters: "Do you know that I looked you up in the *Guide to Catholic Periodicals* at school and GOOD GRIEF, why do you write so much?"

No doubt Michael Mott, himself a fairly active poet and novelist, must have asked himself that question as he studied Merton's papers. Mr. Mott's *Seven Mountains of Thomas Merton* is the authorized biography, which was to have been done by Merton's longtime friend, the writer and photographer John Howard Griffin, who died before he could accomplish the requisite research and writing. The girl in California would surely have been even more in awe of Merton's prolific pen had she been given access, as Mr. Mott was, to Merton's journals, only parts of which (edited, of course) saw the public light of inclusion in his various books.

An important evaluative moment in the biography offers this explanation of the meaning a torrent of confessional prose had for a particular Christian: "The journals were a method of sabotaging the ideal Merton. If they preserved the spontaneity, they preserved the scandal, the whole man (whole, sometimes, to the point of exhaustion). The pages on God, on prayer, on humility, would distress some; the pages of criticism of the Church would worry many; the praise of the Church, others; references to drinking, to dreams, to periods of depression—references to his own evasions, to his capacity for kidding himself, to his being less than an honest lover, to costly mistakes of fact and judgment. When he was used, or used up, the journals would speak of him without editing, crossings-out, polishing—a place where the narrow-minded, or those who had made a cult of him, would flounder and where the seekers of truth without pretense would find him."

He was, in a sense, one of those "seekers"—anxious and determined, throughout his life, to face himself down honorably, an Augustinian task made progressively more difficult, he realized, by the very attempt to do so, insofar as it was shared (through his articles and books) with hundreds of thousands of complete strangers, who yearned to see and worship his every word, even when he was being self-indulgent or wrongheaded or presumptuous—as he knew he, like the rest of us, could occasionally end up being. Again and again he takes himself to task for being prideful, for being too self-conscious, for letting egoism cloud his vision or affect his various involvements. At one point he refers to the "old narcissism," rather as George Eliot used to make mention of the "old Adam."

His biographer refers to "crises of solipsism," after which he attempted "to adapt and identify himself with others." Those "others" for over half of his life were his fellow monks, and much of this book offers a running account of his complex relationship with Dom James, the abbot of the monastery of Gethsemani, who in an earlier life "had graduated from the Harvard Business School at the age of twenty-one," and for whom "the ideal monk was one who lived in anonymity and who died known only to God and to a few of his fellow monks."

In his own way, Merton agreed—hence his solitary side, his wish to live as a hermit within the confines of Gethsemani, his hope at the end of his life to find someplace (he was considering Alaska) where he could once and for all be rid of the press of outside attention. Still, an active, successful literary life made it certain that he would be always tempted: "Merton told them [visiting friends] Don Ameche had telephoned the monastery at Easter asking if anyone had bought the film rights to *The Seven Storey Mountain*. If not, Ameche would like to make the film, presumably playing the part of Thomas Merton himself (Merton had been thinking more of Gary Cooper). Dom James had said no to the film and gone right on to ask if Ameche had made his Easter duty. Don Ameche said he had been to communion that morning."

This amusing anecdote, Mr. Mott knows, is more generally edifying with respect to Merton's Cistercian life than many readers are likely to realize until the end of the book. Merton was much attracted to a secular culture he also fled from; and his biographer does well to give us, in clear and unpretentious and vigorous prose, the many details of that ambivalence. The author also is wise to resist the temptation, surely substantial in this case, to hagiography—

though, if one were to choose a psychological patron saint for Merton, the much-tempted St. Anthony would be more fitting than, say, the austere St. Benedict.

The first chapters offer slow reading because Merton's family and his early life, his youth, too, are presented as they were—a good deal of foolishness and self-indulgence. The reader's attention becomes completely fixed once a somewhat dissolute man has begun to wrestle in earnest with the devils in him. But this is no work of cynical skepticism. The author obviously admires his subject and wants to evoke with compassionate understanding his sometimes heartbreaking difficulties—not only of the child who lost his artist mother, the youth who lost his artist father, the man excited and tormented by his writing gifts, but also of the monk who fell in love with a beautiful nurse who cared for him when he was sick in the hospital, the political activist who had grave doubts about the manner in which various protests were being enacted, and finally, the Roman Catholic ever more strongly drawn, toward the end of his life, to the significance of Eastern religions.

That last interest might have been further pursued had Merton not been accidentally electrocuted on December 10, 1968, while he was attending a conference on monasticism in Thailand. He was fifty-three. His death, of course, attracted much notice, and the depth of sorrow felt by so many people, of such varied backgrounds, is powerfully rendered in *Merton, By Those Who Knew Him Best*, a thin volume of memoirs assembled by Paul Wilkes, who directed a recent public television program devoted to Merton's life. In no way, one begins to sense, has Merton left his friends; they talk of him as if he will always be near at hand, smiling broadly, roaring his infectious laugh, sharing with them his thickly textured knowledge, his penetrating wisdom, and his urgent idealism. (He was an early supporter of the Civil Rights movement, a tough critic of our Vietnam involvement, and an eloquent opponent of the development of nuclear weaponry here and abroad.)

In his final year, Mr. Mott tells us in the biography, Merton declared himself taken with "the idea of starting out into something unknown, demanding and expecting nothing very special, and hoping only to do what God asks . . . whatever it may be." By now, one hopes and prays, he has found the answer to that implied question, the all-important one for him. Meanwhile, on the occasion of this long, detailed, affectionately knowing but stoically unsentimental biography, a good number of readers will reach a conclusion about an aspect of God's design for his eager, ardent servant, Thomas Merton—that his words and deeds were meant to touch many of us deeply, instruct us significantly, and reveal to us in various ways a divine grace as it came, wonderfully and mysteriously, to inform a singular, memorable life.

New York Times Book Review, December 23, 1984

Gravity and Grace in the Novel
A Confederacy of Dunces

Simone Weil was a brief, visionary presence whose gifts to us of the twentieth century are still being sorted out and estimated with a certain surprised awe by her various critics and admirers. She combined, in a life of only thirty-four years, a radical social and cultural disaffection with an intense, conservative yearning for certain elements of the past that she hoped to see given new life in a world whose moral contours she tried to imagine and describe in various essays—while all the while (it can be said) dying the death of someone who had a profound skepticism of what the future offered this terribly endangered planet. She ached for the poor, the humble, the hurt, the ailing, the vulnerable; she scorned what in the Bible gets called derisively "principalities and powers"— those who earned the outspoken contempt of Jeremiah and Isaiah and Amos in the Old Testament and, of course, of Jesus Christ himself in the New Testament—the smug, pompous, and self-important ones whose merciless and vain extortions are done at the expense of the rest of us.

On the other hand, she saw precisely, and early on (she was, indeed, a prophet), how mean, vicious, and dangerous some of this world's so-called reformers are—full of pride and its consequences: the ruthless, arrogant failure to consider anyone's point of view, unless it serves the purpose of a particular (ideological) cause. Simone Weil needed no reminder that original sin is far from a quaint term, entertained gullibly and in ignorance by those who lived in earlier times. She looked relentlessly, candidly into her own mind and heart. She observed others closely. She concluded that no political or economic changes, no matter how well intentioned, will take from us our humanity, our moments of doubt and disappointment, envy and truculence—aspects of our very condition. We are, as Lord knows our novelists and philosophers have been telling us over the generations, the many-sided creature who (through words and ideas) looks at the stars but who rivals—arguably, outdistances—any and all so-called animals or beasts when it comes to such behavior as rage, rapacity, and even wanton murderousness.

Her torment, then, resided in her intellectual, if not spiritual, breadth—a stubborn, idiosyncratic, original-minded, personally devastating capacity for, even insistence upon, living marginally, and thereby embracing ambiguities and inconsistencies others shun as intolerable. Through her marvelous, hard-won spirituality (a gift to her as she became physically sicker and sicker), she managed to find, ironically, a strong interest in the concrete, particular world, the day-to-day routines and objects of involvement that, she knew, tell so much about us. "No ideas but in things," William Carlos Williams has reminded twentieth-century urban Americans in his poem *Paterson*. Simone Weil knew how dangerous it can be for a Christian pilgrim to ignore one or another version of that injunction. The penalty turns out to be the Gnostic heresy, a direct challenge to a God who willingly, if not ardently, assumed "the flesh." And gnosticism is related to other fatal splits—that, for instance, of ideologues who assume they can spend hours, days, a lifetime with the seductive, self-serving pleasures of theory, while putting aside as unworthy or of lesser significance the countless pressing details of this life. I remember, for example, when Harvard's buildings were seized in the early 1970s, I stood watching the assault with Erik Erikson, who wondered this out loud: "When they leave the building, will they help some old person trying to cross the street and in danger of being hurt? For that matter, will you and I do so—as we do our arguing or meditating or analyzing?"

As I read John Kennedy Toole's *A Confederacy of Dunces*, I found the above train of thought gripping my mind constantly. Simone Weil gave us an unforgettable polarity: "gravity and grace." By gravity she meant the ever-present "weight" of our minds and our bodies. (She was a great one for seeing the poetry of physics and mathematics.) We are, inescapably, acted upon by the atoms and molecules, the muscles and hormones, the synapses that make up, in sum, ourselves. And, too, we are constantly acting upon one another: asking, taking, beseeching, demanding, telling truth and telling half-truths, and lying, and manipulating, and exhorting, and imploring, and loving, and demonstrating fearful possessiveness, angry petulance, sly displeasure, open resentment—as the expression I keep hearing in church puts it, "world without end." But there are moments also of transcendence, strange moments, unexpected moments, even unearned ones—unless one will have God to be a Puritan, a vigorous bourgeois. "Grace is everywhere," Georges Bernanos has his curé saying at the end of *Diary of a Country Priest*, and surely Jesus Christ, as he walked through Galilee and as he suffered in Judea, taught that lesson to "all sorts and conditions" of human beings—if I may again, and conservatively, call upon the "old" Book of Common Prayer I remember so fondly. As Dorothy Day used to put it, for "the lame, the halt, the blind," not to mention the skeptical, the loony, the extremely vulnerable, even the strenuously condemned and the exiled—grace becomes theirs, and not through the laws of state, and not, either, through the arbitrary, rigid classification of the Church, but through an unexpected, a mysterious, an utterly providential arrival: Him. Dunces and doubters, men and women demeaned by political and religious doctrine—grace lifted them all, gravity having been decisively defied.

In New Orleans, the novelist Toole is determined to show us the unyielding pull of gravity. We are all dunces, of course, and that certainly includes any would-be prophet who happens to know how to spin a yarn. But what, exactly, is a "dunce," or indeed, a collection or "confederacy" of them? All of Toole's characters are dim-witted, driven, distended by their maker's insistence upon satire. They are true to the biblical moment of Mark: the Gadarene swine, repositories of the madness of a legion (and, alas, waiting in the wings, historically, have been thousands of other legions). They are the blind leading the blind, or conniving or manipulating, or ruining altogether. It is Toole's contention that Freud missed not a trick about our silliness, our pretentiousness, our hell-bound lustiness, and our feverish, egoistic possessiveness with respect to one another. It is Toole's contention, further, that a "walk on the wild side," as the saying goes, will give us, finally, ourselves—all of us who seem remarkably *unlike* Mr. Toole's various comically exaggerated men and women, until, of course, we stop and look closely at those warts and more that we have learned to conceal from others, not to mention ourselves.

New Orleans has long been a cosmopolitan city, so it provides a natural and splendid setting for Mr. Toole's moral and spiritual purposes. He knows that no high-minded critique of humankind of any

value can do without the devil, under whatever name, and needless
to say, Freud's "death instinct" was one such name. "The devil has
slippery shoes," I often heard black people in Mississippi's Delta say
as they contemplated, in the early 1960s, the workings of our nation's political life, and Mr. Toole has his particular black friend,
Jones, tell us that again and again. Jones's running commentary is,
actually, a strangely sane, earthy, shrewd, and knowing one, a valuable and activist counterpart of Astor and Sulk, those two "handy-
men" Flannery O'Connor gave us in "The Displaced Person."
Faulkner started it, I suppose, with Dilsey, the most powerfully developed, noble, and sustaining of all the characters offered us by
white Southern novelists. The Compsons fall apart in *The Sound
and the Fury*; Dilsey retains her dignity and offers what little she
has, which turns out to be rather a lot. I detect a similar irony in *A
Confederacy of Dunces*. The whites, all of them so much better off,
supposedly, than Jones, by virtue of their skin color, turn out to be
collectively out of their minds and especially incapable of sensible,
pointed, and appropriate social and psychological judgments. But
he is down-to-earth, clear-headed, and above all, attentive. He has,
in Simone Weil's theological way of seeing things, devoted himself
to seeing the gravity of his, of everyone's situation. (She obviously
uses that word "gravity" in both its scientific and moral senses.) The
result is a curious and winning grace, that of the observer who is not
by any means as weighted down by the grave apprehensions that afflict all those other New Orleaneans. The meek one is certainly not
going to inherit a patch of the earth known as "the city that care
forgot," but he rises above others whose burdens manage to put the
South's racial crisis into the largest possible perspective: *sub specie
aeternitatis*.

   I began my postpsychiatric residency working life in New Orleans
and also had my head examined there—psychoanalysis on Prytania
Street. I was a Yankee alienist (if I may revert to that older medical
designation for ironic purposes) and felt that there were certain advantages to being such at the time—the outsider who can glimpse a
serious crisis (the Civil Rights struggle) with a bit of detachment. But
I was a mere novice in that regard, I eventually learned. It was a
group of black children who began to teach me that perceptual acu-
ity with regard to individuals or the social scene is not necessarily
nourished by education or absent in those who have received *their*

education on the streets, in the alley, on the factory floors, or out in the fields, up the hollows, across a reservation or two. Here, for example, is a six-year-old New Orleans girl giving a not insignificant lecture to a Boston doctor not exactly trained to be humble: "The white folks say all these terrible things to us. My momma says they have bad tongues, and I should feel sorry for them. One woman tells me she hopes I die. It's not even nine o'clock in the morning, and she's there, every day, telling me I won't live much longer! I decided to get even with her. I stopped and told her I hoped she lived for another hundred years! She got all red, and she didn't say another word. The next day she was gone! The [federal] marshal I like best says I really 'got' to her. He asked me who told me to say what I did. I answered him no one. If you're black and you go downtown, and you listen to the white people talking, a lot of things come to your mind, but you can't say them. White people say anything they want. Not us, we listen more than we talk, until we're alone!"

I considered myself privileged to be hearing those words. Soon enough, though, I was told in no uncertain terms not to be so proud of myself: "If you came from here, you wouldn't be visiting us." Then, a significant pause, followed by a canny and candid speculation: "My mother said you wouldn't be in that mob." Again, I felt touched, complimented. But this mere child, just beginning to read and write, knew to add a certain pointed explanation, a qualification: "My uncle works at the Touro; he's there at night, cleaning the floors. He says the doctors live nearby, a lot of them. It's way far from here."

One of those "free associations" Freud told us to heed. Here was an "outsider" who knew how to put another "outsider" right in his place—as Toole's character Jones does in A Confederacy of Dunces with just about all the white people he gets to meet and watch and know. And who are they? A particular city's splendid variety: the rich and the poor; the apparently comfortable and secure as against the quite desperate; the old and the young; the quite proper and the rather unseemly; the all too educated and the untutored, the innocent. They all are seen, rather obviously, through the unifying presence of Ignatius Reilly—a series of refractions emanating from a rather large diamond indeed. He is not quite the narrator, but his sprawling, at times unwieldy, other-worldly thoughts and actions make us wonder, in the existentialist tradition, where he came from, who he is, and whither he goes. Am I stretching things too intolerably when I think of Ignatius as a representation of the Catholic Church itself, struggling in the midst of a crooked and unjust and often enough quite crazy world, struggling through the lives of its members, clergy and laity alike, with all their cravings, conventional and irregular, with all their failings, evident and barely concealed and deeply rooted in this and that kind of past, struggling to survive, to make sense of this world, to live for some purpose larger than the self and its demanding requirements? The Catholic Church Mr. Toole tried to comprehend was the Church of the 1950s, the Church that still yearned, as Mr. Toole keeps putting it, for "theology and geometry." How Simone Weil, with her love for the Greek mathematicians and for the Church of plainsong and troubadours, not to mention an adamant theology, might have loved that phrase with its message of order, hierarchy, structure, and interdependence—all under Heaven's exceedingly alert eyes!

But Mr. Toole knew that the clock was running out, the clock of D. H. Holmes on Canal Street and the clock of the hundreds of Catholic churches in countless American towns and cities, where a commercial ethic belonging to an agnostic, secular age rules supreme. He does not try to foist Ignatius Reilly upon us; we are to be entertained and slyly brought up short rather than preached at or converted. There was, there is, Toole knew, a lot of foolish nonsense in the Catholic Church, among other institutions. If Christ was betrayed by one of his handpicked followers, his earthly representatives over the centuries have shown themselves more than able to keep alive the tradition of Judas. But the Church, like Ignatius, had to keep trying, keep reaching out to the entire arc of humanity, keep hoping in various ways to become a spiritual instrument in the lives of every possible kind of person, as Ignatius, for all his absurdities and tics and postures and excesses, manages to be for the characters in *A Confederacy of Dunces*.

Maybe the word with regard to Ignatius's behavior is follies, as in "fools for Christ," a phrase Dorothy Day used all the time, helped by her beloved Dostoevski, who knew that the "politic, cautious, meticulous" ones, the utterly circumspect and unnervingly "rational" ones, have not ever been, by and large, the ones who live minute by minute with Christ's example in their hearts, minds, and souls. Ignatius is an odd one, if not the biggest of all the "dunces."

He is sexually irregular, to say the least. He is an occupational mis-
fit. He belongs, it seems, to no community whatsoever. His life
seems a messy, hapless one, a dead end. He needs, we have a right
to think, treatment—lots and lots of it. Is he schizophrenic or just
plain loony? As for Jesus Christ and all the saints who have struggled
and died, one after the other, for him and his cause, they too have
made us who are blessed (are we really?) with today's wisdom wonder
about our mental health, our problems, our peculiar if not absolutely scandalous acts, our expressed ideas, hopes, beliefs, values
(what these days one gets used to calling "behavior" or "attitude").

Needless to say, Ignatius is sprung, but where is he headed? Does
grace appear, of all ironies, in the person of Myra? Is the Holy Roman Catholic Church rescued from some of its corruptions, blind
spots, hopeless impasses, and contradictions by the avowed enemy,
secular humanism (to use a contemporary phrase!) militantly es-
poused? Or is Mr. Toole making a less decisive judgment, simply
telling us that the Church of the 1960s had, quite clearly, lurched in
the direction of the Myras of this world, with the outcome of such a
development (the Vatican of John XXIII and early Paul VI) uncertain at best? The author, remember, is a dialectician in the Augustinian tradition, able to envision the devil as a prodding if not provocative ally. A second novel, sadly denied us, might have given us
Ignatius (or an equivalent) in Manhattan on Myra's home territory,
where, believe me, the reservoir of madness, banality, and stupidity—sometimes called by the designations of "high culture," or
"progress," or "contemporary living," or "modernity"—is no less
wide and deep than that of the New Orleans given us by the talented, short-lived, wonderfully astute John Kennedy Toole.

University of Southwestern Louisiana Journal, 1983

Bernanos
The Writer as Child

I do not imagine that Georges Bernanos expected to gain a wide audience for the novels and articles he wrote from about 1925 to 1948. He was French, proudly French, and peasant French at that; he was also a fervent Christian pilgrim. He had no interest in transcending such "limitations," certainly not in order to cross the Atlantic Ocean and become yet another American fad. For that matter, as a person, a novelist, and a political journalist, he challenges not only the secular stranger from abroad but the people of his own country, to the extent that they are inescapably loyal to this century.

Bernanos was born in the Paris of 1888, when the memory of an emperor was still fresh and a republic was in its adolescence. He was educated by Jesuits and later studied law and literature—particularly Balzac and Zola. He became interested in politics and eventually associated himself with Léon Daudet, the novelist's son, who had joined with Charles Maurras to make *Action Française* an all-out nationalist and royalist newspaper. For a while he lived in Rouen and edited a monarchist weekly, but by the autumn of 1914 the war drew him to the battlefield, where he was wounded and decorated. In the midst of the awful futility of trench warfare, he met up with the melancholy, furious, apocalyptic message of Léon Bloy, who so decisively influenced Jacques and Raïssa Maritain. Bloy had little use for the hypocritical, deceitful politicians of the Third Republic, but his outrage was nonpartisan and certainly fell hard upon the manufacturers of the day, who worked children mercilessly, as well as upon the decadent counts and dukes, who never seemed to be done with pretending. Though by temperament he was not as fierce and stern as Bloy, Bernanos sensed in him a kindred spirit. They both were Catholic by precarious faith rather than ritual or inheritance; they both were emotional; and each of them by nature was tied concretely to the poor—in contrast, that is, to being wordy, theoretical advocates of the proletariat, advocates who preach "humanity" but cut down anyone in sight with highly refined thoughts.

After the war, Bernanos found himself increasingly at odds with the purposes and tactics of *Action Française*. He became inspector for an insurance company and in that capacity roamed France. He had married in 1917 and by 1933 was the father of six children. To all outward appearances, he was exactly the kind of humdrum, petit bourgeois person who applauded conservatives like Daudet, though something in him seemed to say no and, more significantly, to drive him to write out his own position.

He wrote and wrote, in hotels, railroad stations, and cafés, wherever there was a table for paper and pen, so that by 1930 he had published three novels (*Sous le Soleil de Satan*, *L'Imposture*, and *La Joie*). They were not overwhelming successes, though they revealed a sensual, poetic, and religious mind in search of a congenial literary form that would enable coherence and control. To some extent, Bernanos had already made that discovery as a journalist. By 1932, he was contributing one emotional but pointed article after another to *Le Figaro*, which allowed him considerable freedom to say what he wanted about politics and literature.

Money was still scarce though, and in 1933 he was badly injured in a motorcycle accident. He wrote a detective novel (*Un Crime*) to become solvent and all the while kept traveling, unhappy with this place, dissatisfied there, sick and in need of rest, outraged at what he saw, and so compelled to move on. By the midthirties, he had long ceased to be anything but a writer—a novelist, a critic, a journalist, and a pamphleteer, whose output was steady and incredibly diverse in character.

In 1934, he left France for Majorca, the first of repeated exiles he would undertake. For three years he stayed there, and they were the three most productive years of his life. We owe to them *The Diary of a Country Priest* and *Mouchette*, which has just now been translated into English. The two are companion pieces, and together they are an almost unbearable experience for any reader even remotely susceptible to the vision of this world that drives Bernanos to such agonized expression. In a sense, they are one book; in different ways they treat of pride and innocence, those two states of mind and soul that struggle within us for command of whatever destiny we may have in this universe. In both books, the reader is taken to the same world—bleak, isolated villages, whose air is always damp and land always mud-soft and covered with leaves. The rain comes down thin and steady, or it pours so hard that the author has it lashing away at people who, anyway, are beaten through and through. They are poor. They are ignorant. They are cruel to one another. They hate and lust without the decorative guile and pretense that money and clever ideas enable. They are no better than kind and sensitive aristocrats and no worse than the pompous, self-sufficient owners of a galaxy of electrical gadgets and some bank books that—you can be sure—will never get wet in *any* rain. For Bernanos, they are like all people, the occasion for God's presence and absence on this earth.

In *The Diary of a Country Priest* Bernanos found the perfect form for his digressive way of handling a few very pointed themes. The young, ailing priest can write down his thoughts openly and naturally without feeling any need to tailor them to the particular demands of conversation. The novelist is not so tied to his scenes and characters and is less tempted to use them gratuitously as his own mouthpieces, so that by no means are we confronted with a thinly disguised personal journal, another version of the various letters and private notebooks Bernanos published—or others did for him after his death. The priest is an unforgettable person, and so is his encounter with a grieving countess, whose dead child has provided her with the excuse she needed for that peculiarly disarming kind of pride that clothes itself in tragedy and uses self-pity as a bludgeon. The author's desperate and fierce religious struggle, lived out on three continents, against a background of revolution, war and death camps, submerges itself almost miraculously in the novel's discouraging, inauspicious countryside—with its raw weather everyone's fate at one time or another, and its peasants, clergy, and nobility as mean and driving, as ordinary and self-congratulatory, or as vulnerable and decent as their equivalents in other places.

To Bernanos, Christ's Sermon on the Mount contained so much irony and paradox, so much pitiless contempt for the vanity of our institutional life, that no one can feel safely Christian, though a case can be made for some more easily than others. That is the writer's challenge, as he saw it, to allow each of his characters to make his case. In *The Diary of a Country Priest*, and even more tersely in *Mouchette*, he sets out to create them, supplicants all, and give them their circumstances, in the sure knowledge that whatever they do he will be there—observant, surprised, and horrified. Like Mauriac, he both entreats and abandons the reader. The novels are suffused with spiritual concerns, but the mystery of Christianity, of salvation and damnation, remains almost austerely beyond analysis or even speculation. By the same token, human motives are not fixed upon and scrutinized as ends in themselves; to do so would be sacrilegious. What matters is how we act, and specifically how we act toward one another—always against the background of a perplexing Sermon that seems particularly foreboding to people of authority or apparent success, among whom can be found successful novelists.

Bernanos cannot forget Christ as the child and the passion of the cross. Childhood and death are the themes that came up again and again in his writing, and they are inevitably joined together. The priest is a child, not one of our successful, competent (those are indeed the words) nursery school children, whose parents are cramming the whole world into his brain for the sake of *their* salvation, but a defenseless child, who is nevertheless capable of hurting both himself and other people. Bernanos has no interest in what Rousseau or Wordsworth saw in childhood—a sort of *tabula rasa*, or a shelter where only lambs and doves live. Nor is he interested in the psychoanalyst's idea of what makes a boy nervous or a girl worried. He assumes all along that one can be vulnerable and hurtful, patient and capricious, forgiving and predatory—and be a child. More radically (and here I think he is very much with Freud, whether he likes it or not), he assumes that childhood is a continuing state of mind, a terribly important one that is never outgrown or left behind but murdered, yes, by being thwarted, stifled, or terrorized.

The priest, like a child, tries to do what he is told but feels within himself all kinds of confusing, urgent wishes. Like a child, he embraces, then pulls back; like a child, he can walk perfectly well one minute and then stumble, without marking that fact down in a ledger and making it part of some overall count or "evaluation." In fact, Bernanos ingeniously splits the reader, the writer, and the priest from one another. The priest's reactions are not ours. If he could see himself and write about himself as we see him and read of him, through his own words, he would be damned not saved, just another self-consciously "aware" man. Through the use of a diary, Bernanos can bring out the child in the curé, his fantasies and doubts, the flow of fear and desire he experiences, the impromptu conversations with himself that in later life we come to call daydreams or reveries, or in a doctor's office, free associations. The lesson seems clear: self-knowledge and reflection are obligatory for anyone who seeks God (hence the effort of a diary), but a certain kind of "distance" on oneself (and others) can lead to arrogance and pride, to the kind of mind found in mature, "grownup," and educated people who make guns and order them used. If the reader feels himself judging the priest, and thus uncomfortably close to acting like God, Bernanos can only smile wryly. He distrusted intellectuals, himself included. Eventually he fled them, himself included, by leaving France.

In Spain he saw Franco's work. The man who started as a follower of the right-wing Maurras was on his way to being claimed by the leftist readers of *Esprit* as a Catholic humanist, a radical fighter for the rights of the poor. One day in Majorca, he saw trucks moving up a road and in them "miserable human beings, their hands on their knees, their faces covered with dust, but sitting up straight, very straight, holding their heads high with the dignity Spaniards have in the most atrocious situations." What he saw—the men were republican hostages being driven to their execution—had the following consequences: "Naturally I did not deliberately decide to make a novel out of this. I did not say: I am going to transpose what I saw into the story of a little girl tracked down by misfortune and injustice. But what is true is that if I had not seen these things, I should not have written the *Nouvelle Histoire de Mouchette*."

We are fortunate to have this particular translation of the novel, done by J. C. Whitehouse. Bernanos loved the French language and took advantage of all its subtleties. His words are simple and plain, like so many of the people he describes. He sets phrase upon phrase, again all done very directly but in the interests of achieving his intricate design. His prose is lyric and open, not densely metaphorical, and would have been damaged by even a capable translation. Whitehouse has done a lovely job: "The dark west wind, the sea wind, was already scattering the voices in the darkness. It toyed with them a moment and then lifted them all together, dispersing them with an angry roar. The voice which Mouchette had just heard hovered in the air a long time, like a dead leaf floating interminably."

Mouchette is fourteen years old, and so solitary that she has never felt lonely. She has a sharp, cutting eye for the insincerity and intrigue in her classmates and for the nervous self-importance of her teacher. She has been ignored or beaten by her drunken father and her tired and sick mother. There are many children in this peasant family, and they all are part of a village whose life seems timeless.

The story is deceptively brief: the girl, both timid and proud, walks home alone from school in what turns out to be an unusually severe storm. She meets Arsène, a poacher and braggart, who has been hurt in what he claims to have been an encounter with an enemy of his, the forest policeman. He is running from the law, she from a world never really entered. The confession she hears from a murderer is ironically the first act of trust, the first intimacy she has ever known. Rather than find Arsène frightening, she is drawn to him. They have taken shelter together, and she admires the way he forthrightly cauterizes his wound with a burning brand. She reaches out for him, and suddenly finds herself able to sing. For only a second can he return her gentle trust; drunk, basically a coward, he rapes her. She goes home to find her mother dying, and in a heartbreaking scene tries to tell her secret. The mother dies. Mouchette learns of Arsène's deception, and even worse she realizes that her family and the town can offer her nothing—except the spectacle of death, which slowly seizes the girl's imagination as something to be achieved in the absence of love. She leaves a village that forced her to close in on herself, that made a mockery of her effort to be generous, and she drowns herself.

Bernanos was obsessed with the betrayal of one person by another. It is not stretching things to connect Mouchette's death with the crucifixion. In Spain he saw where the twentieth century was headed, with its "realism" and its "progress," its Chamberlains, Hitlers, and Stalins. In a letter to him, Simone Weil wrote: "Having been in Spain, I now continually listen to and read all sorts of observations about Spain, but I could not point to a single person, except you alone, who has been exposed to the atmosphere of the Civil War and has resisted it. What do I care that you are a royalist. . . ."

He had long since stopped being a royalist when those words were written in 1938. He had just returned to Paris, only to leave that same year for Paraguay. From there he went to Brazil. He tried farming. He supported de Gaulle and the resistance, attacked the

Vichy government in a torrent of articles, and returned to Paris in 1945. Two years later he was in Tunisia, disappointed with the Fourth Republic—and a year later he was dead.

A restless, turbulent man, drawn to politics but impatient really for Armageddon, where he would fight to the death, Bernanos has very little to offer today's world. Like Péguy, he can be "summed-up," labeled as reactionary, naive, impractical. He had no "workable" political or economic vision; he knew little about any "existential crisis," and he didn't seem to care about the workings of the unconscious, though he did say this once: "As soon as I take up my pen, what comes back to me immediately is my childhood, my quite commonplace childhood, so like everybody else's and from which I draw all that I write, as from an inexhaustible source of dreams."

When he died, he was quite lucid and anxious to admit that he had enjoyed his life on this earth more than he ever dared acknowledge. Like any honest but shy child, he had complained only about what he loved, and now the time had come to say thank you, say good-bye, and hurry home.

New Republic, April 15, 1967

Bernanos's Diary
A Country Priest as Everyman

No book has meant more to me than Georges Bernanos's *The Diary of a Country Priest*. I have read it and reread it, and I keep it in front of me on my desk. At times I do Bernanos a sacrilegious injustice; something particularly provocative or troubling has taken place, in my own life or in the larger world that we all share, and I am drawn to *The Diary*, drawn to a number of well-marked passages, which, I suppose, have a scriptural significance for me.

I first read the book while in college, but at a friend's suggestion rather than any professor's. At the time, I was hungry for answers, the more clear-cut the better, and to my frustration I found precious few in *The Diary*. Years later, though, while taking my training in psychiatry, I went back to the novel—after hearing Paul Tillich refer to it in a lecture sharply critical of secular America's almost religious interest in the human mind. Anyway, the second reading marked a turning point in my life. Tillich's message came across all the more strongly—so that thereafter I could manage a smile when I heard yet another bit of psychiatric theory proclaimed as the way to the New Jerusalem.

Bernanos was a French novelist and essayist who died in 1948. He told powerful, haunting stories in a lean, self-possessed style that carries over very well in translation. He is unfortunately not well known here, probably because his struggles as a passionate Christian pilgrim simply do not interest most Americans, even those who nominally call themselves believers. Perhaps that is why several of his eight novels and almost all of his forceful, brilliantly argued religious or political essays are not even available in English. But *The Diary of a Country Priest* is very much available, and the film of it, done by Robert Bresson, is occasionally shown in a film series—though each year I find that most of the students I teach have not heard of, let alone come across, either the book or the movie.

The Diary was written in the mid thirties while Bernanos lived in

Majorca, an island he loved. There, as well as on the Spanish main-
land, a civil war was already under way, and the sensitive novelist
felt personally and philosophically challenged by the terrible injustices he witnessed. He also felt driven to words, to an effort that
would give a life to his doubts and anguish and make them subject to
the scrutiny of others.

His essays burned with indignation that human beings could
make other human beings suffer so; that politicians and generals
could be as wretchedly cynical and corrupt as they were in Spain
and in his native France; and, worst of all, that the Church, the Roman Catholic Church he loved with all his heart, could betray
Christ and stand beside a collection of decadent, greedy nobles and
landlords. In his novel, *The Diary of a Country Priest,* the same
sense of disgust and shame appears again and again but far more unforgettably—because the priest and others are carefully developed
characters in an almost unbearably delicate and touching story.

Bernanos made a crucial and inspired decision when he chose to
put the novel in the form of a diary. The priest can say what he
pleases, openly and honestly and directly and unashamedly. In a
sense he is given complete freedom—from the presence of the author. As a gentle, troubled, inward man, the priest has a right to
think about all sorts of things: the value of prayer; the nature of
childhood; the effects of poverty on the mind and spirit; the only too
apparent flaws in the Church, and, indeed, in every single institu-
tion—whether social, political, or religious. But he can also act,
abruptly and spontaneously; and, above all, he can act unselfconsciously. We as readers can judge him, and later he can judge
himself.

Almost miraculously, though, Bernanos has removed himself
from the novelist's great temptation to cheat on his characters by
not taking care that their speech, their ideas and ideals have been
earned—that is to say, that they must emerge as naturally the property of the person portrayed. Not once does Bernanos call attention
to himself as the author. When *The Diary* is over and its author
dead, we feel we have met him: an ordinary priest whose parish is
"like all the rest"; a tempted priest, who inevitably succumbs repeatedly to the sin of pride; a sad and confused priest, who drinks and
almost stumbles his way through a short and apparently unremarka-
ble life; and finally, a man of God, perhaps a saint, whose faith we
can appreciate, even as he doubts it until the very end.

Obviously, *The Diary* has no formal or coherent plot—any more than a real-life diary would. But lives have their particular trends, and in the long run what seems aimless, haphazard, or accidental can figure as all of a piece. In this case, the curé from the beginning is old beyond his years, in almost constant physical pain, and alive in a town that itself seems stagnant if not damned outright. The rain beats the land incessantly. Constant fog makes it hard to see beyond one's feet. The village seems like a hasty afterthought, something that was never meant to be. As for the parishioners, they are tired and lonely and bored. Yes, they go through the motions, even work up appetites, preferences, hates; but their priest hears something else: the fears, the misgivings, the self-lacerations, and worst of all, the pride that masks itself in fake piety and in a slyly boastful resignation to "things as they are."

The curé knows how awful it is for everyone, and he himself has little to offer—to them or himself. He can only find himself wanting, lacking, doomed perhaps to the exquisitely poignant but inert wisdom he writes down in his diary. In one crucial episode, he confronts the town's leading citizen, a countess, with her pride. Her son died as a child, and she still wears a medallion that contains a lock of his hair. Her husband seeks the company of other women, and she is desperately unhappy, but no matter: what seems like a stubborn inner strength enables her to appear always correct, always dignified, always able to endure her fate. All of which the curé slowly exposes for the pride it is. A kind of stern, moralistic stoicism is not quite what Christ had in mind as redemptive; and certainly he did not die so that others would continue to nail themselves to a succession of private (hence idolatrous) crosses.

Not that the curé is some cool, carefully trained technician who knows how to pace himself and make his "interpretations" (always authoritative and correct, of course) at just the right moment. One moment he can be rude, tactless, himself insufferably priggish. Then he turns, catches himself, and speaks in an honest, strong, and clear way that can only be called revelatory—and particularly so because the diary, which tells us what happens, is full of exactly the mixture of self-doubt, genuine humility, and blindness that even inspired saints necessarily demonstrate. In fact, it can be argued that the curé is meant to be a saint, meant to be a man whose holiness is unknown to himself but instructive beyond all words for those of us who read the diary.

Though a writer, Bernanos profoundly distrusted words, which he knew to be the money that intellectual confidence-men put to a million corrupt and murderous purposes. In *The Diary of a Country Priest*, the words are plain and strong, the talk almost unbelievably pure, down-to-earth, unadorned. Quietly but relentlessly, the curé goes about his struggle, and eventually—so Bernanos must have believed—all who read *The Diary* must choose, must find that struggle either compelling or trivial, since from the very beginning Christ insisted upon making *choice* humanity's inescapable right and burden.

But beyond esthetics, beyond *any* choice, the self-serving ones of everyday life or the literary ones or the exalted and agonized religious ones, a kind of peace can come after the choice has been made: "True grace is to forget oneself. Yet if pride could die in us the supreme grace would be to love oneself in all simplicity—as one would love any of those who have loved and suffered in Christ."

A saint and the grace he or she somehow receives are presumably everywhere to be found, though in *The Diary* one does get the impression that some places and some roads are better than others. More than anything else, Bernanos fought the temptation to ignore life's uncertainties and ambiguities, its built-in mysteries, its setbacks that can mean so much and its victories that are nothing, nothing really. For years he succumbed to sin and raged against those he believed to be his enemies—the clever, self-serving intellectuals who have a name, a label for everyone and anything, and who kill one another every day with words sharper than any knife could ever be.

But the author of *The Diary of a Country Priest*, like the curé in it, may have at last and unwittingly achieved his particular moment of grace, of sanctity. "Does it matter?" the priest asked as he neared the end. One can almost hear Georges Bernanos asking the same thing: Do they matter, all the shrill and confident ideologues around? No, the curé would say, and wryly smile; and no, Bernanos at last could say to himself.

New York Times Book Review, November 3, 1968

The Pilgrimage of Georges Bernanos

A
mong French novelists of the twentieth century, Georges
Bernanos is one of the least known and least appreciated
by English-speaking readers. Even the relatively sophisticated ones who are likely to have read many of the novels
or essays of Camus or Sartre or Gide and who may know Mauriac by
reputation draw a blank on mention of Bernanos. In France and,
indeed, throughout the Continent, it has been otherwise—Bernanos's novels and his social or political essays were widely appreciated during his lifetime (1888 to 1948), and they still command the
strong interest of a literate public, especially that segment of it with
religious and philosophical interests. As for his *Diary of a Country
Priest*, it was a great success among both general readers and critics
when it was published fifty years ago, and it has been, unquestionably, the Bernanos novel that has earned the most lasting interest of
readers, no matter what their background or nationality.

Bernanos was born in Paris and brought up in a middle class, de
voutly Roman Catholic home. He came of age at a time when
France was deeply divided culturally and spiritually—a division that
the Dreyfus Affair only served to accentuate. On the one hand, Paris
was a cosmopolitan city of international renown—a home for early
twentieth-century secular thinkers, artists, and writers. On the other
hand, millions of French citizens (those living in rural areas, especially, but also the social elites of Paris) were still very conservative—
devoutly religious and, significantly, monarchist in sympathy. In the
early years of this century, that split threatened the stability of the
nation. Demonstrations and street fights were by no means rare,
with the Dreyfusards and anti-Dreyfusards at each other's throats,
republicans taking on monarchists and agnostics challenging Catho-
lics. The young Bernanos was then a fiercely conservative Catholic
royalist, deeply suspicious of those so-called progressive forces that
claimed to speak for a new century and way of regarding this life,

forces that were man-centered, optimistic, and wedded to social change, political reform, and cultural experimentation.

As he grew older, Bernanos tried to figure out what to do with his life. He had been educated by the Jesuits and had taken courses in law and literature. He had joined the notoriously conservative, if not reactionary, Action Française movement headed by Charles Maurras and Léon Daudet. Indeed, just before World War I he was editing the royalist weekly *L'Avant-Garde de Normandie*. During the war, he fought in the French army and was wounded and decorated. In 1917, he married Jeanne Talbert d'Arc, a collateral descendant of Joan of Arc; they would eventually be the parents of six children. After the war, he began a gradual reconsideration of his social and political views that culminated in a decisive break with Action Française. He did so in response to his craving for ideas, fiction, and moral reflection. In the 1920s, when he was in his thirties, he found himself noticing the poor, the humble, the scorned, and wondering why his beloved Catholic Church was so deeply connected to the powerful and wealthy people of France.

At the time, he was working for an insurance company. He was always on the move, from train to train, hotel to hotel. As he moved, he looked carefully and took notes, and he felt a strong and continuing desire to write—stories, novels, literary essays, political jeremiads. By the early 1930s his early novels—*L'Imposture*, *La Joie*, and a detective story, *Un Crime*—had earned him modest recognition. By 1935, when the last of those three had appeared, Bernanos was a frequent contributor to *Le Figaro*—a thoughtful conservative writer with a strong Christian conscience who wavered between his respect for established religious and political institutions and his fiery individualism and anarchic contempt for those earthly powers that both the Hebrew prophets and Jesus had so roundly condemned.

He was a loner, too, utterly contemptuous of the literary salons so many other writers delighted in frequenting. A motorcycle accident in 1933 only made him more reclusive. He was partially crippled for the rest of his life, and by the middle 1930s he had become a full-time writer, though by no means financially self-sufficient.

In 1934, Bernanos had moved with his family to Majorca, and soon enough two more novels, *Un Mauvais Rêve* and *Monsieur Quine*, appeared. He was a witness to the human consequences of the Spanish Civil War and eventually went through yet another personal and political transformation. Even as Simone Weil and George Orwell were horrified and disgusted by what they saw in Spain on the left—the betrayals, deceptions, lies, and cruelties of various Communist leaders and organizations—Bernanos had come to realize how murderously vicious Franco and his henchmen were turning out to be. He did not hesitate to speak out and thus risk the condemnation of his fellow Catholic conservatives.

It was at this point that Weil addressed her famous letter to him. In 1938, Bernanos published *Les Grandes Cimetières Sous la Lune*, and the Vatican itself was shaken by his searing, powerfully rendered account of the terror Franco's legions were inflicting on innocent men, women, and children, all in the name of Catholic nationalism. "I recognized the smell of civil war, the smell of blood and terror, which exhales from your book; I have breathed it, too," Weil wrote. But she recognized that in Bernanos's literary hands a new clarity, honesty, and decency had been reached, an exceptionally edifying and inspiring level of political writing: "I must admit that I neither saw nor heard of anything which quite equalled the ignominy of certain facts you relate, such as the murders of elderly peasants or the Ballillas [an Italian Fascist cadre] chasing old people and beating them with truncheons."

In that same letter, Weil praised *Journal d'un Curé de Campagne*, which had been published in 1936. Bernanos wrote that book too in Majorca, and it would turn out to be his most celebrated one, justly so—a masterpiece, really, whose wisdom will never become outdated. *The Diary*, as many have learned to call this singularly affecting novel, is the simple story of an obscure, rural French priest who seems virtually overwhelmed by what he judges to be his own inadequacies, not to mention the isolated, woebegone nature of his parish, which he describes in one of his entries as "bored stiff." This humble curé tries hard against such odds to minister unto his obscure, lowly flock.

It is a stroke of genius, of course, for Bernanos to give him to us through his journal, because the priest is not apologizing or boasting, scolding or excusing. All through Bernanos's writing life he tried to comprehend saintliness, holiness, and it is in *The Diary* that he most nearly approaches that complex and forbidding subject with evident success. Saints, he knew, do not give discourses on saintliness, and authors who attempt to do so risk rhetoric and sentimental bombast. But the literary device of a diary permits a candor, a lack of self-consciousness and self-importance, so that gradually this ailing, seemingly confused, melancholic young priest becomes to the reader a virtual incarnation of divine grace. His unpretentious, stumbling, honestly earnest manner, his mixture of knowing sadness and naiveté, his moments (and longer) of self-doubt, followed by quiet spells of prayerful trust in the Lord's intentions for him and for everyone, all are evidence for the reader of what a true *homo religiosus* is like inwardly.

As the curé goes from home to home, from situation to situation, we witness his brief, painful, unimportant life, so full of conflict and uncertainty, and finally we begin to realize how spiritually triumphant this life has been, no matter the opinion of the one who lived it. Not that there are any obvious victories in the conventional sense. This young priest dies of cancer, having felt himself to have failed both his church and his own personal ideals. We know otherwise, however, we who have been exposed to this diary, this account of one soul's arduous ascent toward its Maker. What we read, of course, is Bernanos at his most brilliant, daring to assert in this century of agnostic, materialistic skepticism a fervent plea for religious faith and also for a humane social ethics that is worthy of the lives Isaiah and Jeremiah and Amos lived, the life that Jesus lived.

"How little we know what a human life really is—even our own," the curé writes. Then he makes this declaration: "To judge us by what we call our actions is probably as futile as to judge us by our dreams. God's justice chooses from this dark conglomeration of thought and act, and that which is raised toward the Father shines with a sudden burst of light, displayed in glory like the sun." A little further on, the curé notes that "the wish to pray is a prayer in itself," and he even dares to remark that "God can ask no more than that of us." Later, the temptation to prideful self-righteousness is acknowledged: "He who condemns sin becomes part of it, espouses it." Then, toward the end, the disillusioned Georges Bernanos (who would wander through Brazil and Paraguay in the late 1930s and, after fighting Hitler as a friend of de Gaulle's, would leave for North Africa and die at the age of sixty as much a loner as ever) merges with the curé in this fashion: "The Pagan State: the state which knows no law but that of its own well-being—the merciless countries full of greed and pride!"

Nonetheless, despite a few such harsh and grim asides, this novel, with its account of various meetings, incidents, and chance encounters, with its small victories and defeats, is steadily true to the essentially forgiving and redemptive message offered the world some two thousand years ago in the incarnation of Christ. The curé exclaims at the end: "How easy it is to hate oneself!" Then he turns himself around: "True grace is to forget. Yet if pride could die in us, the supreme grace would be to love ourselves in all simplicity—as one would love any of those who themselves have suffered and loved in Christ." This is no cult of contemporary narcissism or of salvation on the cheap. By the time we have read that last entry in the diary, we have ourselves made a pilgrimage of sorts—with our guide and mentor, of course, a particular novelist who was himself an ever-seeking pilgrim and who, one suspects, died rather as his curé did, glad at last to be headed home.

New York Times Book Review, June 8, 1986

Minorities, Art, and Literature

Human Nature Is Finer

Seven years ago, I was taken to a tenant farmer's cabin in Clarke County, Alabama. I was taken by a young Civil Rights worker who was born in the cabin. Though his parents had died, his grandmother and an aunt and uncle still lived "on the place," and he wanted me to get to know them somewhat, which I did—somewhat. We talked. We didn't talk. We tried to make talk. We were at our most comfortable when talk wasn't expected or necessary—in church or out in the fields or walking through the woods, where I could, the grandmother said, "take in the scenery" or "sit myself down in God's house," and see and hear and not feel constrained to think up things to say or get others to say something.

At the end of a weekend, the young man and I went on to Mississippi, where he was working to get his people the right to vote and I was talking with relatives of several black children I knew. (They were the first black children to enter white schools in New Orleans, amid something less than "law and order.") As we drove, we talked about the circumstances under which blacks live in the rural South and the road ahead if changes were to take place. I had seen extremely poor people living hard and brutish lives. I had seen the illnesses, the fearfulness, the weariness. And my friend, on leave from a small, all-black college in Alabama, at twenty embittered because in the early sixties his people couldn't even vote in this richest and strongest of the world's democracies, had only one retort to my expressions of sympathy; he wanted to let me know a thing or two: "I don't recognize myself or any of the people I grew up with in those articles people write. I decided to major in sociology because I thought I'd really learn about my people that way. But you read and you read and you say to the author: Listen, man, you're lost. You're looking at the trees, and a lot of them are in bad shape, but there's a whole forest, too, and it's still around, after all the fires we've had, and all the trees they've cut down, and the drought, and everything else bad. We're standing, and we're going to keep on standing. People should come around and see *that* and explain *that* and write about *that*—just for a change."

For a change, his wishes have been realized. He probably would not agree with everything Albert Murray has written in *The Omni-Americans*, but the book's argument will be welcome to the many black and white political activists who know how cleverly a government intent on foot-dragging can utilize all the reports and findings, all the data from all the research projects—so many of them supported by federal money people could use for food or clothes. Mr. Murray is not primarily a political person. He commands no cadres, no followers. He speaks for himself, and he speaks as a literary critic, an essayist, and a short-story writer. But he also speaks as a man who is proud of his people and their considerable achievements. In *The Omni-Americans*, his purpose is to set forth those achievements and to warn against America's "experts," especially what he calls "social-science survey technicians"—people who ask a lot of questions and tabulate the responses and proclaim without modesty or qualification lots of conclusions and prescriptions. They do not, says Mr. Murray, see the richness, the complexity of the black experience in America (or, for that matter, any group's experience); they merely contribute to the caricatures that so many of us cannot get out of our heads. Mr. Murray says that social scientists are most comfortable seeing the problems people have, not the people: the fears, the tensions and hates they feel compelled to reveal, the hesitations and infirmities, the exhaustion and despair. He does not deny that millions of blacks have had the worst possible life. He was born near Mobile, has taught literature at Tuskegee Institute, and has lived in Chicago and New York as well as the rural South, so he has seen how political discrimination and economic hardship produce the mean lives that some men and women live—and then hand on as an awful inheritance to their children. Nevertheless, he insists that black people have never been as used up and shattered as some of their more hysterical observers have maintained. He sees and hears in Alabama and in Harlem things quite different from what most of us are accustomed to read in newspapers and magazines and books. He sees people who have shrewdness and toughness and style and a liveliness that three centuries of American history have been unable to destroy. He sees children who can run and sing and dance and laugh. He sees youths who are thoroughly in tune with concrete realities. He sees men and women who have "soul," who do indeed have rhythm, who swing, who throb with a vitality, a responsiveness, a spirituality that will not be denied. He hears jazz and the blues and work songs and spirituals and gospel songs. He hears people who have no trouble testifying and signifying, who have no "communication block," who have long known about "dialogue" and "group support" and "emotional catharsis" and "interpersonal relationships." And from all he has seen and heard, he has decided that his people can demonstrate an elegance of taste, can live intense, glowing lives, can have a gusto that certain observers and social scientists naturally *would* miss—given their limited, dreary outlook, their pretensions, their insistence upon submitting everything to a theory or a conceptual system. Mr. Murray simply wants to balance things out:

> *The Omni-Americans* is based in large measure on the assumption that since the negative aspects of black experience are constantly being overpublicized (and to little purpose except to obscure the positive), justice to U.S. Negroes, not only as American citizens but also as the fascinating human beings that they so obviously are, is best served by suggesting some of the affirmative implications of their history and culture.

Those implications are spelled out forcefully. The heritage that enabled a Bessie Smith, a Coleman Hawkins, and a Duke Ellington is not an "adaptation to stress" but the distillation of a particular human experience—one that has inspired people as well as discouraged them, for black people have never been as far removed from America's "higher" world as they have seemed to be. Neither Mark Twain nor Melville nor Faulkner could escape black people, any more than the blacks could escape the whites' religion, habits, values, and language. Anyone who has spent much time on a plantation manor sees (or struggles not to see) how much rich Southern whites have learned from their "help." A decade ago, when I lived in Mississippi, I was told by a lawyer in Pass Christian that his daughter was "as sassy as a nigger." Mr. Murray would have wanted me to notice that the lovely belle in question was brought up by a black woman, liked her way of preparing food, used a lot of her words, even walked a little like her, and was "sassy" like her, which means that she had the same intense and unyielding spirit. Mr. Murray would wish all of us to remember that those thousands of young white people came to the Woodstock festival so that they could talk in a certain way, sing in a certain way, respond to a particular kind of music, and that the songs and words and responses showed how close we can be to each other, how black in spirit and culture many white-skinned Americans are.

This book contests "the systematic oversimplification of black tribulations" to be found in the press and in the journals and books social scientists fill up with their special prose—a prose that certainly lacks the direct, strong, lucid words "disadvantaged" children use every day. In the eagerness to examine black parents, black youths, and black families, the serious problems and flaws of white people are nearly ignored. To Albert Murray, it is as if white hypocrisy, duplicity, boredom, crime, and family instability were off-limits for those interested in "pathology" and "deprivation." Sometimes Mr. Murray states his complaints against social scientists so sweepingly and angrily that he undermines his own important argument. Blacks who live in either Alabama or Harlem *do* have serious difficulties, as do whites in the fanciest of our suburbs. Sensitive psychologists and historians like Kenneth Clark and C. Vann Woodward have to dwell upon the sad and bitter and painful moments (in the life of both individuals and a nation) even as they pay respect to the fact that, after all and through everything, those people and this country are still very much alive. The best of our social scientists— such as Oscar Lewis and Elliot Liebow and Allison Davis—know that the people they work with (and, incidentally, feel very close to) are not the absurd caricatures that come out of many "studies." All the same, *every* American reporter and critic and social scientist could profit from this book. If Mr. Murray can get too outraged, too fussy, too insistent, he can also grin and enjoy himself and write provocative, intelligent, original prose. This is how he talks about the "new" effort by certain blacks to achieve "self-esteem," which is one of many questionable abstractions that this book mocks:

> If U.S. Negroes don't already have self-pride and didn't know black . . . is beautiful, why do they always sound so good, so

warm, and even cuss better than everybody else? Why do they dress so jivy and look so foxy, standing like you better know it in spite of yourself? If black people haven't always known how beautiful black is, why have they always been walking, prancing like they'd rather be dancing, and dancing like everybody else is a wall-flower or something? If Louis Armstrong doesn't know he has black beauty to spare how come he can create more beauty while clowning than them other people can giving all they got? How come a hard-boiled cat like Johnny Hodges got so much tenderness and elegance left over? And what's Coleman Hawkins doing turning the blues into such finespun glass, and what were Dizzy Gillespie and Yardbird Parker doing all them acrobatic curlicue lyrics about? How come Count Basie and Lionel Hampton think they can make a hillbilly jump, stomp, and rock— and almost do it? Why does everybody take it for granted that Duke Ellington can wipe out anybody anywhere, anytime he wants to?

Though everybody acknowledges Duke Ellington's abilities, many of us are less willing to give him and Ralph Ellison and Langston Hughes and Alain Locke and Arna Bontemps and W. E. B. Du Bois and James Weldon Johnson and John Hope Franklin their place in a particular culture, which is black and yet which draws widely upon this nation's traditions and customs, its folklore, its idiosyncrasies and ceremonies and values—thus the title of the book. Albert Murray thinks that we should be mindful of that culture· built up and tested and strengthened in the rural South, then brought into the cities, where "Walkin' the Ground Hog" and "Fishing in the Dark" and "See That My Grave Is Kept Clean" gave way to "Harlem Air Shaft" and "Concerto for Cootie" and "Sepia Panorama." Himself a Southerner, Mr. Murray knows his people's muscles and nerves, knows how attentively they can listen, how closely they can look, how artfully they go about their business, how keenly they judge their blustery "betters"—who are so sure of themselves and of everything around them and yet so unaware of a whole world of sharp eyes and ears and intelligent minds and hearts, torn and saddened but capable of generosity and hope and devotion. "Scenery is fine, but human nature is finer," wrote young John Keats to a friend. Albert Murray, whose love for the poet's language, the novelist's sensibility, the essayist's clarity, the jazzman's imagination, and the gospel singer's depth of feeling is so apparent, would no doubt agree with that nineteenth-century white man's strange suggestion that no matter what distracts us from each other or about each other, *we* are what really matters—each of us and all of us.

New Yorker, October 17, 1970

More Exiles

T he exile is no stranger to history, and certainly not to our time. The story of the Jews is so familiar that it is difficult for anyone to try to tell it again. The exile of the Negro in America is just beginning to be known by the society that once allowed him little travel and no entrance to its social or cultural life. Whether the exile is enforced or claimed, its very definition is its detachment, and from this condition arises both the yearning and the anger.

Blues People is a book of large ambitions. LeRoi Jones, poet, essayist, story writer, and jazz critic, will not confine himself to the history of the development of the blues as music. He will not simply talk about blues people, how they felt in their double exile—as Negroes and as artists—from a country they never left. He subtitles his book *Negro Music in White America*, and from the first page we are informed of his larger sociological and anthropological interests and of his intention to show us the roots of blues in a people and their fate.

Yet the book is at its best when Jones is less concerned with these large questions and traces the history of early blues and their relationship to early jazz, to purely instrumental blues, then to the more classic blues, sung as formal entertainment rather than as an expression of a person's private life or a people's social tragedy, and finally, to the emergence of boogie-woogie, ragtime, and dixieland. We are next led through what the author calls "the modern scene." We see big-band jazz marching to its death in the "watered-down slick 'white' commercializations" of swing. We hear about the *separation* (the author italicizes words like this) of the Negro musician from both white and Negro middle-class culture. Beboppers restore jazz, but their *antiassimilationist* sounds antagonize white America; and the middle-class Negro emulates his white "bossman" again, "trapped in the sinister vapidity of mainline American culture." Finally, in the

origin and development of progressive and cool jazz, the white musician comes into his own—and jazz, of all things, is split into two
mutually segregated forms. Thus, the progressive jazz of Stan Ken-
ton comes from a white, upper-middle-class cerebral tradition, and
cool jazz is most suitable for "white musicians who favored a 'purity
of sound' . . . rather than the rawer materials of dramatic expression." But the bebop of Charlie Parker "re-established blues as the
most important Afro-American form in Negro music."

Mr. Jones falters when he leaves this study of Negro music and its
various forms for extensive forays into history, sociology, psychology,
and ethical judgment of class values. For instance, he tells us that
narcotics users, and particularly heroin addicts, are really a rather
self-assured and aristocratic group. His incredible words are: "Heroin is the most popular addictive drug used by Negroes because . . .
the drug itself tranforms the Negro's normal separation from the
mainstream of the society into an advantage (which I have been saying I think it is anyway). It is one-upmanship of the highest order."
Such talk is nonsense of the highest order. The medical and psychiatric agonies, the sickness and desperation of the addict, whether
he is high, low, or withdrawing, do not deserve such ill-informed
sentimentality.

It is ironic that this gifted young poet, bent on fighting middle-
class American culture in all its shabby superficiality, yields so
willingly to that very culture's most vulgar jargon, its narrowest,
pseudosociological mode of thinking. A writer who has written fine
poetry to honor Charlie Parker tells us in this book that "the ver-
ticality of the city began to create two separate secularities, and the
blues had to be divided among them if it was going to survive at all."
Scattered through the book are phrases like "pseudo-autonomous
existence" or sentences like "the lateral exchange of cultural reference between black and white produced an intercultural fluency."

If Mr. Jones plans to persist with such talk, and if he really wants
to pursue his lay sociology and psychology, he should be more careful about the tone of some of his descriptions. I am not recommend-
ing that he follow the model of those heartless social scientists whose
work so often panders to those who want abstractions about people
rather than the truth of their actual lives. But the sociologists, the
psychologists, and the anthropologists whom he so much admires
have a serious job to do, gathering information about people and

their societies and trying to make sense out of it. Their concern must be strong, their values real, their work passionate, but none of these to the detriment of their curiosity and good sense as observers. They may not like what they see, but surely they cannot confuse their hopes with their study. At times one finds in this book less concern with information than polemical writing disguised in the latest jargon of the social sciences. And often this jargon is not even used to communicate or describe but to condemn.

The book is most effective in its simple, direct information about blues music and its people and in its willingness to relate the suffering of generations of Negroes to the tenaciously redemptive power of their music. What was one kind of hell, the author says, now turns into another as Negroes succumb to the blandishments of the white middle-class world. The blues and their successors in the several forms of jazz are thereby threatened. No less so, however, than the writer—living in that same world—who tries to do them justice.

Dan Jacobson clearly felt himself enough threatened by *his* world to leave it. The longest essay in his *Time of Arrival and other Essays* tells of the author's arrival in London. His childhood as a South African Jew weighed heavily upon him. His youth and its choice of loyalty to this past or departure from it was very much his challenge. The possibilities of his manhood as a writer, as a person with friends, family, and a place to live cropped into his mind at almost every turn in the great city of London, a city movingly appreciated by the young émigré. He comes to it like a cook, an artist, a musician—savoring it, noticing its bulk and its more subtle shapes and forms, responding to its light and shadows, hearing its various sounds.

Jacobson obviously enjoys travel. The book has four parts, three of which are given the names of countries: England, South Africa, and Israel. These three nations in their customs and traditions are closely involved in the writer's life and identity. He writes about each with a special intimacy, and where there is desolation or agony to describe it is done clearly and with compassion. We are taken to the Jewish ghetto in London, dying yet twitching still with life and with memories for the susceptible visitor. In four essays, we are exposed to South Africa's uniquely tragic and disastrous racial situation, and in two more we hear about Israel from one of *its* exiles. The author is at his very best in dealing with ironic situations, as in the resemblance of a crowd lunging after visiting royalty to a racist mob; the reactions of whites as they watch a native African festival; the strange twist of history that makes Israel no solution for the problems of the Diaspora, making in certain ways Jewish identity—in the continuing "abroad" that is the world outside Israel—more emphatic, even less defined, still puzzling. All through these three parts, the essays are both simple and tightly organized, the decency and charity of the writer always present, and his essential good sense and lucidity of mind a pleasure to encounter.

Of *Uncle Tom's Cabin* Jacobson says: "I am not sure whether we can learn more from the book's faults than from its merits; but I am sure at least that we can learn something from our own misguided insistence, over these many years, that the book has no merit at all." He goes on to wonder whether "our revulsion from Tom doesn't spring in part from an uneasy fear that his way of asserting his humanity might be as effective as any other way open to him—or to us." He goes on to make his critical judgment: "Stowe never fully imagined that the day would come when Negroes would read her novel and comment upon it . . . [and] this failure of imagination is a crucial one; and one for which she is less and less likely to be forgiven in the future." Yet, he concludes wryly with these words: "We can trust her sufficiently to say that she would not have minded this at all."

These are the words of one who understands the relationship between the individual and the historical moment. We act out of our lives and make history; but we act *in* history, too. To denounce from the perfections of a later period the "failure" of a book that was itself striving toward that period, to see its malicious "influence" retrospectively rather than its contextual meaning, its still partial relevance, and certainly its integrity, is to abandon, Jacobson feels, one's vision and one's humanity.

Jacobson's feeling for the humane comes through again in his treatment of Mark Twain and *The Adventures of Huckleberry Finn.* The dismaying misapplication of psychiatric theory and nomenclature to literature has hardly left the relationship of Huck and Jim untouched. Who can ignore the provocations of a jazzy, doctrinaire criticism, plucked from psychoanalysis, and thrown foolishly, accusingly, sometimes with unbridled sanctimony at the lives of writers or the characters of their books? Here is Mr. Jacobson on Huck and Jim:

By any definition of the word, the relationship between Huck and Jim on the river is considerably more "civilized" than any relationship which they can enjoy with anyone else or with each other, on the shore. The relationship between the two on the raft demands from them both the sacrifices which civilization demands from us all, and which we frequently find most burdensome to make: it demands mutual responsibility, self-abnegation, and moral choice. . . . The tragedy of the book is that the fineness of Huck's relationship with Jim is impermanent; it cannot survive on shore, as the last chapters dismally demonstrate. Though he did not realize it, this is the saddest and fullest judgment that Twain was ever to make of "the damned human race."

The essays are very much like Orwell's in their clarity and warmth. And their author's mind is both sensitive and sensible, an unusual combination these days.

Partisan Review, Winter 1964

To Try Men's Souls

We all know that America's cities are in trouble, especially because blacks have fled to them in mixed hope and fear. We know, because we are constantly told, that the whites don't understand the needs of the blacks, that we will go from bad to worse, that it is too late because another apocalypse is at hand. But almost no one has tried to tell us about the early lives, the *inner* early lives, of black people, the particular ways that black children in a rural setting grow, only to leave and become the urban poor, the "social dynamite" we hear abstractly described again and again. The tragedy had to be documented, yet social documentation and political prescription can be static and flat and self-defeating when the men, women, and children involved become merely part of something called "a history of exploitation and oppression." And books and thinking that carry on in this fashion will not, unfortunately, really be counterbalanced by Alice Walker's *The Third Life of Grange Copeland*. Novelists and poets (Miss Walker is a published poet, too) are not the people we look to for help about ghetto children and racial violence in our cities. Moreover, Miss Walker was born in and has spent most of her life in the Southern countryside, and she is now a writer-in-residence at Tougaloo College, a black Mississippi school that is not in a city. What can she know of the crime and violence, the drug addiction and alcoholism and despair we have been told exist so significantly in our urban ghettos? What can she volunteer about the attitudes of black children or their problems?

In her own way, she has supplied some answers, but she has not written a social novel or a protest novel. Miss Walker is a storyteller. A black woman from the farmlands of Georgia, she knows her countryside well—so warm and fertile and unspoiled, so bleak and isolated and blood-soaked—and especially she knows the cabins, far out of just about everyone's sight, where one encounters the habits of diet, the idioms of speech, the styles of clothing, and the ways of prayer that contrast so strikingly with the customs of the rest of us. Fearful and vulnerable, rural blacks (and whites, too) can at the same time be exuberant, passionate, quick-witted, and as smartly self-displaying as the well-dressed and the well-educated. She knows, beyond that, what bounty sharecroppers must hand over to "bossmen," and how tenant farmers struggle with their landlords, and how subsistence farmers barely get by. But she does not exhort. In *The Third Life of Grange Copeland*, the centuries of black life in America are virtually engraved on one's consciousness. Equally vivid is Grange Copeland, who is more than a representative of Georgia's black field hands, more than someone scarred by what has been called "the mark of oppression." In him Miss Walker has turned dry sociological facts into a whole and alive particular person rather than a bundle of problems and attitudes. Character portrayal is what she has accomplished, and character portrayal is not to be confused with "motivational analysis."

Grange Copeland is a proud, sturdy black yeoman who has the white man on his back. He picks cotton, lowers his head when "they" appear, goes through the required postures a segregationist society demands—the evasions, duplicities, and pretenses that degrade black people and make moral cowards out of white people. Underneath, he is strong enough to hate, and without rage a person like him might well become the ingratiating lackey he has to pretend to be. His anger is not really political or ideological. He sulks, lashes out at his wife, his young son Brownfield, and her illegitimate infant. He sees too much, feels too much, dreams too much; he is like an actor who has long ago stopped trying to estimate where he begins and his roles end. He works backbreaking days in the field and then comes home saddened and hungry for sleep but tense and truculent. ("By Thursday, Grange's gloominess reached its peak and he grimaced respectfully, with veiled eyes, at the jokes told by the man who drove the truck. On Thursday nights he stalked the house from room to room and pulled himself up and swung from the rafters of the porch.") He is nearly consumed by his contempt for the white landowners, the bossmen, but he and his wife struggle tenaciously for the little integrity and self-respect they can find. Eventually they conclude that they are losers and take to drink and promiscuity, followed by hysterical efforts at atonement on Sunday mornings. Then Grange abandons his wife, and she poisons herself and her illegitimate infant. Brownfield, the child of their hope and love, is left to wander across the land, left to learn how much a child has to pay for the hurt and pain his parents live with and convey.

I suppose it can be said that *The Third Life of Grange Copeland* is concerned with the directions a suffering people can take. His first life ends in flight, and his wandering son takes flight, too, becoming in time a ruined and thus ruinous man, bent on undermining everyone who feels worthwhile and has a sense of pride and dignity. For a while, the lives of father and son converge on the establishment run by Josie, a sensual, canny, generous, possessive madam whose café and "rooms" full of women feed off the frustrations men like Grange and Brownfield try to subdue. There are complications, accidents, sudden and surprising developments. And always there is the unpredictable and potentially violent atmosphere of the small Georgia towns and the dusty, rutted roads that lead from them into the countryside.

Grange's second life, in Harlem, is equally disastrous. He becomes slick, manipulative, unfeeling—the thief and confidence-man our respectable world (which has its own deceptions and cruelties) is shocked to find and quick to condemn, yet not wholly unfeeling: he tries to help a white woman in distress and is rebuffed. His hatred of whites presses more relentlessly, and so he goes South to find escape from them at any cost. Josie is waiting for him. Brownfield has married her niece, a charming girl, "above" her husband in intelligence and education and sensitivity, but step by step he goes down, systematically destroying his wife and daughters. Yet Grange finds at last—in his third life, as an exile returned home—the freedom he has asked for. The whites are everywhere still powerful, so it is not political and economic freedom he achieves. But he does take care of his son's youngest daughter after her mother is killed by her drunken husband, and, finally, he can say to his beloved granddaughter, "I know the danger of putting all the blame on somebody else for the mess you make out of your life. I fell into the trap myself. And I'm bound to believe that that's the way the white folks can corrupt you even when you done held up before. 'Cause when they got you thinking that they're to blame for *every*thing they have you thinking they's some kind of gods!"

Brownfield tries to get his daughter back, and to prevent that Grange kills him. What goes on between that daughter, that growing child, and her grandfather is told with particular grace; it is as if one were reading a long and touching poem. But Alice Walker is a fighter as well as a meditative poet and a lyrical novelist. She has taken part in the struggles her people have waged, and she knows the struggles they must yet face in this greatest of the world's democracies. She also knows that not even ample bread and wine or power and applause can give anyone the calm, the freedom that comes with a mind's acceptance of its own worth. Toward the end of his third life, Grange Copeland can at last stop being hard on himself and look with kindness upon himself—and one wonders whether any achievement can be more revolutionary.

New Yorker, February 27, 1971

A Dream Deferred

No one who was involved with SNCC and CORE in the 1960s will read *The River of No Return* without a good deal of nostalgia, sorrow, and bitterness—not a very pleasant mixture of emotions, but things haven't turned out so well, either. The author, Cleveland Sellers, is a longtime Civil Rights activist. He comes from a small town in South Carolina, and is of a middle-class family. He needn't have worked so long and hard on behalf of his people. He might easily have become yet another member of E. Franklin Frazier's "black bourgeoisie." Instead, he joined up with SNCC in the early 1960s and to this day is working as an organizer and political activist. As he himself says, "I don't have a personal life anymore."

Much of this book is appropriately impersonal. We are told less about the author's life than about the life of the Civil Rights struggle in the South. Especially evocative, haunting at times, are the recollections of the "old days," when it was "black and white together"; when it was "we shall overcome"; when a relative handful of students could think of taking on the whole segregationist state of Mississippi—and do so with more success than they dreamed possible. (They never underestimated the dangers, the lives that would be lost, the beatings that would take place.) Success, of course, meant the vote for previously disenfranchised people—along with a seat in a Howard Johnson's or a movie house, if one had the money. Yet by no means have the region's Eastlands given up their economic power. By no means, either, have the rural poor Mr. Sellers knows so well had any reason to give up their heritage: fear, extreme poverty, constant anxiety, and a sense of vulnerability that no SNCC or CORE can remove—not when a Voting Rights Bill or a Public Accommodations Bill is followed by an administration such as we have now. So Mr. Sellers expresses his rage and confusion. He persists, tries to do what he can, feels hopeless one minute but on the whole determined—and utterly selfless about his dedication. What matters is his people, still at the bottom of the ladder, still at the mercy of sheriffs and landowners, and yes, high government officials, who right now are cutting the heart out of valuable domestic programs (ones that *do* work but have been denied proper funds, and now will lose all funds) but making sure that all those military bases in states like Mississippi and Alabama stay well supplied with a "cash flow." Mr. Sellers is not surprised at all that, but then why should he be? He has written his book, presumably, to tell the rest of us that our surprise and chagrin are matched by his people's daily pound of flesh—and more.

New Republic, March 17, 1973

Through Conrad's Eyes

I remember going to our nation's capital during the late 1960s to testify before various congressional committees. I had been working in the South, and in Appalachia, and in our Northern ghettos, and presumably I knew something about matters then of significance to the country as a whole and to the men and women who represent us in Washington, D.C. I went before one Senate committee and talked about what I'd seen in some of the worst urban areas of the Northeast. To another committee I described what I'd seen of the life migratory farm workers must live. To yet another committee I reported on the findings a group of us physicians had made while touring the Mississippi Delta—widespread, severe hunger and malnutrition in children. I was becoming, I suppose, one more American expert, called to make his definitive statements, to come up with his appraisal of what has been, is, and ought be—a heady but not altogether rare experience for people in my profession, to whom so many in our contemporary world turn for suggestions and advice, if not a dose of consolation.

In the course of such journeys, I came to know one person fairly well; he was the junior senator from New York, Robert F. Kennedy. I first met him in 1965, when I testified before a committee whose concerns (ghetto problems) were very much his. He relentlessly questioned us witnesses about those problems, and so doing, he seemed to be getting away from the usual facts-and-figures approach. The senator was wondering about how people who are extremely vulnerable regard not only themselves and their neighbors but this life—its purposes, its ethical underpinnings, if any. Later, he took us to lunch, and as we talked I could again feel the moral intensity of the man, a certain thirst and hunger in him as he probed and probed, those blue eyes always staring directly at one's face, and the ears never missing a single word, and for that matter, hearing the silences, too, the remarks not made, whether out of ignorance or stupidity, or arrogance, or shortsightedness. Toward the end of the meal, he suddenly turned to me and asked me what I'd recommend that he read if he had the time for one book, only one—with respect to the racial question in this country. I paused and seemed unable to answer. I remember the blank in my head, his stare continuing, my sense that I was once more going to flunk a course, and then my mind's desperate summons of my wife's views, her often expressed opinions, her way of looking at things, her sensibility. She is a school teacher, and I suppose a pupil in bad trouble was calling for whatever assistance he could find. I heard her say, in my head, *Invisible Man*, and then I heard myself say it: "*Invisible Man.*"

Right off, the academic arrogance, the condescension of my kind asserted itself: better tell him the author's name and say something about the book. But say what? Why had I, anyway, passed over dozens of sociological and psychological studies in favor of a particular story? This man opposite me was a busy, tough, shrewd, demanding, hardheaded, and practical man, who needed concrete, specific answers to concrete, specific problems. What would *Invisible Man* offer him? In any event, as that line of thinking crossed my intimidated, awestruck, ingratiating head—the eager social scientist-hustler glad to be within sight of a mighty empire's world-famous legislative and executive buildings—the senator did an end run around me. I remember my sense of frustration as he told me how much he admired that novel. Did I have any idea whether Ralph Ellison was working on a second one? I readily reported that I was sure Ellison was, then quickly added the obvious, that Ellison was taking his time. I'll never forget the comment that followed, which I can offer almost word for word: "There was so much in that novel; it'd be hard to know what more to say."

Well, we had no more to say on that subject, at least then. An aide of the Senator's approached the table, there were some whispered exchanges, and soon enough he was on his way and the rest of us on ours. When I got home (we'd just moved back North to Massachusetts, after living in Louisiana and Georgia for five years), I told my wife of that moment, and she wondered at *my* problem, never mind the problem (racial turmoil) we had discussed at that lunch. I could only say that I didn't think, at the time, that *Invisible Man* was quite the kind of book the senator had in mind for me to suggest. He was clearly upset terribly by what he'd been seeing in his visits to various American cities, and he very much wanted to figure out how to change this nation's social and economic direction so that our poor and so-called working-class families would be getting a better deal. He had a razor-sharp mind, I'd discovered, and was vigorously pragmatic in his nature—qualities I'd not only observed but had occasion to feel as I tried to respond to his thoroughly alert, conscientious, and independent-minded manner of posing questions and discussion. I was glad when our preliminary discussion of *Invisible Man* and its author had been interrupted. What would I have said, I kept wondering, had the question (which single book to read?) been put to me yet again? Surely the asker had not been seeking the kind of answer I'd offered.

My wife said she certainly hoped he *had* been· seeking the very answer I supplied. I became annoyed; one doesn't seek an answer to something if one already has the answer, unless one is being rhetorical, and that was not the case then. Not necessarily, my wife persisted. We may have our own ideas, but we do want to know what others think. True, I realized, but this was an extremely busy man, who wasn't summoning experts to Washington or talking with them at lunch in order to have a "great books" or "important ideas" discussion. No Senate committee needed me (or anyone else) to come and tell them that Ralph Ellison had written an extraordinary novel, which in its own way said as much as (well, quite a bit more than) the honorable legislators were likely to hear from the collection of social scientists then testifying and (given this nation's culture, its values, and habits) likely to continue testifying.

My wife knew that even anyone as sure of himself and willful and well-read (and versed in Sophocles, Shakespeare, the nineteenth-century romantic poets, all of whom Robert Kennedy often quoted) as the senator was not about to declare war on such objects of secular idolatry as psychology and psychiatry, sociology, anthropology, economics, and political science. She knew, too, that such disciplines had their own particular truths to offer, and the point was not to blame them without qualification for what all too commonly happens—the overestimation of their usefulness, these days, by so many of us. Still, she was not going to relent on her central point—that there is a crying need in this country for a persuasive moral vision and that it is a pity people such as Ralph Ellison aren't the ones testifying before congressional committees, in as much as they seem far more knowing, far more eloquent and savvy with respect to what ails us, what we have been and are and might be, than those who constantly arrive in Washington, D.C., with their "data" and their theories and their "policy proposals." Soon enough, she added another novelist's name as the sort of person she'd like to see talking with our nation's legislators, and she reminded me of a book of his, published a few years earlier, which had meant a lot to us: *Who Speaks for The Negro?* by Robert Penn Warren.

Today the use of the word *Negro* is unwelcome to many —though not to Ralph Ellison, as a matter of fact, who for his own stoutly maintained reasons, keeps using that word. Back then the word *black* had (almost overnight) become a powerful claimant upon the (ever-anxious) white liberal vocabulary, even as black radicals were just that, suddenly—*black*. But at the time it was not the word *Negro* in Robert Penn Warren's book that had bothered many readers. It was a certain point of view, perhaps best explained by one of the (white) Civil Rights activists we knew who had read the book and turned against it, as had happened with *Segregation*, an earlier book of Robert Penn Warren's I'd also once recommended to him and others: "You like these literary folks! They look around, talk with people, then say this is a very confusing world, and it's complicated (they're *always* saying that!), and no one really knows the answers to a lot of these troubles, and so all we can do is try to see as much as we can and write as honestly as we can about what we do manage to see. Right?"

I could hardly say "wrong"; but I did try to amplify his own remarks by asking him whether there wasn't, actually, room for (and need of) precisely that kind of tenaciously reflective and aspiringly evenhanded manner of inquiry. Maybe there was for such as me, he agreed reluctantly and with some accusation (I felt) in his voice, but not for those who were in the middle of a serious social struggle to end, at last, the South's segregationist power. Why need such a struggle preclude paying attention to the helpful observations of a Robert Penn Warren, not to mention Ralph Ellison? He took on Robert Penn Warren, and a black friend of ours, sitting nearby, took on Ellison, and together their argument went like this: Listen, buddy (if such you are!), we are involved in a big fight, and we want to win, and we have a clear idea of what we're fighting for (the vote, access to everyone else's schools, moviehouses, restaurants, and so on), and why we're waging that fight, and how we plan to achieve our victory. Along you come, preaching at us through these novelists who (we'll acknowledge) have strong social interests, a strong desire to help change things for the better, racially—but who also come up with nothing to say that will help us in this war of sorts we're waging, and who even come up with a lot that makes it damn hard at times to go out and take the risks of being a soldier, because when you keep getting told that life is almost infinitely complex, and that ambiguities are everywhere, and ironies, and troubling inconsistencies (namely, in you and your comrades as well as in the enemy's camp), then by God, you're in danger of becoming so "weighed down" (they both used those words) you just feel like surrendering.

This summarizes a long, long series of conversations—of the kind, I knew at the time, Mr. Warren himself would have wanted (talking about irony!) to put into his book, which did, indeed, show how *various* the views of black people were, hence how utterly human their situation: not a herd, a "them" for racists (or supposed friends who had endless amounts of advice to give, aid to offer, and in the clutch, with disagreement, that same aid to withdraw) to hate but the almost infinitely diverse human beings we all are, no matter our racial, religious, ethnic, social, or cultural background, once one pays attention to the words and deeds of particular men, women, and children. I must say that I wasn't inclined to argue too strenuously with those two friends. As in my meeting with a given senator, I knew how important a struggle those two youths were waging, how tough the odds were at times, and how precarious the victories achieved. Is it not under such circumstances a luxury (of certain writers, and the college students or comfortable members of the bourgeoisie who make up their major audience) to take the long and reflective view of the humanities?

Of course, soon enough, the Civil Rights movement, once a band of brothers and sisters, no matter the skin color of anyone, had become torn apart, with all sorts of voices in exhortation and condemnation directed at all sorts of targets. Who *does* speak for "the Negro," everyone was beginning to ask—and who, for that matter, speaks for the white people, whether those who belonged to, say, SNCC and CORE and SCLC (abbreviations for the three major Southern activist groups: the Student Nonviolent Coordinating Committee, the Congress of Racial Equality, and the Southern Christian Leadership Conference), or those who were, simply and not so simply, ordinary Americans? The country was seriously splintered, and we needed all the perspective we could find, each of us, if we were to be able to figure out why that division had happened and in what direction we might turn. Moreover, Ellison's story had turned out to be uncannily accurate—the way, for instance, people long persecuted learn to imitate their persecutors, even to the point of visiting upon themselves the old, familiar responses learned from "the man."

I remember, by 1967, thinking that Ralph Ellison and Robert Penn Warren not only knew "everything" (as poets or novelists at their best seem to) but had reserved for themselves some special gifts of prophecy. They'd both made extraordinary judgments about the manner in which white and black people get caught in blindness even as they struggle to catch sight of what is true and significant and valuable, and not least, worth upholding, worth fighting for—no matter the temptations of envy, rivalry, greed, ambition, and egotism, those qualities none of us ever manages to shed; no matter our skin color, our success, the number of years we've undergone psychoanalysis, the articles and books we've written, and yes, as both Mr. Ellison and Mr. Warren would remind us, even the fine poems and novels we may have by the grace of things managed to compose.

By late 1967 and early 1968, I was having the chance to see Robert Kennedy talk with people I knew in the Mississippi Delta, in the hollows of Appalachia, as he made his restless trek through America, fueled by his burning desire to help others far less fortunate than himself. I remember another talk, similarly brief, about books. Now we were in the rural South and had just seen some extremely hard-pressed tenant farmer families struggling to get by. They were black people, and they possessed within themselves a mix of desperation and dignity that a privileged outsider could find awesome, intimidating, accusing, and unnerving. Suddenly the busy senator started talking about the hurt and ailing people we'd met and about the strange effect they'd had on him, on us. He was searching for words, for a way of putting what he saw and felt. He was searching in vain, it seemed, for a while. He had such moments, one knew—when he stopped talking altogether, or his stream of talk sputtered, and came in fits, starting and stopping and starting and stopping. All of a sudden he mentioned Joseph Conrad, how much it had meant to him, back in college, to read *Heart of Darkness* and

The Nigger of the Narcissus. We talked about the novels, about Conrad's personal life—and I had in my distressingly single-minded way concluded that we were now diverting ourselves, trying to find relief in intellectual talk, in the life and work of a man long dead who lived far from the state of Mississippi and had no great interest during his life in America's racial difficulties. The senator kept talking about Conrad, though; and soon enough those two stories were under surveillance once more by both of us—the greed and despair, the nihilism of the imperialist West, its "darkness," and the effect that James Wait, the dying black man, had on the crew of the freighter the *Narcissus.*

This United States senator (thank God) was no pedant or psychiatrist. He had no interest in pushing his interpretations on anybody, himself included—no interest in dressing them up in fancy, portentous language, the better to dazzle and, eventually, command the obedience of the listener. At one moment in our talk, though, he did say this: "You look around you here, and you can see the point of seeing the place and the people through Conrad's eyes." I was now able to think again of that black man in *The Nigger of the Narcissus,* of the fear and the hate he inspired in others, of the "weight" of James Wait as he waited for death, and of the "weight" we all can be to one another, even as we can inspire and uplift one another, too—as Conrad did with his story. Now, fifteen years later, I hear my sons discuss those stories, and not rarely my mind goes back to that late afternoon of a warm and humid Delta early autumn day: the car speeding to the airport, the press of politics exerting a toll, the presence of suffering nearby; and suddenly Conrad's eyes, his heart and soul, his mind and spirit, upon us in their mighty power to instruct morally—world without end, one hopes and prays.

American Poetry Review, January/February 1984

James Baldwin Back Home

James Baldwin will turn fifty-three on August 2. He was born and grew up in Harlem. He left this country when he was twenty-four for France, where he has, mostly, lived ever since. This summer he returned to New York City but not on yet another brief visit—the expatriate dipping into the forsaken land for a draught of outrage or disgust. He is coming home to live and glad to be back. But if one presses him a bit on the virtues of this country, he is quick to spell out his particular point of view: "I left America because I had to. It was a personal decision. I wanted to write, and it was the 1940s, and it was no big picnic for blacks. I grew up on the streets of Harlem, and I remember President Roosevelt, the liberal, having a lot of trouble with an antilynching bill he wanted to get through the Congress—never mind the vote, never mind restaurants, never mind schools, never mind a fair employment policy. I had to leave; I needed to be in a place where I could breathe and not feel someone's hand on my throat. A lot of young Americans, white or black, rich or poor, have wanted to get away as a means of getting closer to themselves. For me, France was the beginning of a writing life; I wrote *Go Tell It on the Mountain* there. It was there I began the struggle with words."

He is not at all sure, however, that he would go to Paris now if he were a young, black, would-be writer: "I think I'd probably go to Africa, to some part of Asia—the Third World. I love France; I know it well, have good friends there. But it is a *hermetic* place, in certain respects—plenty of arrogance and smugness among its intellectuals and upper bourgeoisie. History brings changes to countries and continents. Exiles, wanderers, refugees find different havens, from generation to generation. I still love France; I do not want to repudiate a former mistress. But Europe has changed. I went there to get enough away from the American Negro Problem—the everyday insults and humiliation, the continual sadness and the rage—so that I could sit down and write with a half-clear head. Now many of the former slaves of the Western colonial empires have come to Europe: blacks, Mohammedans, Pakistanis, Moluccans. A Harlem is rising in Paris."

He talks some more about his life in Europe and again resists, partially at least, an opportunity to clothe himself in the garb of the repentant critic who has finally come around and is effusive with praise for what he once had only scorn: "This country has experienced important changes. When I've returned on visits, over the years, I've gone South and seen how different it's become there. It's still no paradise for blacks in Alabama or Mississippi. Let's not start sounding like chamber of commerce boys in Montgomery. I've seen the same wretchedness in the rural areas—broken-down shacks, and fear in the eyes of people who have to watch out every minute for the bossman and the sheriff, the whites who run the show. And there are urban black slums in Atlanta—the same high unemployment and poverty that millions have to accept as 'life' in Harlem or Chicago's Southside. But in the South, the black man and the white man still get on personally—haven't yet become strangers. I think there's more hope in the South, right now, for the people of both races. It's too early to know whether that hope will turn out to be justified. I don't wish, at this point in my life, to turn into a Southern romantic. The region has been badly served by its apologists—and there's always an interesting market up North for such people. There's little hope in Northern slums, where nearly half the black young people can find no work. Would America's white people stand for that—unemployment figures like those in the ghetto?"

He is somewhat drawn to Jimmy Carter. In an open letter to him Baldwin said that "you, in my lifetime, are the only President I would have written." He sees Carter and Andrew Young as products of a similar regional experience. He is not at all surprised that during the election year blacks turned so quickly and overwhelmingly to Carter. He does not expect the statements of either the president or his roving black ambassador to change very much the concrete realities of power as it affects the lives of millions of malnourished, virtually starving people in the underdeveloped countries, or for that matter, the victimized people of Eastern Europe. Still, he is a writer and not completely down on the value of words, though not, also, without his moments of doubt: "Words can be disguises for inaction—a smokescreen. But words can open up possibilities too. I think Andy Young knows what he can and cannot do. He's sending out signals. The people meant to hear them are listening. They are no fools, don't expect miracles. But they are waiting too. What will come next? How committed is the United States to the poorer countries? We sent billions abroad to rebuild Germany, twice our enemy. Is there an interest of that order in countries who have never fought us and whose resources we have taken when we have needed them, at no great profit for 'the natives'? I think Andy Young is giving it a try; he's waiting to see what will happen, as a writer does when he pours out the truth as he sees it and wonders if some people will sit down and read, and read, and then say: Yes, by God, *yes.*"

He hopes the president will be able to live up to the populist side of his instincts, but he points out repeatedly that the presidency is but one part of a given political and economic system. And besides, there is a history we all have to contend with: "For a long while, liberty was a privilege in this country Blacks had to learn, growing up, a severe interior rigor—to the point that they didn't need the state's police on patrol to keep them in line. In Eastern Europe there is austerity for the masses and the constant presence of the police, the military. Here it is different—if you're doing well, you can say a lot and get away with it. If you're poor, you can shout to your heart's content, provided no one starts listening to you and your message doesn't threaten too many people. I think blacks have to say to themselves something like this: We will act as if this is a free country, until the white people tell us it's not by jailing us or killing us. And a lot of us have been locked up or murdered over the centuries we've been here. It's a hard thing to talk about, the Iron Curtain and its significance. I know that my books have been very popular in the Soviet Union. But *Giovanni's Room* cannot be published there. And why have the Russians been so eager to read and praise me? On the other hand, it's no credit to this enormously rich country that there are more oppressive, less decent governments elsewhere. We claim the superiority of our institutions. We ought to live up to our own standards, not use misery elsewhere as an endless source of self-gratification and justification. Of course, people tell me all the time in the West that they are trying, they are trying hard. Some have tears in their eyes and let me know how awful they feel about the way our poor live, our blacks, or those in dozens of other countries. People can cry much easier than they can change, a rule of psychology people like me picked up as kids on the street."

In France, or elsewhere abroad, he hasn't been able to stay away from the events in this country. The Patty Hearst case prompted him to think of the Weathermen and others like them, the enraged products of privileged homes who turned so bitterly and violently on America, and finally on one another. He would like, one day, to write about such matters, the disenchantment of people who have so much and yet, it seems, so little. He has been reading *The Possessed* again. He has been thinking of the nineteenth-century Russian intelligentsia, among them the political activists who became so fiercely against the status quo and at such a high cost to their personal lives: "It's ironic—some black kids know that their fathers are criminals, have been arrested, have been in jail again and again. But what to think of a Patty Hearst, or others like her—though they never went as far as she did—who begin to think that *their* fathers may be a bit 'criminal' too? Whites and blacks have met at that point—an awakened sense of the subtleties of injustice. Each time I come back to this country, I travel-lecture on several campuses. The races are less obsessed with each other than was the case in the 1960s. Many black students tell me they pay no attention to whites— though indifference may conceal many other emotions. We hear that whites have gone on to other concerns—themselves and their careers. But I have met many white students and hear by mail from others, and they seem bewildered, troubled, at a loss to know what to do, where to go. I'm not sure they're as passive and inert as some social observers say, or wish. Maybe some of them have learned a lot, as a result of the Civil Rights movement, the Vietnam War, Watergate, the assassination of beloved leaders, and so on. Maybe those young people are trying to figure out what's right, what ought to be done, now that they've seen before their eyes what's wrong. Inertia, even despair, can be a stage in one's growth, a way of coming to terms with what one has gone through and learned."

He is insistently the "native son" essayist, full of strong-minded, if not polemical, comments of a social or political nature. But he is a novelist, and when asked about that important side of his life he becomes more guarded, more tentative, less inclined to speak in a forceful, even provocative, manner. A book of his meant for young readers, and already published in England, will come out in September: *Little Man, Little Man*. It tells of a short time in the New York City lives of a seven-year-old boy and another boy and a girl. He has for some time been working on a novel, one that means a lot to him. It will actually take up where *Go Tell It on the Mountain* left off. He has, he thinks, been skirting the subject all his writing years—the life and death of a gospel singer, a man: "I have a few more months of work on the novel. I'm going back to France in a few days, because that's where I can best finish the novel. *Then*, I guess, I'll be able to come home. People stop me and say: 'Coming home, Jimmie?' I say yes, soon, but I've got to go back and finish something. Maybe it'll be the end of more than the novel—a long apprenticeship, I sometimes think. It was in France that I could start a career of writing English because there I was not able to speak French and so I was driven to recognize myself as an outsider *that way*: not as a black man, but as an English-speaking person. In Harlem, as a boy going to school, I also felt myself an outsider. I knew a language different from the ones teachers were trying to make me learn—the language of jazz, spirituals, the blues; the language of testifying and signifying; and the language of cool black cats, street kids, holding on to life by their fingernails while they heard their parents screaming up to their God in heaven, asking him what's going on, and what's going to happen, and when, oh Jesus, when?"

He is asked to tell more but pulls back into a writer's self-protective nervousness. He hopes, but cannot be sure, that he will do justice to a subject that has haunted him: his people's struggle, through the passion of religious faith, for some understanding of what life means, if anything. His hands, ordinarily on the move rather constantly—grasping for words, slicing up sentences, swinging at enemies, reaching for agreement or pushing strenuously in the face of disagreement—become strangely still. As he talks about the character of the gospel singer he is trying to evoke, as he talks about the preachers he has known, the messages they have handed down, as he remembers the Holy Rollers, remembers Billie Holiday in a green dress sustaining one evening a mixture of irony, detachment, sadness, and terrible, mocking amusement at the spectacle of her own celebrity, he loses the physical intensity he has had and willingly spent. The hands knock gently on the table's wood. He doesn't want to talk about the novel he is trying to achieve; he wants to leave the country, finish it, and come back to live in America, a country he insists he has never really left, only crossed the ocean to look at more intently. He hopes he can capture sharply and suggestively the "pacing" of a certain kind of desperate spiritual life: "I remember in those Pentecostal churches when I was young, the tension, the drama, the struggle for a handle on life. I hope I can remember *well*. A person would get up and he'd say, she'd say, to begin with: 'I'm going to step out on the promise.' I guess that's what I'm trying to do. I look at Andy Young on the screen and see the frustration and hurt in his eyes—all the pain he's seen here and now sees abroad, but there's a glow in his eyes too—a smile that says he's going to keep taking a chance, one more and then one more after that. And some of the black kids I see in Harlem or elsewhere, the same goes for them— they're stepping out on the promise, and that's about all I guess they can do, each one of them."

New York Times Book Review, July 31, 1977

Behind the Beyond

We are removed from many people on this planet by more than distance, and we are apt to judge them by our standards. Neither planes nor television nor any other technological achievements have turned the world's population into understanding friends and neighbors. One can go everywhere without losing a self-centered view of the world; one can watch a thousand travelogues or *cinéma vérité* documentaries and still distrust people who look or act "different." The tug of our own lives often is too much for us, and if anyone tries to pull us toward "them"—Asians or Africans, or our own Indians or Eskimos—we are quick to react: our informant is merely an anthropologist, who has made a career out of tribal observation, or a polemicist. Occasionally, an observer who has ventured into regions unknown to nearly all of us can educate us in the most disarming way—informally and patiently, without any academic or ideological agenda. One thinks of James Agee among Alabama's sharecroppers in the 1930s, of George Orwell doggedly pursuing the "lower depths" of Paris or London. They bring fellow human beings so close to us that we can recognize them as brothers and sisters under the skin, no matter how unlike us they seem; a hard-driven Alabama field hand comes across clearly, a man on skid row whom Orwell happened to meet is conveyed to us in a compelling manner.

Sheila Burnford's *One Woman's Arctic* is in that tradition. She tells what she has observed in strong, straightforward prose, and she organizes her ideas and observations so that the reader learns more than he or she may realize; she avoids didactic insistence: the people I studied have certain traits and can be categorized in a certain way. She has spent years in the out-of-doors of her native Britain and in Canada's sparsely settled north woods. In her fifties, she is still active, adventurous. During the Second World War, she drove an ambulance. She hunts and fishes; she sails; she has a pilot's license; she wanders far and wide taking note of the natural world. Her first book, *The Incredible Journey*, is at initial glance a tale for youthful readers—the trek of a young Labrador retriever, an ancient bull terrier, and a Siamese cat through the Canadian wilderness. What distinguishes the book is the author's special understanding of animals and the terrain these ones traveled. In *The Fields of Noon*, she presents the reader with tender, knowing sketches of dogs, of a canary, of open countryside, and deep woods—in Scotland, in Spain, and in Canada. More recently (1969), Mrs. Burnford turned her attention to human beings—the Cree and Ojibwa Indians of Ontario, whom she describes with empathy and shrewdness in *Without Reserve*. Now she tells us of people in the Northwest Territories well above the Arctic Circle, where she spent two summers with the Innuit Eskimos, mostly in Pond Inlet on remote Baffin Island. With her was Susan Ross, an equally hardy older woman.

Mrs. Burnford was there, she says, not to preach to the Eskimos, teach them her values, convey her kind of knowledge, buy anything from them, or enlist them as hunting guides: "I was there 'just to be there.'" She acknowledges "mild amateur interests in birds and wild flowers, animals, and artifacts." And she is sure that the Eskimos were puzzled by her: "We were two Kabloonahs, white women *d'un certain âge*, as the French so happily put it, with grownup families." It took a while to get used to the twenty-four-hour days of the Arctic summer. A visitor loses a sense of time: it is for others, far away, to look at watches and clocks. Not that the life of Pond Inlet is static or uneventful. The day has its rhythms—all related in the mind of the Eskimo to the movement of the sun across the sky, but not fitted into a strict chronology. One responds to Nature's moods with no notion of schedules or quotas to be met within a given time frame. For the Eskimo, the world is awesome, people small and vulnerable; one tries to survive and to stay in touch with the environment rather than subdue it.

Mrs. Burnford is quite aware of the subtleties of the changing landscape:

> Now the strait was ice-locked to silence and there were no birds; soon there would be the sound of open water and shifting, groaning, creaking ice floes, the air filled with the music of dozens of different gulls and waterfowl. Now the rocky hillside was covered in snow; in a few days it would spring into brilliant

life, carpeted with myriad wild flowers. One moment the glaciers opposite would seem remote as another continent; next time I looked it would seem that I only had to walk a mile or so across the ice to be at the end of their thousands-of-years-old road. Or the mountains would be cloud-wreathed, the sun striking in silver shafts across the ice below; then a pure white peak from the ice cap would rear through the clouds, catch the sun, and so change light and color again.

As for the Eskimos, "like a piece of blotting paper I simply absorbed whatever came my way, content to be given bits of information, not to question or inquire, more interested in the land, and in the people as villagers and friendly faces, than in their relationships, or in the workings and economy of the settlement." Yet we have an excellent account of how a community overcomes a vast range of obstacles. We are brought close to that community. "It was impossible to feel shy or a stranger for long." The Eskimos of Pond Inlet, like Eskimos elsewhere, are generous, hospitable, helpful to outsiders in whatever way, and no questions asked. Perhaps people constantly reminded of their extreme vulnerability are not carried away with themselves, or perhaps they are simply by nature gentle and easygoing. It is as if they regarded themselves as brief guests on this earth, with an obligation to help one another and to be prepared at any moment to leave. In the vastness of the Arctic, the entirely white mountains that appear so near seem to recede as one approaches. A strange and haunting medley pervades—the wind sweeping across the land, the ice moving, groaning, "the cries of gulls and long-tailed jaegers overhead; the excited, rushing patter of a flock of a hundred guillemots' feet on the water; the high-pitched scream of terns; sometimes geese calling far out, snows and white-fronts, or the amazingly melodic gossip of old squaws drifting across the water." Then the clouds that have been threatening vanish, the noise abates, the silence becomes a noticeable presence. "I felt suddenly overcome with the magnitude of it all compared with the infinitesimal dot that was me standing in the middle of a frozen sea; so infinitesimal that it seemed ludicrous that anything so nearly invisible could have cold hands or feel hungry—could do anything in fact except just *be* and no more. I have seldom felt so utterly content. I was often to experience this most peaceful acceptance of my microscopic unimportance. I think I began to understand then how this land binds so strongly, and is bound up with, its people. The two are one."

From Mrs. Burnford we learn who settled in the Arctic and what befell them, what it is like now, as more explorers, surveyors, engineers, and officials arrive. She raises a vexing issue that is a constant presence in every one of her books: How is one to regard the Eskimos or the Indian tribes who live to the south of them? Are they our moral superiors? Are they hopelessly isolated and primitive people who barely hold on to life? Are they ill suited to another life situation? Only by implication do we learn that her attitude is essentially admiration and practicality: live and let live. The Eskimos have never wanted to move south, acquire land that is somebody else's, or insist that others conform to their way of life. They have received all visitors and have been patient listeners and observers, if not the most willing and compliant of hosts. Whalers and hunters have come to the Arctic, and adventurers, gold-hungry explorers, missionaries, misfits, geologists looking for oil, and surveyors to plan wells, roads, and pipelines. And the reward for the willingness to extend a helping hand is the shantytowns of Alaska and northern Canada—inhabited by a demoralized people who have lost touch, who no longer have a purpose, who spend their time in bars or in the lineup in front of government agencies. Mrs. Burnford acknowledges that the white culture can bring the Eskimo a longer life, a more comfortable and secure existence. But she speaks, too, of "laziness and greed, loss of skills, and eventually loss of racial pride."

This has not yet happened in Pond Inlet. There the author saw a people of enormous vitality and resourcefulness go about their chores. To stay alive is a constant achievement: today's supply of food, or bearable weather may be followed by near-starvation, wind, snow, and cold of an intensity we of the Temperate Zone cannot comprehend. The Eskimo is clever, alert, ingenious, quick of reflex. Mrs. Burnford, mother of three children, notes that the Eskimos do not make the child an object of veneration; children are allies, successors who need to learn quickly how to survive, even though by trial and error. A child perpetually protected cannot survive.

"Thirty years ago Rasmussen observed," says Mrs. Burnford, "that he had learned from an old Eskimo 'It is generally believed that white men have quite the same minds as small children. Therefore

one should always give way to them. They are easily angered, and
when they cannot get their will they are moody, and, like children,
have the strangest ideas and fancies'—a somewhat sobering estimate, and one that time does not seem to have modified." But what
the famous Arctic explorer said then can apply to the Eskimos as
well, they, too, can be "small children," susceptible to blandish-
ment. Six hundred miles from Pond Inlet lies an enormous base
built by the United States Strategic Air Command. The base has
been closed, but the city that arose around it remains, and so do
many of the Eskimos who worked there before the airmen departed:

> "Difficult to judge how many millions of dollars thrown away
> when they left," I wrote in my journal after wandering the site,
> still surrounded by its towering fence, the catwalks on stilts in
> case of "whiteouts" still intact, the Operations Room with
> tiered seats just like the movies. All electrical radio, radar, etc.,
> equipment burned or hacked to pieces, shed after shed of
> twisted, broken remains. The cars and trucks were put into gear
> and sent over the hill to the gravel pit below, then bulldozed
> over, so that no one could possibly benefit from them. Yet they
> left canteen furniture, bunks, etc. With such an example of
> white wastefulness to a people accustomed to making some-
> thing out of nothing, everything out of something, perhaps it's
> small wonder that the Eskimos exposed to it were never the
> same again. . . . Small children asking for "pennies," tarty-
> looking teenage girls emerging from the Palace Theatre, one
> memorable character with the shortest of sawn-off shorts, pur
> ple fishnet leotards, and a small dirty baby in a filthy *amouti*
> on her back—puffy-eyed, flabby-faced boys shouting unin-
> hibitedly Anglo-Saxon badinage after them.

So it goes: a great nation moves to defend itself, and a scattered,
defenseless, but brave and sensitive people become, in a way, casu-
alties of a war they never saw or understood. Perhaps some Arctic
travelers would, instead, emphasize the marginal nature of Eskimo
living, the many infants who die because no medical care is available or grow up to live needlessly risky lives. Mrs. Burnford, it is
true, sought out a particularly sturdy and self-reliant community of
people and became a comrade and a partisan. She was a guest in
their cabins, a welcome friend who ate their raw fish, their seal

meat, their muktuk (the skin of narwhal), and traveled with them behind a dog team. Her Arctic is a place where genial people come to respectful terms with a splendid stretch of unspoiled land; and for all its challenges of weather, it is a safe land—no robbers, no assault, no pollution (at least in Pond Inlet) of air or water.

As one reads Mrs. Burnford's books, a question comes up that she has anticipated: What did the Eskimos or the Indians with whom she spent so much time think of this not so young woman, the mother of grown children, who wanted to see and photograph and tape-record birds of the Arctic? But the Eskimos, reticent and polite as they are, do not question other people; people are entitled to privacy. Perhaps Sheila Burnford was one of the more pleasant surprises for Pond Inlet. However isolated, however resigned to "fate" or accepting of "Nature," they have learned to live with a modicum of white visitors and no doubt to expect lectures, sermons, questions, instructions, even commands. Instead, two women arrived, stayed some months, demonstrated the most intense affection and concern, even a bit of envy, and then left in obvious sadness. One wishes that this book could be read by those whose land, character, and spirit the author conveys so well. But surely her Arctic friends know how much she hopes, for the sake of all of them, that there will be a middle ground between the precarious, brief, but dignified life of the hunter or fisherman of Pond Inlet and the life of the Eskimos she saw near that Air Force base only a few hundred miles away.

New Yorker, September 23, 1974

Outsiders

As Martin Luther King kept reminding his black compatriots at a time when simply going to hear him was a risky business, there were people all over the nation who shared their social and economic condition. To my knowledge, he never included Asian-Americans, the subject matter of a book, assembled as an "anthology of Asian-American writers" under the unusual title of *Aiiieeeee!*, by four anthologists—Frank Chin, Jeffery Paul Chan, Lawson Fusao Inada, and Shawn Hsu Wong. These men are all Asian-Americans—a term they apply mostly to those who were born in America to parents of Asian ancestry, those "who got their China and Japan from the radio, off the silver screen, from television, out of comic books, from the pushers of white American culture that pictured the yellow man as something that when wounded, sad, or angry, or swearing, or wondering whined, shouted, or screamed 'aiiieeeee!'" They are, as we all must be well aware, a substantial and hurt and troubled group, deprived of their rights and liberties by both law and prejudice and by a process of exclusion that has brought about poverty, unemployment, inadequate education, and a high incidence of preventable diseases. These people cannot easily turn back to China, Japan, or the Philippines; they are, after all, the children, the grandchildren, even the great-grandchildren of American citizens. Their ancestors helped build this country, especially the West—doing menial jobs others considered beneath them but that had to be done if the nation was to carry on. There has, it is true, been some movement back and forth across the Pacific, especially by the somewhat better-off Asian-Americans, whose small businesses have enabled a modest accumulation of cash. Then, there are some in this country who were born in China and came here, just as there are Asian-Americans who have spent a lot of time in Asia. And there has been assimilation, too: the *Pacific Citizen*, a newspaper put out by the Japanese-American Citizens League, reported in 1972 that about half the Japanese-American women and

Chinese-American women are now marrying men of other races. (We are not given any statistics about what the Japanese-American and Chinese-American men are doing.) That also troubles these editors: Will their people slowly disappear, become absorbed?

The editors of this anthology struggle, besides, with the problem of deciding what is genuinely "Asian-American" literature. For seven generations now there have been Asian-Americans, yet to many of us, we are told in the introduction, an Asian-American still means a laundryman or someone who lives near or works in a restaurant in an area called Chinatown. And to most of us, the term "Asian-American literature" brings up memories of Fu Manchu or of Charlie Chan, who, said his creator, walks with "the light dainty step of a woman." The editors of the anthology see him as the literary figure who represents to millions of us the "best" of the Asian-Americans. They also regard him as the precursor of a whole literary genre—the *Chinatown Book, Father and Glorious Descendant, A Chinatown Family,* and volumes with titles like *Inside Chinatown* and *Chinatown, U.S.A.* The editors deplore all this, and most especially Charlie Chan, "the fat, inscrutable, flowery but flub-tongued effeminate little detective"; if some white people regarded him as intelligent, observant, and inventive, these Asian-American editors consider him to be emasculated and passive, one of the all too familiar Chinese men who are pictured as "worshiping white women and being afraid to touch them." For a long while, many of us never distinguished among Japanese, Chinese, and Filipinos; they were all "Asiatics," as in "Keep the Asiatics out." (There is something of that sentiment today, as the South Vietnamese refugees wait in their encampments.) And keep them out we did—after the hard work of opening up the West was completed, so much of it by "coolie labor." For a while, too, "Japan and China, as well as Japanese America and Chinese America, were one in exotica." During the Second World War, when thousands of American citizens of Japanese ancestry were interned in camps in denial of their constitutional rights, a distinction was at last made: "Chinese-Americans became Americans' pets, were kept and groomed in kennels, while Japanese-Americans were the mad dogs who had to be locked up in pounds."

That opinion may seem a brutal way of confronting what can indeed be brutal in American life, but the stories, the excerpts from novels and plays, and the autobiographical essays in this book have quite another tone—not the dreaded passive attitude but a wry, thoughtful detachment, even in the face of hardship and misery. One of the most touching of the lot is the work of the Filipino-Amerian poet and short-story writer Carlos Bulosan, who died in 1956, at the age of forty-one. For years, in California and elsewhere, he was a migrant fruit picker, riding freight trains between jobs. Eventually he became a labor leader, but, worn down by many years of bad food, unsanitary living conditions, and lack of medical care, he succumbed to tuberculosis just as, after several books of his had been published, he was becoming a political and literary spokesman for his people. "I tried hard to remain aloof from the destruction and decay around me," he wrote in *America Is in the Heart.* He did not always succeed. Despair and a desire for vengeance sometimes overcame him. But his descriptions of the farm workers in California, of the subtle differences among his own people, the Chinese, and the Koreans, are sensitively rendered. He summons up humor when he happens upon adversity, and he resists self-pity. He wishes to evoke the world he has seen, not to deliver polemics. The Japanese-American novelist John Okada, who also died young (in 1971, at the age of forty-seven), likewise manages placidity under difficult circumstances; in his *No-No Boy,* part of which appears in this anthology, a youth, Ichiro, is trying to understand the behavior of his strange, remote mother, who dreams of a triumphant return to Japan, and of his father, good-humored, tolerant, willing to come to terms at any cost with the demands made by America on its outsiders. To the mother, Japan is a beautiful, strong, proud country; its people are noble, refined, honorable. She has ignored Pearl Harbor, the imperialism that prompted it, and the postwar industrial resurgence of capitalist Japan. In her Japan, people are more concerned with how they behave toward one another and with the state of grace they may one day obtain for themselves through a life of devotion to others. The real Japan arrives in a letter from her sister, and her husband tries to impress the facts it contains upon his wife, but she moves even deeper into fantasy, and he pulls back, gently begins to help her maintain her illusions. The son becomes enraged at his father, at his mother, at having to live a life quite different from the one his parents, in their separate ways, have contended with.

The younger writers who appear in this book are more interested in the relationships between their own experiences and the experiences of other Americans. The Chinese-American novelist Jeffery Paul Chan, thirty-two years old, offers a tense, unsettling story, "The Chinese in Haifa," that tells us how "integrated" Chinese-Americans can be when they become part of America's suburban professional class, with its drinking, its pot, its nicely furnished homes, its divorce rate, and its mixed feelings about having children. There are brilliant exchanges between a recently divorced Chinese-American schoolteacher and his Jewish neighbors, one of whom observes that since "there are Jews in China, there must be Chinese in Haifa." The dialogue between the Chinese-American and his neighbors is sharp, ironic, painfully revealing. None of these people is hungry or jobless, and yet there is so much suspicion, so much prickly self-consciousness. An outsider, aware of the raw nerves and the vibrant perceptions of these Chinese-Americans (and, for that matter, of their Jewish neighbors), might wish he could enter the scene, offer comfort, reassurance, affection, and suggest that the past be forgotten so that we all can join in a common effort to make do on this increasingly endangered planet. But the past does not yield so easily to the demands and the realities of the present. The past, with all its class tensions, racial animosities, and ethnic antagonisms, remains part of the present, as this book poignantly reminds us.

New Yorker, June 2, 1975

Children and Literature

Lost Generation

For years Ned O'Gorman, a white man, a poet, an essayist, has been working with Harlem's young black children in a storefront nursery and children's library he founded. He has already written two books about the nursery: *The Wilderness and the Laurel Tree* and *The Storefront*. This latest book, *The Children Are Dying*, with its grim, admonitory title, is not meant to describe the further educational observations of an especially dedicated and honorable man. He is at this point in his life desperate, sad, enraged. He believes that isolated efforts such as his mean little in a world he comes close to writing off as a living hell, populated by an American *lumpenproletariat*:

> The children who come to me are children who exist in a colonial "outpost" of the American empire. I have been eleven years in Harlem, *eleven full years:* I have watched a place on this earth decay while the nation in which that place exists grows in power and wealth. It is as if Harlem, like Biafra or the gutters of Calcutta, had become a dispensable part of the fabric of national life. Nothing has happened in eleven years to make one jot of difference in the lives of the children conceived during that time or in the lives of the children who came to my nursery since 1966.

At another moment he is even more drastic and unqualified: "The wreckage in Harlem is almost total, and the possibility for change now, as I write, is almost nil. I think that the generation I teach in my little school is lost, and I think their children will be lost, too."

The beginning of O'Gorman's book is less gloomy. He sounds like the James Agee who wrote the scripts for *The Quiet One* and *In the Street*, earlier views by a white poet of Harlem. A thirteen-year-old black boy, already a liar, a would-be rapist, and God knows what else, prompts in the author rage but also words like these: "But I

187

thought, too, of his beauty, of his childhood and of those years that had come to him since birth with all the human plagues. I wondered what he was like when he was a year old, when he lay in someone's arms, watching the light and dark hover over him, bringing the seasons and music but bringing, too, the attendant swells and hammerings of death. . . ."

Such soaring, touching words soon yield to plain autobiographical detail, followed by brief narrative accounts of young lives in the process of rapid, fatal deterioration. The author tells us that he does not live in Harlem, that he can come and go as he pleases; he was born lucky and has "lived always in the midst of beauty." He also tells us that he knows that he will stir many to anger and scorn: yet another white man, some may say, peddling his noblesse oblige, his clever generalizations, and his self-dramatizing stories, meant to alarm but in a curious way reassure liberals—because bad as things are, and modest as the author appears, surely he is living proof that one decent, kind-hearted soul can make a difference, even in Harlem. Moreover, in the book's early pages the author may seem a familiar young existentialist, a source of inspiration to those troubled bourgeois souls in the throes of an "identity crisis":

> I came to Harlem because I simply had to decide what to do with my life. The task I was ready for was teaching in a college, but I did not want to traipse about forever clutching English literature anthologies in my arms. I did not want to rot away in academia, and the two years I spent in it were sure signs that if I did teach, I would rot. Harlem drew me.

No doubt some blacks will be offended by such vulnerable self-description and even more put off by the evidence of psychological abuse and degradation so relentlessly presented in this book. The author has no interest in protecting himself. His work is dangerous; on upper Madison Avenue he daily has to face down threats in a neighborhood where knives or guns are used all the time. This book will earn him additional enemies. He attacks those who "romanticize Harlem, a task some black intellectuals have taken on as their special mission." He also attacks a "cruel power elite" that (in the case of New York) he does not flinch from spelling out: "Catholic, Jewish, Black, Protestant, Religious, Judicial, Educational." Like many truly religious people, he abhors the pretensions of priests and ministers who, calling upon the name of God constantly, hold hands with the prevailing powers. Harlem is full of people claiming to be God-possessed yet willing to turn their backs on their down-and-out neighbors.

Ned O'Gorman's "problem," apparently incurable, is that he can't act in that way. He detests what he calls "abstract calm": that of intellectuals, all too ready to mull, sift, sort—and have it both ways by advocating political changes while living high on the hog; and that of various bureaucrats, church authorities, and school officials who offer pieties and banalities by the bushel to a people dazed and broken. He wants for the spiritual life of Harlem's children what he calls "the fury and the passion of revolution."

The author is not without his own fury, which he tries hard to control as he tells us of suffering. Child after child appears in this book as wounded, in deep pain, ready to give up emotionally and spiritually. After a while, the reader wants to say *basta*—enough of all this. And no doubt many of us will resort to the old rationalizations, the pain-saving psychological deceptions we have learned to use. We may remind ourselves that there is equal or worse suffering elsewhere in the world. Surely one could find hurt, betrayed children in other neighborhoods (white and better off), if one was of a mind to do so. Surely one must recognize that some racial progress has been made in recent years. Meanwhile, nations spend billions so they can blow up the planet, whereas Harlem's thousands of children waste away daily and the pleas of Ned O'Gorman go unattended. Those who talk of complexity, the long haul of history, and comparative economic or social analysis are dealt with as harshly in this book as are O'Gorman's liberal friends, from whom he has come to expect much sympathy but no action.

Sometimes the author comes close, maybe closer than he really intends, to saying that Harlem is hopelessly mired in "a culture of poverty":

> You see, I think the cycle of poverty becomes almost a physical occurrence in the oppressed people. It establishes in the blood a weakness and a tendency to capitulate, just as in some families, mine for one, liquor lurks in the shadows to grab up the best of our minds and destroy them.

He hastens to add that he is not embracing a "genetic weakness" but rather "a psychic-imaginative one." But a few pages later he returns to the same theme, however cautiously: "I tread carefully here because I must ask if the children of the oppressed—black, poor white, North African, Indian—generation after generation do not inherit a *faiblesse* toward failure, toward despair, toward annihilation."

Do they "inherit" such a weakness—a fatal tendency "toward" the destiny the author mentions? In fact, the blacks of Harlem are predominantly recent comers North who inherited the workings of centuries of painful experience: abrupt, enforced removal from one continent; an awful passage to another; generations of slavery, in which explicit, socially acknowledged family life was legally forbidden, and in which children were often treated as chattel; additional generations of vigorously enforced segregation, accompanied by extreme deprivation, exploitation, lynchings, and a virtual denial of education; and starting in the second decade of this century, the trek. toward Detroit, Chicago, and New York, there to be the last hired, the first fired.

Of course such a chronicle is known to the author, known to those who (unlike him) peddle far more ambitious and categorical notions of how blacks are culturally, even biologically, "impaired"—an impairment, so it is claimed, "responsible" for the apathy and cynicism and bitterness and disintegration of spirit to be found in places such as Harlem. But those same places also suffer from unemployment rates of fifty percent for young people. They have received people systematically beaten, confined, despised—for a long time defined by the glorious Constitution of the United States as property.

In any case, the author is no theorist bent on making a point at all costs. He sometimes comments on the strength and vitality he has also seen in Harlem, especially among black women, the mothers and grandmothers of the children he correctly describes as in extreme danger of losing their mental and spiritual lives. And he does, here and there, give us specific instances of lives being saved—almost always the result of intelligent action: a child was taken from one unpromising or sordid situation and placed in an environment that gradually exerted a redemptive influence. The boy or girl in question, he believes, must have to begin with at least some valuable sides to his or her psychological "inheritance," qualities often lacking even in well-to-do white families where childhood psychiatric disorders may prove intractable to changed circumstances and concentrated psychiatric care. "I have seen the loveliest of children turn into animals," the author declares. And he adds: "I have seen beautiful, caring women turn into passive mothers who transmit to their children the malignant despair that had bent their own lives out of shape." The strength and dignity have been passed on—but still they are overwhelmed by what happens in the wretched streets of one of the world's richest cities.

A man working against such awful odds, and doing so voluntarily out of his persisting decency, will not forever keep cool and retain in the forefront of his mind the long-range political perspectives that others manage to summon up so handily. At times this gentle and giving man, this Harlem poet, becomes bitter and scornful. He turns on almost everyone in sight—even the families of the children he loves and works with, not to mention those of us who proclaim good intentions but are not able to live the life in Harlem he has chosen for himself. There are lapses of logic and overstatements: "Harlem, as is true of all the cities of the dispossessed, is a completely unpolitical, nonpoliticized community." *Completely?* "An open classroom always praises the genius of a child's imagination." *Always?* And there are passages that seem to suggest the writer's premature intimations of death, as if he has caught the disease he set out to conquer. He tells us he may well be in mortal danger himself, and he warns of the possibility of future collective violence. Reading these premonitions of large-scale disaster, we may remember the slogan "Burn, baby, burn," heard when the accumulated grudges of a people erupted into a death cry—aimless, futile jabs of vengeance. Soon enough an obituary appeared: there was a flurry of sympathy mixed with reprimands and disgust from those cross-town whites who were on television cameras or wrote newspaper or magazine columns.

Now and then this book turns guardedly encouraging. We are told what we might do if we were a different society—more democratic-socialist and less democratic-capitalist. Resources would move toward what amounts to an underdeveloped nation within a nation. Instead of celebrating the personal life of a singular man, Ned O'Gorman, and instead of feeling pleased when we learn from him that a boy here, a girl there, has been "snatched totally" from a decaying, foul tenement and an aching, dazed family, we would as a country take active notice. The author refers to a needed "corps of field-workers," who would work with entire families on their many problems. He talks of a "community of healing." He dreams of local "twenty-four hour clinics," with not only medical concerns but larger social and economic interests. But he recognizes that there is no likelihood that the kind of drastic political change he has in mind will take place in the foreseeable future. He falls back, instead, without much hope, on the prospect of a "whole new body of laws" that might take a given "oppressed child *away from* the forces of oppression."

He gives such laws impersonal, Orwellian names: what seems needed is the imposition of "the surrogate will" and "the monitoring intelligence." He acknowledges the dangers such concepts pose—"an alien notion to this democracy." He is being both ironic and furiously rash. No doubt he has heard of those in the past who felt the awful risks of dictatorship preferable to certain death from hunger for many people. In the late 1930s, my mother's uncle, a politically conservative American missionary in China, became "disturbed" one day after hearing the illustrious Madame Chiang Kai-shek speak about the threat that communism presented to the "tradition of liberty" in China. He is reported to have lost all sense of decorum, to have raised his voice and asked the beguiling Wellesley graduate: liberty for whom? An old and vexing issue for the morally upright who go out to save others, hopelessly damned, in the name of Christ or of simple human equity. There are occupational hazards to such endeavors, a price to pay emotionally. But from them, perhaps, one obtains an occasional flash of revelatory insight, no doubt quickly cut short, lest yet another person become a "revolutionary."

The last word in this book is given to Edna Driver, a pseudonym for a Harlem mother overwhelmed, driven to near madness, but eloquent and knowing in her capacity to look both inward and out toward Harlem's dreary streets. "Life is a strange thing to live with," says this thirty-five-year-old woman who is haunted by mysteries, obsessed by complexities no less worthy of attention than those that are debated in universities: the terrible psychological importance of fate and circumstance; the enigma of God's, of nature's purposes, if any; the question of whether or not to struggle for bare, mute survival in the face of frightful daily burdens. Is this woman "hopeless," by virtue of a "culture of poverty," or does our country, by virtue of what it permits, still, in such places as Harlem, have a morally impoverished culture?

Ned O'Gorman, surveying Harlem, does not dwell upon its twentieth-century cultural renaissance—the achievements of Langston

Hughes, Zora Neale Hurston, Countee Cullen, or Claude McKay. Still, his point of view is not unlike McKay's, whose *Home to Harlem* gave us a vivid glimpse into a city's black "lower-life." McKay was a teller of sensual and erotic stories. Ned O'Gorman is a poet who has for the most part lost hope and is attending to the world he sees rather than the one he can conjure up with a pen put to paper. When he talks about the Harlem he works in every day, about the "fortresslike aloofness" of its buildings, he brings to mind Ralph Ellison's "Harlem Is Nowhere," written to plead for the harassed minds of a community whose "blues," whose fiercely assertive jazz, like Ned O'Gorman's book, become, finally, voices of resignation or torment that are heeded aesthetically by us fortunate outsiders—the only response possible, we tell ourselves, as we think about our own constraints and frustrations.

New York Review of Books, September 28, 1978

The Holocaust and
Today's Kids

F orty years ago, the murderous Nazis were well on their way to achieving what would later be known as "the Holocaust," a genocidal assault on European Jewry, as well as on other men, women, and children whose background, interests, views, or activities made them enemies of the German state of the early 1940s. Since the end of the Second World War, the entire world, in one way or another, has lived in the shadow of that unspeakable tragedy. No longer would Europe's cultural and scientific advances hold the promise they once did: signs of civilization's advancing possibilities. The Germany of the 1930s had no group that we might have called "culturally disadvantaged" or "culturally deprived." Nor did that Germany have illiteracy as a burden. The Gestapo and the concentration camps emerged in the nation of Goethe and Schiller, Beethoven and Brahms; in a nation whose people, in impressive numbers, had a thorough mastery of science, philosophy, art, psychology, and sociology. Moreover, in no time Hitler and his henchmen were quite able to count on the support of professors, doctors, lawyers, journalists, architects, and, I regret to say, many of my kind—psychiatrists and psychologists—who submitted with no protest to the dictates of those who ran the Third Reich.

We will, one hopes, never stop contemplating that set of events— the rapid accommodation of a once exquisitely civilized nation to a political regime whose explicit purposes, from the very start, were declared to be viciously hateful.

John Milton, the seventeenth-century poet, once told us that the power of truth would make men free. Yet there was no absence of truth in Weimar Germany. Freud's truths were available, as were Einstein's and Thomas Mann's. And in art, expressionists were much concerned with the nature of German social reality. In engineering, in the social sciences, and even in the contemplation of religious and moral issues, Germans excelled mightily. Still, the devilish fascist thugs took power quickly in January 1933 and consolidated their rule without great turmoil. Within five years, a nation went through an enormous transformation—a descent into hell; and nothing at home (or even, alas, abroad) seemed likely to change that state of affairs.

How are we to comprehend such a turn of events? One hastens to insist that such a question not only be turned into abstract speculation but also be grounded in real, human situations—parents informing their children, teachers doing likewise with their students. There is, in any case, no series of sociological or psychological abstractions that explains, definitively, the emergence of Nazi power, the hypnotic spell Hitler exerted over so many people, the murderous behavior his followers demonstrated openly by 1938.

In *retrospect*, we see everything: the trickery, the lies, the bluffs that, tragically, German politicians, church leaders and, ultimately, the political leaders of other countries failed to call. In *retrospect*, we know that the Hitler who became Germany's chancellor in January 1933 became a mass killer, conquered much of Europe, presided over the utter destruction of his own nation—and, all the while, commanded a fierce loyalty from thousands of followers.

As one goes through the newspapers of the 1930s, the magazines, the news documentaries made for the movie houses, and yes, the personal letters and diaries of all sorts of people—Jews and Gentiles, the rich and the poor, the educated and the less educated—one finds no such clear, collective awareness of what awaited the people of this planet: an unparalleled spectacle of our capacity for bestiality. Rather, even among the vulnerable Jews who lived under Hitler in the mild 1930s or maybe *especially* among them, given their desperate situation—there never ceased to be hope.

In *Never To Forget: The Jews and the Holocaust*, an excellent historical account of Jewry's fate under Hitler (an account that was written for children and that draws heavily on recorded memories, firsthand observations, and fragments of letters, diaries, songs and poems), Milton Meltzer asks: "How could anyone have overlooked the signs [of the coming Holocaust]?" He hastens to answer his own question in this instructive way:

> With the advantage of hindsight, it is not hard to ask that question. But the Jews living through the experience could behave only on the basis of what they knew then. The German Jews,

the first in Europe to fall victim to Hitler, could reach no real agreement on the nature and extent of the danger threatening them. Nor could they agree on what to do about it. We must realize that there was no historical precedent for the Holocaust. It was a *new* event in world history; the mechanical mass-murder system of an Auschwitz had never happened before. Like any person anywhere, each Jew thought and acted on the basis of his own level of understanding, his own degree of courage, his own moral judgment.

Those last two words, of course, challenge all of us: What capacity does each of us have for "moral judgment"? How might we react in the face of political evil and madness such as that which came to prevail in Germany during the 1930s? And that latter question, of course, cuts both ways: How might we have acted had we been Jews, or had we been so-called Aryan Germans? Meltzer does not shirk asking such questions even as he conveys for his young readers the enormous outrages, the bloodthirsty excesses of the Nazis—who, by the late 1930s, were acting like craven animals of the lowest kind, yet also like mischievous and canny human beings, able to play on the inevitable mix of optimism and despair we all have as our psychological inheritance. Meltzer is at pains, in that regard, "to indicate how hard it is for anyone to resist a ruthless totalitarian power which commands modern weapons and employs elaborate means to crush opposition."

I have read a fair number of books written for young readers, and among such books, Meltzer's is especially edifying. He has no interest in brushing the complex truth of his subject matter under this or that ideological carpet. The Jews of central Europe had to face a devil hitherto unknown to humankind: the modern, technologically buttressed state as an instrument of wholesale terror and murder. Under such circumstances, the resistance of even a handful becomes a major miracle.

Given the singularity and atrocity of the events, one appreciates the challenge to any historian, any writer. Several storytellers, nevertheless, have aimed to convey to children what it was like—for, say, boys and girls their age—to witness hell itself unfold. Similarly, those who were actually there, Jews and non-Jews, have used autobiography as a means to reach youngsters today. Finally, some essayists have aimed at prompting reflection in young people through narrative exposition, accompanied in some instances by questions meant to provoke moral self-scrutiny.

In *The Holocaust: A History of Courage and Resistance*, Bea Stadtler takes her youthful readers, step by step, through the rise of Hitler and the subsequent horrors visited upon the Jews. The narration is strong, lucid, compelling, and it is interrupted by powerful personal accounts—remembrances of men and women of what they saw, heard and not least, experienced. On the evening of November 9, 1938, for instance, the Nazis struck at Germany's Jewish people. Synagogues were destroyed; the Jewish sacred books were burned; thousands were arrested, hurt, and killed. It was called *Kristallnacht* (Night of the Broken Glass), because glass was smashed all night long, the glass of Jewish homes and businesses and places of worship.

Sentence after sentence confronts today's schoolchildren with one of the worst nightmares mankind has ever experienced. Then "things to think about" are presented, and surely to good effect. The "things" are a mix of statements and questions, as in these two examples:

> Many Jewish homes were robbed, looted, or destroyed; and many Jewish men were hauled to concentration camps during the night and morning of *Kristallnacht*. Do you think it was possible that the Nazis alone were responsible for such a terrible event?
>
> We have heard of people in large apartment buildings watching a person being robbed and murdered in the courtyard and not even calling the police for help. Is this any different from the attitude of Germans who watched their Jewish neighbors being taken away, or beaten, or robbed, without saying a word? Would you be able to sleep through a "*Kristallnacht*"?

Given what takes place in all too many of our schools, one can only be grateful for such a line of moral inquiry. How many of our schoolchildren, one wonders, have been asked to read about and ponder the significance of the Holocaust—or for that matter, of some recent events in our own nation's history: the Civil Rights struggle of the 1960s, for instance? How many of *us*, young or old, know how to answer the question of responsibility? We realize that the Nazis somehow had to enlist the active complicity or passive acquiescence of millions of fellow citizens to accomplish the Holocaust. Might we have been among those citizens, had we been Germans? Might we even have been one of the many neighbors who watched silently as Jews were threatened, attacked, and forcibly removed to camps? We know that in any society a criminal assault upon one is, in effect, a criminal assault upon all; and we know that the person who does nothing to interfere with such a collapse of the legal and moral structure of a democratic nation is himself or herself made a criminal. Still, each of us wonders how we might have acted, had we been living, say, in Berlin during the 1930s, as neighbors to Jewish people. The Nazis were quite shrewd on that score, understanding our self-protective and self-enhancing instincts. They comprehended brilliantly the workings of fear and greed and guilt: how we lose self-respect as we clutch at what little privileges we have and then turn on those less fortunate, on victims of all sorts, with scorn, because they remind us of our flawed and corrupted morality.

One wants with all one's heart and soul to say, confidently: "No, I'd not sleep a wink though *Kristallnacht*. Never! Nor would I merely stay awake. I'd run into the streets, try to save my neighbors, help them in any way possible. If necessary, I'd fight the Nazis to the death." I have, in fact, asked children I know about such hypothetical situations: What would you do if you saw a Klan mob attacking a black child, say, or a grownup? How would you sleep if you heard the police on a rampage outside against people you believed to be innocent—a family, perhaps, condemned by virtue of their background, their skin color, their accent, their religious avowals? Almost invariably, the children respond as I would hope they might: they declare their (hypothetical) willingness to fight directly and hard in the cause of justice. I put that word in parentheses not out of cynicism but rather out of a sad doubt about all of us, for each and every one of us must travel a considerable distance between moral reasoning and the achievement of a moral life that is grounded in particular actions.

To be sure, it helps us, helps our schoolchildren, to read these historical accounts and to reflect upon questions that connect the lives, for example, of Jewish boys and girls living under the Nazis in the 1930s and 1940s to our own lives as we attempt to live them in America in the 1980s. The brief but stirring book *Joseph and Me: In The Days of the Holocaust* is explicitly written for such purposes. The author, Judy Hoffman, lived through the terrible darkness of the Nazi reign—in Germany and in Holland. She understands only too well what it means to be separated from one's parents, to live in daily terror, to be snatched and sent to a concentration camp. She tells her story in such a modest, straightforward, and touching way that one can only sit back and wonder what significance this life can possibly have, given that it is a tale of tragedy but also, ironically, a tale of good luck, when compared to the sagas of millions of others who never lived to tell of their experiences. At the end, in anguish and sorrow, the author addresses the young reader this way:

> There is more, but you don't have to know the rest. What is important is that I have shared my story. It was not an easy story to tell. As I told it, many sad thoughts came back to me, and I felt much of my pain again. But pain is a small price to pay when I think that perhaps you will see to it that such a horrible thing as the Holocaust never happens again. No one believed it could happen, but it did. Please, *please* try with all your might to see that it doesn't happen again. Please!

The book is accompanied by a pamphlet, *A Guide for Teachers*, which offers questions and topics for written and oral discussion. Readers are asked: "What would it take to survive in these [concentration] camps?" And: "How can the people of the world prevent future Holocausts?" I have no doubt that such questions prompt—at least in some sensitive youths—all sorts of honorable responses. Yet surely, we all must wonder, in considerable humility, what we would do *if*—and what we can truly do, *now*, about this or that political and human tragedy. And so wondering, we may join hands, maybe, with a young black child, whom I met in Mississippi in 1965, and heard speak in this fashion about her experience:

> I have a cousin, and she had to go by a mob, and they were standing in front of the school, and they told her they'd kill her, and she was scared to death, and she wanted to run away, but she knew if she did, they'd catch her, and when she came over to see me, she asked me if I wouldn't just take her place, and I said I'd do it, I'd be scared, but I'd try, and she said I can't, and I knew I couldn't because she's she and I'm me; and she said if she was me, she'd say what I said, she'd volunteer, but because she's she, she knows she wouldn't volunteer, not if she was me!

Then, she said what the minister said, that no one can be someone else; God makes each of us different, and there's only so
much *we* can do, and *we* can know, and no one can take our
place, because it's *us* we are, and someone else is walking down
a different road, and there are as many roads as people.

Such explorations into the nature of selfhood are the task of philosophers, teachers, doctors and, of course, all of us, including children. How will we ever know our moral worth—until we are tested
by this life's events? Yes, we must indeed pose questions to ourselves
constantly, ask ourselves what we believe, what we hold dear, how
we would respond under any number of circumstances. But the
question for teachers, always, is one of method: how to prompt such
inquiry in a manner that truly engages a child's imagination, intelligence, and thoughtfulness. I have no easy answers to such a question—especially when it is asked in connection with the Holocaust
as a subject for schoolchildren to contemplate. All I can do is recall
how Anne Frank's moving personal story stuck with me for months
and longer; how a recent story by Jana Oberski, *Childhood*, also
pulled at me, stayed with me; how the autobiographical account of
what it meant to grow up as a sensitive Aryan in Nazi Germany,
Howl Like the Wolves by Max Von der Grün, kept reminding me
that Hitler betrayed thousands and thousands of Germans whose af-
firmed Christianity was, for *der Führer* and his Gestapo cohorts, the
worst possible sign; how Ilse Koehn's *Mischling, Second Degree*,
which describes what a "mixed" child (part Jewish, part Gentile) endured under the Nazis, kept stirring memories in me of people,
places, incidents; and very important, how a brilliant novel by James
Forman, *Horses of Anger*, managed to evoke, better than anything
I've read, what happened to young people during the Nazi period.

Not that a novel such as *Horses of Anger* gives the reader any specific categorical answers. It is a story about four of the Hitler Youth
and how they respond to a dictator's leadership and the horrible consequences this had for Germany. The Holocaust is not specifically
explored for the reader who goes through Forman's story. Yet the
author works hard to illuminate a world black with evil; he tries,
really, to push us, in mind and heart, closer to the German situation
of a half-century ago—in the hope, surely, that we will thereby be

able to gain some sense of what *we* are, what *we* might be, what we can only beg God that *we* never become.

Whether or not we live a decent life depends upon what our moral imagination makes of us. As that black child told some of us nearly twenty years ago, it is all too easy to *say* what one ought do, what one would do, or even to know, confidently, what one should or should not do; it is quite something else to *learn*, in the course of a given life, what chance and circumstance, fate and luck (good or bad) have encouraged or enabled us to do, and discouraged or prevented us from doing. We ought, forever, all of us, to be haunted by the Holocaust. Without question, its lessons ought be taught, with factual recitations and thorough, intelligent discussions. Toward this end, the good novel is an invaluable moral resource. Through it, the texture of experience can be rendered so truly and forcefully that we are, for a while, transported into quite another world and thereby challenged by its messy (but quite realistic and terribly scary) ethical choices.

Forman has a Nazi youth emerge as morally tortured, confused and, in the end, aghast at where (and with whom) he's found himself—even as Jewish children have wondered, understandably, what kind of meaning or purpose this life can possibly have, given this century's history. To evoke moral conflict convincingly when it is present in the belly of the beast, so to speak, is, needless to say, no easy job—and yet, one is strangely grateful for the effort. Why? For reasons known to those who formulated the explicit questions in the books mentioned earlier, Hitler knew that he not only had to win a political office but that he had to convert the people of a nation. In due time, it came down to "the neighbors" of Germany's Jews; and it comes down to those "neighbors" for us, too. Will "they" help us in one or another clutch? And most important, since all of us are "neighbors" to others, what will we do when tested by fate collaring us and forcing us to choose?

Those who write for children about the Holocaust have embarked upon a bold, often fierce effort at moral analysis. Their point, again and again, is this: you who read must have the following ultimate question in mind: How could "they" have done what "they" did? I fear Forman and others give us the answer in their moral fables: once the devil obtains power, he bewitches many (oh, so many!) he approaches, exposing a vulnerability none of us can presume to be absent in ourselves. One can, then, pray not only for the strength to resist one or another devil but for the luck to be ineligible (as a matter of fate) for his beckon. One can, too, keep reading about others who stood up to the devil, who lost faith in him after being bewitched, who died innocently in the wake of his wretched visitation. One can pray and pray, and read and read, and as that black child implied, hold one's breath in hushed and worried awe.

Learning, November 1983

Children's Stories
The Link to a Past

In November of 1960, amid the terrible strife of school desegregation in New Orleans, I found myself talking with a black child, six years of age—a pioneer of her race, and every day coming close to being a martyr, because she had to face mobs and threats of violence, all to enter a school boycotted by whites. I worried about her. I wondered how long she could endure the constant harassment; the severe threats, repeated daily; and not least, the spectacle of a crowd of mean-spirited people denouncing not only her but her people in the vilest of terms. But she proved strong, astonishingly so; and she proved resourceful. Her parents, her kinfolk, her neighbors, her teachers, her friends, all would at one time or another wonder about her. How did this child, the daughter of former sharecroppers, manage to do so well, over the long weeks and months of a particular social and racial crisis? It would take me some time—weeks turned to months, then years—before I would begin to sense a few answers to that question. Yet I now realize that the young lady, at six and seven, was more anxious to help me than I was able to realize at the time.

She told me stories at the age of six. And when she was able to read fairly well, at eight or so, she read me stories given her by a black minister friend of the family's. They were stories of black rural people, Mississippi sharecroppers, stories handed down through the generations and carried ultimately from the Delta (Greenwood) to the eastern, industrial section of a cosmopolitan Southern city. They were stories of canniness and grit, of cleverness used against an adversary powerful and unpredictable. They were stories of victories and defeats, of miscegenation and lynching and racial hate and frustrated populism, and, always, of a Christianity that would not die and that is, I believe, considerably misunderstood by both Marxists and those psychiatrists who place too much stock in Freud's *The Future of an Illusion*.

I recall one of those stories—an account of a near lynching in the

1920s. The child had no specific dates, but she knew it was in her grandfather's time and after the First World War. He'd come home from the army, and a white man was sure he had a rifle he should have left behind in some military camp. Her grandfather was an "uppity nigger." So the child emphasized to me—as she explained what that expression meant and what happened to the man who was the occasion for such usage of the language: "My momma's daddy was tall, and it made the white ones jittery. He was light, as the colored people go, and *that* made the white ones even more jittery. And now he'd been out of the South and in the army—no telling what he'd come home and do!"

That was as far as the girl could go for a start. She paused and seemed a bit lost. She had an Oreo. She washed its crumbs down with a Coke. Her listener, once more, started worrying about her sugar intake, her teeth, her general nutritional intake. She smiled, seemed withdrawn. Was she "anxious"? Was she then, on a Sunday, anticipating tomorrow's street bedlam? There is a "story" in *that*, too: the cultivated psychological "awareness" that can't let anything or anyone just *be*, and what such a frame of mind does to others— say, a girl of six trying to be a narrator. In any event, Ruby Bridges of New Orleans, Louisiana, resumed her account after a few moments: "My grand-daddy had a bad habit. He didn't move off the sidewalk and onto the road—the dirt road, it was—when a white one came along. They'd been telling him to do that before he went into the army, all the Negroes who knew him. When he came back, they told him again, only they were really worried. And you know why? [No pause for anyone's answer.] Because they'd heard what the white ones were saying."

Then she paused, shrewdly. Her guest had all sorts of guesses as to what those "white ones" might have been saying. However, her guest was being given a calculated rest: end of chapter; settle yourself and turn the page, please. Another Oreo, another sip of that bad, bad sugar-saturated, dark, fizzy drink, and a resumption: "The white ones said there was one of them who was protecting my grand-daddy, and he was the most important person, the bossman of all the bossmans. He was a good man. But there was a bad man, and he came into town in a truck and he had a gun, and he said he was going to 'get' my grand-daddy, no matter what."

She stopped, looked me right in the eye, made sure she'd got out

of me exactly the response she'd hoped for; and when she was sure
that she had, indeed, obtained my complete interest—to the point
of rather elaborate, lurid fantasies—she continued her story, now
briskly: "He shot my grand-daddy. He hit him, but it wasn't a bad
hit. He drove off. My grand-daddy fell on the sidewalk. The white
ones stood there, and the colored came and they were going to drag
him to the road and put him on a wagon, but he was wide awake,
and he said they mustn't. They had to come over and talk with him,
and when they did, he said they should never stand aside for *anyone*
on that sidewalk, ever more; and the white ones heard him, and a
couple of them said amen. And my grand-daddy became the one
who went and talked to all the bossmans, from that day on."

The end she indicated by a knowing look. She was her grandfather's granddaughter, she told me, through another look. Did I
want an Oreo? Had I ever been to Greenwood, Mississippi? How old
was I? Those were questions meant to tell me that she was, indeed,
through with her story—and so now *I* could eat, rather than sit
transfixed, listening, watching her replenish her narrating body with
food and drink; and tell me, as well, and rather tactfully, that I probably didn't know the Delta all that well, and in any case, couldn't
(given my age) have possibly known the Delta her grand-daddy lived
in and tried to come to terms with, as best he could. As for her, she
was following suit, and she was also letting a rather inquisitive (and
terribly naive and all too self-assured) doctor know that if he would
only stop asking her his constant questions about how her appetite
was holding up and how she was sleeping and what she was *feeling*—well, then, she would do what any child, in the course of
time, would do: tell him something, perhaps, through one or another kind of story.

Later on, Ruby would read stories as well as relate ones she'd been
told. We've heard, many of us, of the oral tradition among certain
"primitive" or outlying people; and it is true, among rural folk, or
urban people newly arrived in the city, that there is a strong tradition
of talking, of storytelling—and yes, of tall talk. But education is not
necessarily a damper to that inclination. I know Indian children,
Appalachian children, Eskimo children, Chicano children, and
yes, white middle-class suburban children who have all sorts of
stories to tell (family stories, tribal stories, personal experiences) and
who *also* have learned in school to read and thereby gain possession

of even *more* incidents to relate: quite often to others of their age, and without the knowledge or applause or intervention of their parents. The truth is that many of us (certainly many in my field of child psychiatry) don't give enough credit to the natural, normal, everyday development of narrative interest, narrative sense, narrative response, narrative competence in boys and girls of all backgrounds—and all that not out of any mental pathology, or to solve some emotional conflict or problem, but as part of the mind's developing capacity to comprehend what is taking place in the world. To be sure, stories heard or read, and told and told again, often help children to resolve in their minds worries or fears or anxieties—to come closer to a difficulty through a story of which that difficulty is the subject matter. But the mind is not only fueled by traumas or turmoil. We are a perceiving creature: we want to know, to understand; and not least, we are, distinctively, a talking creature. We are the ones (as little Ruby was letting me know back then in a city seized by near insurrection) whose nature it is to use words, and more words in the course of our lives—in good moments and bad, and be we rich or poor, black or white or brown or red or whatever.

Eventually I would begin to realize how important a clue I'd been given then, at the start of my fieldwork with children. Years later, in a small coastal Eskimo village of Alaska, I would hear this from a nine-year-old boy I'd come to know fairly well: "My father took me fishing, and while we stood there and waited for the fish to bite, he told me the story of our people. He said we were going to be put here to fish, and the spirits asked us where we'd like to be. We could have our choice. We chose here, near the ocean and the Kobuk river, because we'd *have* to fish. In the Lower Forty-eight, the teacher says, you fish when you want to fish. A long time ago our people thought of moving south. They got together and decided they'd leave here. They started out, but they got hungry, so they stopped and began fishing. They ate the fish. Then an Eskimo said: What if we walk and walk, and it gets warmer and warmer, and we decide to stop and make houses for ourselves, and we are happy, but we look for a place to fish, and there isn't a place? What will we do then? We'll stop being Eskimos then. We'll be like the white man. So, they never left; and here we are. I told the story to our teacher, and she said it's a 'nice story.' I told her it's what our people decided. She said it's a 'nice story.' I told my father what the teacher said. He said, 'She's a nice teacher.'"

So much for irony, wry humor, and the difficulties of Eskimo life, Eskimo education. But that Eskimo boy had noticed something important: a white teacher's lack of understanding, her failure to see that when she dismissed an earnestly told account of a people's collective experiences, apocryphal or not, as a "nice story" she was not doing justice to the intent of a people—to clarify their condition with a good deal of ingenuity, detachment, implied humor, resignation, pride, and, yes, regret. They are people who, after all, must pay dearly for that decision to stay and fish rather than flee to a less circumscribed environment. They haven't explained their fate in order to hear themselves say "nice" things—or be told by others that such is their way of storytelling. It is a matter of some importance for them that they know what they live by and, also, what they live for. Put differently, they are no less inclined than Gauguin was in the far warmer world of Tahiti (the same ocean, though!) to ask those unforgettable and universal questions: Where do we come from? What are we? Where are we going? Those are not only the questions of artists in exile, or of philosophers, or of this century's knowing analysands. Nor are they questions that necessarily bespeak an Oedipal complex or some other evidence of neurosis. They are the eminently reasonable questions that it is in our nature as human creatures to ask. Call them cognitive or existential questions; the point is not wordy, showy characterizations but a recognition on our part that each one of us is so equipped that we use language to ask, to try to contrive an explanation, an important one indeed—on a matter of life and death to us: the whys and wheres of our destiny.

It is to such a purpose that the story lends itself, in my experience, at a very early age and to all children in America, no matter their racial, social, cultural, or geographic situation. Children don't only crave information; they don't only seek facts. They have every intention of pulling together what they see and hear and wonder about and what others have seen, heard, wondered about, and passed on. They do so by putting words and ideas and speculations and incidents and worries and hearsay and sayings and jokes and admonitions into a series of stories, some ever so brief, others a bit longer, still others rather long indeed. They can be heard all over the country passing on received wisdom as Hopi tales, Eskimo legends, Southern country stories, ghetto jokes; and they can be heard passing on news of what happened in a suburban school, in a small town neighborhood, not just yesterday, but *there* and *then*—the amplified incident that has become the shared story of boys and girls on a yellow bus or at play in a backyard, a street, a pleasant grassy knoll. For some of those children there will be, soon enough, the encounter with other, more experienced and ambitious storytellers, ones who get called writers; but I doubt any child has ever heard a story read, or come to read one himself or herself, who hasn't already heard various unwritten stories and also told more than a few of them. Stories connect children to the past of their parents, their people; stories also enable children to connect themselves to something even more fundamental, their very essence as talking, listening, thinking creatures, who are anxious to fit together, as best they are able, whatever they learn about human experience. Soon enough they will begin to sense the limits of such knowledge. Soon enough they will appreciate the mysteries of the world—the stuff of another level of storytelling.

In *Children's Literature*, 1980

The Poetry of Childhood

They're hungry. / So hungry, they bark the pain. / They would eat me / Down to the last meat / On the last bone. / But they'd still run and growl / So, it's lucky the police have a chain on them / The mad white dogs!"

Those were the statements of Ruby Bridges, a black girl of six in 1961; she faced viciously threatening segregationist mobs every day for months as she desegregated (all by herself) a totally boycotted elementary school in New Orleans. Many Americans may well remember her—escorted by federal marshals past the howling men and women. She knew they wanted her blood. Yet she smiled at her tormentors. She even told me she prayed for them. Why? Because her grandmother told her that "they were to be pitied—as Christ pitied his assailants." But Ruby was not one to bury her fears in the sands of nightly appeals to God. She was plain scared. She was also plain smart; she took careful, daily estimate of the dangerous world around her. She tried to understand what was happening and why. No student of history, no political scientist, and bless her, no psychologist or psychiatrist, she yet was able to come to a conclusion or two and assert her humanity by putting her sense of things into the instruments of a particular language: words.

I have taken some remarks made to me in February of 1961, in the course of a few minutes of innocent afternoon talk, and put marks between the various sentences that followed one another, just as they do above. Ruby intended no poem: yet she was calling upon a sustained image, and her brief, pungent sentences, punctuated by occasional moments of silence—pauses that possessed great power—were not easily forgotten by my wife or me. Nor by one of the federal marshals, a big, burly, somewhat morose fellow, who only gradually overcame some of his strenuous white, Alabama prejudices enough to take an obvious, if reluctant fancy to "the kid," as he always called Ruby. One day the marshal, often ravenously hungry himself, had a comment for my wife and me: "She's right, the kid. They're crazy, those people on the street; and they're hungry—for her. They *would* eat her up alive if we weren't there to protect her! She's a smart one. She's like a poet; she says these things, and you don't forget them. I tell my wife what I've heard the kid say, and my wife asks how come our daughter doesn't talk like that, and she's nine, three years older. Maybe our daughter *does*, though; maybe we don't hear her."

I got to know his daughter, eventually, and a number of other ordinary white Southern children, who, like Ruby, had to go through the confusions of historical change—which had become for them everyday life. A white girl, a year older than Ruby, and a member of a family that lived on the same street as the federal marshal just mentioned, had this to tell me one day in 1962: "It's over, the storm. / The black clouds came / The white clouds came / Then, lightning and thunder, a bad rain / We almost drowned / Fire and noise and water / Now the sky is clear / The sun shines on both races / Like the Bible says / The rain falls on the just / The unjust, too—some of us white folks / I pray for all people / In this city, not God's: New Orleans."

She spoke those words in May of 1962, already a hot and humid day in that old, cosmopolitan port city. I've not pulled sentences out of context. I've not really left out much—a few stray words, a few oh's and ah's. She was telling my wife and me a story of sorts. She was remembering. She was trying to make sense of what she'd gone through. As she talked, she used her hands, her arms. She used her voice: ups and downs of excitement, sadness, fear, bewilderment, all those emotions my kind talks and talks about. But she had no interest in going from personal experience to the abstractions of the social sciences. She had been through a lot of difficult, perplexing moments, and she wanted to evoke them, to do justice to their continuing, collective significance in her life—and not only hers. She called upon abstractions all right, but they were the kind a novelist or a poet rather than a psychologist or psychiatrist would likely summon.

I am not anxious to call her a poet or to insist that she had a rare and beautiful mind, as yet unspoiled by the incursions of our wicked (adult) world. There is no point figuring out one more way to romanticize children, to make them the chaste repositories of all that is clean and uncluttered and clairvoyant in this otherwise earthly hell (save for a few grown-up poets!). In fact, the girl quoted immediately above was, often enough, a cranky, demanding child, all too willingly able to say mean and nasty things about—yes, the girl quoted at the start of this essay. By this time, one hopes, we have learned that one can be a child who is sensitive and thoughtful and unspoiled by various social ills but also be a child who is willful or self-centered or indifferent to the pain of others—or quick, even, to add some of one's own malice or mischief to the total supply around. So with the rest of us—including poets, whose marvelous perceptions, given strong and touching expression, do not preclude narrowness of vision, spite, arrogance (and on and on) when it comes to this life's everyday behavior.

A white girl saw her world changing, and out of her humanity, her mind's struggle to figure things out and put the result into words, came a few vivid, earnestly felt remarks. Because my wife has taught English composition (prose and poetry) to children, she had a particularly responsive way of listening to such statements made by the boys and girls we were getting to know. She heard them all, really heard them. I was too busy, alas, studying them—trying to estimate what was happening in their heads. As we'd play our tapes later, my wife would stop the machine, reverse it, listen again, and then say: "another poem!" I would smile: oh, the well-meaning efforts of school teachers to find a spoonful of honey somewhere, anywhere.

The years of our work would eventually humble me a little. Gradually I learned to stop categorizing "psychological defense mechanisms"—which all of us have, no matter who we are and where we live—and instead pay heed to the particular life I was privileged to see, day after day: children caught up in a moment of significant political crisis and terribly anxious, therefore, to comprehend what fate had put before their eyes and within hearing distance of their ears. I began to listen again and again to what we'd been collecting—those tapes that prove one a scientist! On them, not to mention in our daily life and work, we found ourselves in the cumulative presence of—well—the poetry of childhood, I'll try calling it. That is to say, we heard boys and girls, America's young, singing or crying—through words, images, and symbols, telling us what they had come to understand was happening around them.

Of course, there were not only intellectual, so-called cognitive issues at stake for these children. They were struggling with their moral perceptions as well. I am sick and tired of those theorists in psychology and psychiatry who have the moral life of children all

figured out—on the basis, mind you, of their theories or some experiments they've done: questionnaires handed out or observations
made in "human development" laboratories. It is curious, indeed,
the way this century has treated children, I keep saying to myself as I
try coming to terms with observations in South Africa and, in retrospect, with remarks such as those offered above. On the one hand,
we insist that children are astonishingly knowing—all taken up with
clever psychological surmises. But those same children, sensitive (it
seems, or is claimed) to just about every emotional nuance imagin-
able, are declared moral idiots of sorts. They are described as incapable of being anything but compulsively obedient or fearfully oblig-
ing—with provocative interruptions of hedonism, selfishness, truculence, and so on: a collective evidence of the "developmental stage"
into which they are locked, ever so firmly and conclusively, by (of
course!) the various social scientists who have done their studies.

There certainly are limitations to this life, and surely we experience them in different ways at different times. But there are all sorts
of exceptions, leeways, possibilities for each of us. We are not necessarily bound to be, at every moment, what some psychologist says
we are or tend to be. We may well be a lot of things that one or
another psychologist has not thought to inquire about—even to
think possible. Ruby Bridges was, I suppose, what I rather drearily
called her when I was first getting to know her—a poor child of
black parents, "culturally deprived" and "culturally disadvantaged."
(No poetry to those labels!) But she was also a caring, plucky child—
"one of God's children," her doting grandmother called her; a girl
who was driven as all of us human beings are to make moral sense of
what takes place in this world and to do so through language—a
habit, it seems, for our particular kind of creature. And so, she gave
my wife and me (and herself) various words and images, her comprehension of what had happened and almost (God forbid!) did happen; her hope, too, of what might happen. "There are days / really
sunny days / when I look at the sky / and God is there, I know. / I
don't see him / I see the blue / I make him up / The wind might be
his voice / A cloud, a small puffy one / All alone, his smile. /
Thank God for you / I say to him / And please, I ask, remember my
grandmother."

She did indeed "ask"; she wondered all the time: why do people
act as they do to one another, and why do they act as they do to her

as she goes to school, and when would all that grim and pitiable adult activity stop, and when would the dear Lord, whom she had been taught to love so very much, come and stop such behavior, make New Orleans better, make America better, bring us "the new heaven" and "the new earth" she heard mentioned, time and again, in church? Such a line of curiosity, of apprehensive concern, would become, through statement after statement, a kind of continuing moral inquiry rendered—it can be said, vividly enough, dramatically enough, persuasively and compellingly enough, metaphorically enough, pointedly and suggestively enough, to warrant (from us, the keepers of the keys!) the acknowledgement, I hope not reluctant or begrudging, of poetry. A black child's lyrical utterances, a white child's similar movement of the mind and heart: two girls growing up in New Orleans during a bad spell were finding through words and more words a touch of grace for themselves, for the rest of us.

The Lion and the Unicorn, 1981

The Vision of the Humanities
for the Young

The humanities ought to offer young people in school a means of fitting various pieces of knowledge into a larger view of things—to draw upon a Latin phrase: *sub specie aeternitatis*. The humanities have to do with perspective—the long haul of time; and they have to do also with values, with a sense of what ought to be as well as what is. The humanities begin with language—the distinctive attribute of human beings. We are the ones who become self-conscious, through words; who begin to ask questions as well as respond to reflexes; who gaze and wonder, then put into talk what crosses our minds. With language comes distance, a capacity to draw back and render an account of what is and has been taking place: history. Language is the means by which we keep trying for answers, not only to specific, factual matters but to the mysteries of this universe. The big questions, those asked by Gauguin and written on his famous Tahitian triptych, are the essence of what the humanities try to fathom for us, through poems and stories and plays and essays and factual narratives: where do we come from, and what are we, and where are we going? Such questions have to do with "the meaning of life," a phrase once summoned commonly, but these days all too sadly left unused. The humanities bring us closest to our essential nature, as the ones who speculate: what, if anything, is the meaning of our existence?

Needless to say, a teacher's point of view becomes a student's experience through the mediation of certain texts. Nor did those who wrote, say, the novels or poems many high school students read spend a lot of time constructing theories of education, or guides to accompany one or another collection of stories. A *Tale of Two Cities*, for example, is just that, a tale given us by a nineteenth-century storyteller. Each student who reads Dickens makes him his or her own companion—brings to Sydney Carton, let us say, a particular kind of sympathy, or indeed, lack thereof. Put differently, the humanities do not begin in a student's reading experience but in our lives—the moral preparation we bring to school, to our reading time. Still, there *is* the teacher who uses those books as a means of conversation, speculation, edification, exhortation, and occasionally, imprecation. What goes for the reader, of course, goes for the reader who is called a teacher—a lifetime's preparation for Mr. Dickens. But one need not surrender, yet again, to twentieth-century determinism. *Part* of that lifetime, an important part, takes place in the daily activity of a given classroom, where a teacher can hope for the same transcendence Sydney Carton sought, even as that teacher hopes to spring a few students, each year, from the moral as well as intellectual constraints of their lives.

I feel myself, already, a bit too abstract; and I am not sure that the humanities ought be under such a tether. The humanities have to do with the moral and spiritual concreteness of our everyday lives, as a number of American youths have reminded me in no uncertain terms. Here, for example, is a New Orleans high school student, lecturing a doctor on the significance of another doctor's life—the latter a character in A *Tale of Two Cities:*

> They gave us the book to read and said we had two weeks, and we'd better settle down and read fast because we had to finish, and if we didn't, they'd find out, because we'd be tested, and they'd use "spot identifications." "They" were the two of them: the regular (older) teacher and the younger one, helping out— and learning, I guess. They kept on saying Dickens was a tough writer, and we should pay close attention or we'd get lost in the novel, and we'd lose interest, and it'd be a real disaster for us.
>
> When I first picked up the novel, I was really annoyed: so big, so long! I had a lot else to do! What did they mean, by assigning that book for us to read, and in the spring! I was on the baseball team! I had a job! I had a lot of trouble at home: my dad was sick, and I was the one who took over some of his chores, and I was the one who tried to keep my younger brothers and sisters in line, while my mother was out working, or home cooking. Besides, who can go back into the past that far? They wrote different English back then. Even the teacher admitted that it's hard to understand a writer if you're alive a hundred or more years after he wrote his novel.
>
> I got into A *Tale of Two Cities* fairly fast! I was surprised! I

just picked it up, and I got interested. I now realize that the first sentences are famous, and a lot of people who haven't read the book know those lines: "It was the best of times, it was the worst of times. . . ." But when I first read them, I thought to myself: yes, that's how it is, right now, for me and my family! We're having trouble, but we're fighting this segregation, and we're beginning to win a few battles, so there's trouble, but there's hope, and it more than balances the trouble.

I got involved with that Sydney Carton, and it was he who carried me through the book. If it hadn't been for him, I never would have finished; I would have skimmed, maybe! Also, Dr. Manette interested me: all the suffering he experienced, and yet he managed to stay alive, and when the right moment came, he got better, or mostly better. I kept trying to figure out how he kept his sanity while in prison; and how he recovered his sanity, once his daughter took him away from Paris. He seems to have lost his sanity in between—while he stayed with the DeFarges. Do you have an explanation? If they'd sent him to a psychiatrist in Paris after he was released from jail, would it have helped? What good can a psychiatrist do when a person is being mistreated very badly and there's no way of stopping his punishment, even if it's cruel and unfair? The psychiatrist would have to *rescue* the person, not *treat* him!

Among other reasons, novelists obviously write to give others a glimpse of a particular vision. Here in the twentieth-century American South, Dickens had found a spiritual kinsman of sorts—a fellow human being whose mind was utterly responsive to A *Tale of Two Cities*, and more, to the moral struggles Dickens had deemed to be so important. In fact, one wonders whether the young man's English teacher was similarly responsive to Dickens. Are novels meant to be studied as if they are bodies of factuality, to be taken apart, limb by limb, and identified? I fear I went through—in college, never mind high school—an experience not unlike that described above: a course titled "Dostoevski and Tolstoy," in which we had endless multiple-choice tests, all meant to prove we had read the books, remembered the names of the characters, principal or minor, and, as well, the various deeds they accomplished. Irony is a favorite device of novelists; but life, as we all know, cannot only prompt art but follow it—when, for instance, one reads stories whose purpose is to help the reader (not to mention the writer) go beyond the narrowness and pettiness of everyday life but ends up once more constrained, now by a narrow and petty didactic method. The transcendence of both Sydney Carton and Dr. Manette in A *Tale of Two Cities* is not necessarily available to many of us, who face no revolution or imprisonment as our fate.

The youth quoted above was, however, not only a critic of a given classroom. He had taken pains to question the very nature of the humanities—their significance to us, their peculiar way of addressing the broadest, yet also deepest, aspects of our human experience. Of course, we teachers have a right to demand that our students do, indeed, pay heed—read the books we assign and remember their contents. But such activity is a prelude to reflection, and not only the kind that has to do with textual criticism. A *Tale of Two Cities*, one young reader dared notice, is a story brimful of mystery. Not so much the conventional kind—cloak-and-dagger intrigue—but rather the mystery we all know as we contemplate this life (even elementary school children, one hastens to add). Here, for example, is a white child who lived in New Orleans during the early 1960s and who (at nine) had never heard of Charles Dickens or Fyodor Dostoevski or Leo Tolstoy:

> I see that colored kid walking past the people, and they're all grown up, and they're telling her they're going to kill her, and I wonder why God put her here, to go through such trouble. In our church, the minister is always telling us that God was very unpopular with the important people because he had his own ideas of what was right and wrong, and He didn't agree with the big shots. On television, I heard that colored girl's daddy say he hoped and prayed the white people would think of Jesus when they saw his daughter trying to get into the school. So, I did think of Jesus! Then, I thought of the colored kid. Then I had this terrible thought that she'd die, like Jesus did, only we don't have crosses to nail people on, I don't think.
>
> I asked my mother what she thought would happen, and she said the colored kid is a pawn, and it's the fault of the Supreme Court. I asked my mother about Jesus, and she said Jesus felt sorry for everyone and that includes all the colored, but you

can't live your life like he did, Jesus, because he was God and we're just people—and besides, he was killed, and he didn't mean for everyone to go get killed, and if we all did, there'd be no one to worship him! Then, I asked my mother if God had a plan when he made some people one way and some people another way. I mean, some people are always having pain, or they're in trouble, and some people are always hurting other people, and the ones who do the hurting say they're Christians, and the ones who get hurt say they're Christians, too, and you get confused when you hear the minister talk, and your momma, and your daddy, and the teachers; and they all *are* confused, I guess, and even Jesus couldn't convince everyone so they didn't feel confused, and I guess all you can do is be glad if someone gets you to do some "good asking," that's what my grandma says: "always try to be true to the Lord, and always ask yourself questions, the way the Lord did." So, I try!

So do we all—try to figure out this world, its endless puzzles, paradoxes, and inconsistencies. The essence of the humanities has to do with moral inquiry, done, of course, with grace, dignity, and aesthetic distinction. When I was a boy, my mother took me to the Boston Museum of Fine Arts rather often. (She was an artist.) There, she would not only comment on certain pictures she found appealing, even compelling, but also ask me to let my mind wonder and wander both, prompted by the artists, and yes, by her as their interpreter, my teacher. Her favorite in the entire museum was the powerful triptych (1897) of Paul Gauguin, mentioned earlier—done in Tahiti as he struggled with suicidal despair. The canvas evokes the entire span of this life—infancy to old age. The canvas also evokes questions, not the least three supplied directly by the artist—one of those rare occasions when words are to be found in such a "place." Those three questions, rendered in French and mentioned earlier in this essay, were translated for me, again and again, by my mother until (finally!) I knew them in English by heart—and gladly repeat them here: Where do we come from? What are we? Where are we going? I also remember only too well this pointed observation of hers: "We're the ones on this earth who ask those questions!"

A mother's meditative side! A Boston woman's philosophical affinity with the existentialist tradition. A teacher's insistence that

Gauguin's genius be saluted intently, seriously, with continuing respect. And yes, a teacher's desire that Gauguin not be confined (by a given pupil) to Tahiti, to the late nineteenth century, even to a particular profession or branch of the humanities. Even as he was driven by his anguish—by his talent, as well—to ask the hardest questions in the most enduring manner, a teacher was anxious to pay homage not only to him but to her own humanity, and her student's, by embracing the responsibility that goes with attentive regard, with personal appreciation. Put differently, my mother was doing as that New Orleans child (a mere fourth grader!) was wont to do, as teachers of all levels aim to do; she was aiming to exert her intelligence, her imagination, in the direction of a scrutiny directed inward and outward both.

This life is full of questions—the general kind Gauguin posed and the specific kind generated by the circumstances of one or another life. The humanities are meant to help us *try*, as the child quoted put it, to find useful, decent, appropriate, sensible answers. Not that there ever will be complete, definite, thoroughly clear answers. The humanities are not, at heart, preoccupied with factuality. One turns to George Eliot not for data in its modern sense—the unequivocal information we all learn when we take arithmetic, or science courses, or for that matter, spelling. "The task of the novelist," said Flannery O'Connor, "is to deepen mystery"; and if ever there was both an implied definition of what the humanities are about and a rebuke to a predominant contemporary sensibility, it is contained in that critical observation—one of many shrewd, pointed, often caustic comments that marvelous and all too short-lived, twentieth-century storyteller from Milledgeville, Georgia, gave to the rest of us who continue to make our way toward the year 2000.

Miss O'Connor added that "mystery is a great embarrassment to the modern mind," and with that aside she got to the very heart of what ails so much of the teaching done today in the name of the humanities. Rather more of us in the humanities than we care to acknowledge are all too awed not by this world's mysteries but by those who claim to have banished them rather thoroughly—the confident technicians, the strutting social scientists, the men and women who know how to punch machines, manipulate materials, and come up with a yes, a no, a true, a false, a solution, definitive and final. Our "embarrassment" bespeaks our loss of self-respect, our shame, our sense of frustration, our feeling of incompetence: others manipulate things and prove themselves "practical," whereas we "merely" watch, listen, muse, and acknowledge the strangeness of things. Why, we even cultivate a many-sided, uncertain, perplexed posture with respect to the world's events!

It is, of course, absurd to expect those of us who teach the humanities (in schools, in colleges, wherever) to ignore the powerful thrust of a culture, a historical moment. The issue, surely, is not our "embarrassment" before the power of technology but what we do with that "embarrassment": ignore it, pretend it is of little import, make it of consuming import, pity ourselves on its account—or use it, wryly, to further our own purposes, as the ones who hope, always, to reflect upon the nature of things when confronted with this life's numerous moments of trial or error. One of the first humanists, Socrates, asked us to regard ourselves with exceeding care, not with a self-centered orgy of reductionist psychology, as too often is the case these days, but with the conviction that honest self-scrutiny can reveal much about *others*. In that tradition, O'Connor's "embarrassment" tells us not only about the predicament of the humanities but also about the situation of all this world's people. We are, so many of us, embarrassed by the seemingly endless evidence that we are finite, flawed, and all too clearly fumbling—no matter the computers at hand or the ponderous phrases committed (if I may call upon W. H. Auden's delicious use of that verb) in the name of sociology or psychiatry. ("Do not commit a social science!")

Moreover, embarrassment has many faces, as Dickens or Eliot, Dostoevski or Tolstoy, always knew: arrogance, preciosity, smugness, self-importance, pedantry, narrowness of mind, smallness of vision, coldness of heart. Have I, with that list, suggested a few traps faced by us who want to teach the humanities—the maneuvers we summon in fear and trembling because we dare not come out and say, with O'Connor's candor, how hard it can be to press upon others, press upon ourselves, the vexing, alarming, saddening exhilarations of our visionary writers and artists? I remember a hero of my youth, whom I was lucky to know, William Carlos Williams, putting the above this way: "On a good day I see enough to say enough to scare myself. If a reader tells me how *pleasing* a line I've written is, or a story, I always wonder whether I've failed. I want 'them' to be pleased—oh sure!—but I want to dig below the surface, and there's lots of pain in digging, or in becoming a digger, by sympathy, yourself."

I suppose I'd better not *recommend* pain in our classrooms—not in an age devoted to countless utopian dreams and repeated romances with prophylaxis of one kind or another. These days, we want not only penetrations to all of nature's secrets but protection from all of its hazards and hurdles. Not for us the willing assumption of vulnerability—as in the Christ mentioned by the two children I have brought into this essay, or as in our own nation's forebears, when they eagerly chose jeopardy in order to obtain a greater measure of freedom. For so many of us the point is security, certainty—the eradication of all ambiguity. No wonder we veer strongly to multiple-choice tests, to summaries and more summaries—of plots, of positions, of policies. "I haven't time to read *Middlemarch*," a not so stupid or ignorant Harvard undergraduate once let me know, without O'Connor's "embarrassment," and indeed, almost casually rather than worriedly or apologetically. Where did he learn such an "attitude"? Not, I presume, in the course of going through the "oedipal" stage of his "psychological development." Not in a fancy suburban home or in a ghetto, either. He learned it in a succession of classrooms. The time has come for all of us to stop hiding behind psychology or sociology; to stop throwing our hands up as we contemplate the erosion of literacy in consequence of television, or the "culture of narcissism," or God knows what else.

The black youth quoted above, whom I regarded as his own kind of Dickensian scholar, could have been quickly assigned to some convenient and faddish sociological ashpile—"culturally disadvantaged," say, or "culturally deprived." Instead, a diligent and thoroughly demanding (without "embarrassment!") teacher had grabbed him (literally, sometimes!), collared him (not literally!), and pressed upon him a novel. She read it aloud to him and his classmates. She pointed out what its pages meant. She virtually sang it, as well as singing its praises. She indicated her belief in it, and she persuaded a number of her students to give their assent—to her, to Charles Dickens, to O'Connor's "mystery and manners," which is what, in sum, our novelists, all of them, try to set down for us to contemplate. It is my hunch that the particular teacher in question and her students, too, require neither exhortation nor analysis from the rest of us—what to do or how to do it. They would like, to be sure, our company as delighted, convinced readers—sharers of a burden of work they have assumed and would gladly have us assume. In the absence of our commitment to their kind of journey, they would probably shrug their shoulders, as Sydney Carton sometimes did— not too hopeful about the prospects of all humanity but willing to stand up for its worth by standing up for themselves as readers and, thereby, unembarrassed dreamers.

In Benjamin Ladner, ed., *The Humanities in Precollegiate Education,* 1984

Politics, People, and Literature

Notes from Underground

S ome questions are never old: How could the nation of Bach and Beethoven and Brahms, of Goethe and Schiller, of Thomas Mann and Rilke, of Gropius and Käthe Kollwitz turn to the Nazis? How could a gang of brutal thugs take over a modern nation, its citizens able to read and write, its industry advanced, its technology unsurpassed, its physicians and chemists and physicists and philosophers among the world's finest? Why did a people loyal to Luther's Protestantism and the Holy Catholic Church suddenly accept feverishly and uncritically the pagan and murderous leadership of men like Göring, Goebbels, and Himmler? These questions have been asked ever since the National Socialists (as they cleverly called themselves) began to demonstrate that murderers could assume the guise of Germany's institutionalized political authority and then lie and cheat and blackmail and kill on a scale only a "civilized" nation could sustain. This irony haunted Friedrich Percyval Reck-Malleczewen, whose *Diary of a Man in Despair,* now published by Macmillan in a translation by Paul Rubens, offers future generations a chance to learn what Western twentieth-century men were capable of doing. His descriptions of Nazi Germany are not those of the scholar bent on documentation or of the victim who has been tortured by sadists. Instead, we are offered a diarist's observations, set down with passion, outrage, and almost unbearable sadness— and set down (among other reasons) to show how easy it would have been for him to be a part of what he came to detest. Like confidence-men and cutthroat social climbers, the Nazis had an unerring eye for the weaknesses of those they intended to use and flatter and extoll, then intimidate and rob and kill.

In May of 1936, when this diary starts, Hitler and his men were not the objects of near-universal condemnation they eventually became. They had taken control with the support of powerful industrial, military, and even religious leaders. Outside Germany, the Nazis were considered important allies by many who believed themselves honorable human beings. Particularly among those Europeans whom the left would have called "conservative" or "monarchist" or "landed gentry" or "aristocrat," there was a tendency to look upon fascist governments as bulwarks against the plague of bolshevism. In the midthirties, few leftists would have recognized a man of Reck-Malleczewen's class and background as a likely anti-Nazi. He was, after all, an avowed royalist, born to a distinguished East Prussian family in 1884, who served in the German army in the First World War and finally settled on an estate in Bavaria. It was there that he saw, at first hand, the rise to power of a group of men who must have seemed laughable and harmless to many other well-educated and well-off Bavarians. In the twenties and thirties, while the implausible was becoming the all too real, Reck-Malleczewen immersed himself in literature, philosophy, and religious history. He traveled. He read. And he worried, not for himself but for the whole world, which he felt was caught up in a collective madness of long duration—a madness in which the Nazis were but one of the many kinds of crooks, liars, and cheats who had over the centuries betrayed both humanity and God.

The diary begins with "Oswald Spengler is dead." Reck-Malleczewen admired Spengler but knew his limitations as a philosopher and a man. We are told that Spengler had seen the rot in Western life but had been fatally compromised by the money that businessmen make available for sharp social critics who have a taste for good food, comfortable surroundings, and the applause and favors powerful hosts and elegant hostesses can offer. For Reck-Malleczewen, Spengler's *Decline of the West* was undercut in this fashion: "Halfway through his work, he let himself become dependent on the industrialists, and began to think less well. How else can one possibly reconcile that really magnificent piece of writing he did in 1922, in which he prophesied the coming of a new, Dostoevskian Christendom, with that technocracy-nonsense in his later work?"

Remarks like that are the heart of *Diary of a Man in Despair*, and they make up a conservative political and religious philosophy that I believe a lot of us today in America will find nearly incomprehensible. Nor is the cultivated Prussian ex-soldier and country gentleman any spiritual kin of the many citizens of the United States who call themselves conservatives. He rails against not only Hitler and the corrupt Western governments that were so easily fooled and pushed about by him, but the ordinary, reasonably well-to-do burgher of the West, who pays lip service to God and country yet devotes himself to the appeasement of his own appetites. In this diary, the Germans who shouted *"Sieg Heil!"* so long and loud are declared to be not unlike the French, English, and Americans who in the clutch are capable of stampeding down blind alleys. And it is interesting to note that thirty years ago this strange, eccentric, lonely, brilliant man saw the dangerous, even fatal traps that await us, Hitler or no Hitler: "I tremble for each tree and each woods that disappears, for each silent valley that is devastated, for each stream that these pirates of industry, the real masters of our land, threaten." As Germany's land is virtually smothered by its newly made bombers on parade, the proud airplanes of a great world power, he comments, "Now, still, overhead, these white savages steer their moronic automatons, flying toward brutality and crime, drowning out the peaceful stillness of this spring day." And as National Socialism is steadily ascendant, as Germans see their land covered with more highways, their factories pour out more products, their Army and Navy and Air Force become the envy of less "developed" nations, the author turns more despairing (and maybe prophetic): "Gasoline, as the basis for all motorized happiness, has contributed more to the inner decay of mankind than alcohol." He does not see how "technology and mechanization can escape being relegated to the dust heap, or at least to the periphery of life." He denounces "superfluous bureaucrats" and "totally useless questionnaires." He warns against the dangers of "rabbitlike reproduction." He says that "only the 'New Adam,' a savage who by an accident has a white skin, who today uses all this equipment with an unconcern bordering on impudence; to whom it never occurs that one must replenish the thought-world from which all this technology derives; only mass man can doubt its destructibility."

For Reck-Malleczewen, Hitler was merely the latest one to assume leadership over mass man and to do it in the name of aggressive military preparedness and expansion—buttressed, as always, by nationalist self-righteousness, an ethic of political pragmatism, and the rhetoric of seemingly harmless pieties. Reck-Malleczewen insists that "Hitlerism is only a symptom." For centuries, we had been moving toward all that goes with Hitler (and Stalin and Mussolini and Chamberlain and Daladier and Franco). Before those men were even born, Bismarck and his equivalents elsewhere were setting the stage for the wars this century still endures. Proud, greedy, self-justifying leaders have betrayed one generation after another, leaving us "the bankruptcy of the last five centuries."

It is hard to come to grips with the author of this astonishing, compelling, and unnerving diary. Early in the thirties, he foresaw a terrible Second World War. He was a moralist, a man of candor, a cynic like the Greek philosophers who criticized the social customs and beliefs of their day, and, finally, a German who easily could have prospered under the Nazis but who chose to write against them with devastating scorn and to show his hatred in small but direct gestures and remarks. Eventually, the Third Reich began to burn up— a victim of not only English and American bombs but its own desperate craziness. Reck-Malleczewen was denounced, jailed, sent to Dachau, and shot. His last entry, in 1944, shows him unafraid, devoutly Christian, contemptuous of the riffraff his people were still calling their legal political leaders. It is noteworthy that he did not take part in the plot to kill Hitler, that he never joined any resistance, never fled Germany in order to take up the struggle elsewhere. Perhaps he felt he had nowhere to go; Spengler was right, the diary says: the West is doomed. Reck-Malleczewen calls English culture worthless, no better than Germany's—"with the exception of the old aristocracy." He indicates that his aristocracy includes yeoman farmers, artisans, and the dukes or princes they once looked up to and in turn drew support from (or so he believed). To him, the Nazi seizure of power is additional evidence that an orderly, rational, decently hierarchical world, a world dominated by his kind of aristocrats, is no longer possible: "I am a conservative. In Germany, naturally, this is an almost extinct political species. I derive from monarchical patterns of thinking, I was brought up as a monarchist, and the continued existence of the monarchy is one of the foundation stones of my physical well-being."

Yet he attacks Germany's last Kaiser and the nineteenth-century Prussian military leaders. His own sort of monarchy—valuable and worth believing in—may never have existed. What is to be done when a monarchy like eighteenth-century France or nineteenth-century Germany becomes corrupt? What is to be done when Hitler takes over everything? Like Edmund Burke, the author of this diary has a passion for order and justice. In the tradition of Burke, his de-

spair over the world's evils—the vulgarities and banalities as well as
the gross inequalities—turns into a volley of sarcasm and ridicule
against phony and pretentious politicians, double-dealing industrialists, and crooks who masquerade as professional men and business leaders. Burke was a patriot, a ruthless enemy of crooks and
tyrants, an upright and thoughtful legislator who wanted order and
stability and continuity—not to keep the entrenched power of a few
inviolable but to prevent one form of violence and corruption from
being supplanted by another, world without end. The French Revolution did away with the Bastille and the royal court—only to demonstrate its own viciousness, its own arbitrary, murderous will. And
the czar gave way to Stalin and his gigantic excesses. When is a government so bad and unjust and corrupt and tyrannical that revolution is justified? In 1789, Burke said no to the French Revolution. In
our time, Reck-Malleczewen, despite his hatred for Hitler, never
really suggests sabotage, organized resistance, or a revolution to end
the Third Reich. The issue is not whether such activity was "realistic" or "practical" or even "possible." (Some Germans kept trying
to thwart or even kill Hitler.) Reck-Malleczewen may have confined
his political opposition to a diary because history seemed implacable, because he believed that he could not forestall an apocalypse
so imminent.

This lonely diarist refers to his house as "a very isolated place
more than six hundred years old, which has long been regarded as
haunted." He mentions Knut Hamsun, the brooding, aloof, austere
Norwegian novelist, who had no real knowledge of or taste for politics but did have a clear notion of the corruptions and duplicities in
the liberal democracies Hitler attacked, one after another. Dostoevski is mentioned with admiration. And, no doubt about it, the "man
in despair" who wrote this diary hated violence and cheapness and
meanness. Like his house, he was rooted in a distant past; like Hamsun, he had an artist's sensitivity, which in a flash could spot hypocrisy; like Dostoevski (and his character who speaks so boldly and dev-
astatingly in *Notes from the Underground*), he struggled to make
sense of his religious mysticism, his political idealism, his deep and
reverential love for the earth, for his nation's history and traditions,
for the "soul" of his people—while hating what the Church and
German politics had come to, what had happened to the land and
water and air, and what his countrymen were doing. All *he* could do

was write down the ambiguities he felt with fierce intensity and dedication—and wait for the death he knew he would experience at the hands of the Gestapo. His immediate objects of hate are gone, but his mind had other enemies, and they are still with us. How Reck-Malleczewen would disdain those American "conservatives" who ally themselves with the oil companies that deface our shores, the coal companies that desecrate our land with strip mines, and how he would disdain the rhetoric of those who justify slander and murder in the name of political slogans, however "egalitarian" their message. Still, though he knew exquisitely and unbearably what he was against, he had very little idea of what he was for—and still less of what he might work to achieve. So he simply sat back and put into words his thoughts—as a member of a spiritual underground that the highly industrialized, well-armed, agnostic West has little reason to fear.

An American Prophet

As we march through history, our direction so much influenced by the past, our time and energy consumed by the demands of the present, there always seem to be, thank God, a few visionaries around; they seek the high land and try to tell us, after finding out for themselves, where we seem headed. Not that everyone who talks about the future of this or any other nation is worth listening to. Each century has produced its fair share of moral monsters, third-rate hucksters, or political confidence-men, all masquerading as far-sighted statesmen. Yet, men of wisdom and courage have also been around from the very beginning, though by no means have they had the clout to do much more than speak out or set down in words what in their judgment is going on, and just as important, what ought to be going on, come a better day. And maybe, through some dialectical twist that Hegel and Karl Marx alike could not possibly foresee (neither of them pretended to paint in the details of the huge canvas whose outline both men claimed knowledge of), there is something about a highly developed capitalist society that not only makes for material abundance but a surfeit of prophets, if not idiot-savants; certainly we in today's America have no shortage of social critics and self-appointed oracles, and book publishing being what it is, not to mention television with its talk shows, they have wide access to readers and listeners—us, the hungry and confused and, upon occasion, the thoroughly gullible. So, when a book like Michael Harrington's *Socialism* comes out one wonders not only about the intrinsic value of what has been written but its larger significance. A sign of the times, that such a man and his ideas seem to be reaching more and more people? An eccentric outburst, doomed to change, *really* change, no one and nothing? A brave effort, all right, but one rather quickly destined to be undercut by the apparently limitless capacity of this society to stop a second and savor things, acclaim to high heaven what has come along, then go on to the next moment's opportunities?

Harrington himself must wonder what possibilities might someday appear for America's Socialist Party, of which he now has become a leader, Norman Thomas's successor—if anyone, however gifted and forceful, can quite become that. Michael Harrington may even have a wry sense of detachment about his book: perhaps he hopes it will persuade many who call themselves liberals or progressives, not to mention some who bandy around the word *radical* to suit their own purposes (self-enhancement, self-righteous assault on others, gratuitous and faddish posturing), that the time has come for those who analyze this nation's economic and political life to do so thoroughly and pointedly. For the fact is, as Harrington points out in his book, that the word *socialism* has become an oddly ignored or feared one in the United States; many shun it without even knowing what it stands for, and many know in their bones rather than their heads what it stands for. A mine owner I once talked with in eastern Kentucky gave a good working definition: "It means I'll lose my money and power, and so will the other stockholders, and instead everything that comes out of this place will go into one big common pool, and I'll be a nobody, just another citizen, I guess."

Unlike him, a number of people secretly think socialism is a fine idea, a great thing to dream about—but let's be *practical*, they say, which means reminding oneself that no one can get away with calling himself a socialist and hope to accomplish anything, hence the need for evasive substitute words and the insistence on piecemeal programs, undertaken with the silent and pious conviction that in the end it will somehow come about, the redistribution of money and power people like Harrington have dreamed of and fought for and foretold as a future reality. On the other hand, many who call themselves liberals sincerely struggle for social and political change but just as sincerely shrink back from the implications of socialism, even the democratic kind, which in this book is held to be the only *true* kind. If only, they insist, a greater degree of control might be exerted on the erring, self-satisfied corporations. If only the military were curbed, the FBI (and now, the Supreme Court) rendered more responsive to the spirit of Tom Paine rather than that of the merchants and landowners who also (for their own purposes) fought against England in the eighteenth century. If only, to draw upon a contemporary way of putting the matter, the populist tradition (the better side of that tradition, one quickly adds) were to be revived, this time successfully, so that the White House and Congress would fall under its spell.

Harrington would naturally welcome such developments; he is no ideologue, no arrogant and self-centered theoretician who scorns the immediate, the concrete, the less-than-perfect encounter with the present that those who work for (rather than dream and write about) a utopian future have to take for granted. He is active in a political party and active also as an ally of America's labor unions. Still, there is in him the historian and the philosopher, and maybe, too, the theologian—and in *Socialism* it is those sides he has drawn upon. The result is a powerful and convincing statement, broad in its command of facts, deep in its examination of various economic and political systems, and tempting in its analysis of our psychological capabilities, as they emerge, given favoring circumstances, in the larger world we refer to collectively as "the society"; and finally, it is a statement that can sometimes become unnerving to many of us— because of the implied questions that come across repeatedly in the author's narrative, though he is too kind and tactful to force them upon us. (Maybe he is also resigned in a way Kierkegaard as well as Karl Marx knew how to be: when the time comes for those questions to assert themselves persuasively, they will; any attempt to push them on people or, more grandly, to push up that time is at the least presumptuous.)

The questions have to do with fundamentals, of course, nothing less than the economic and moral basis of the nation's institutions: the profit motive, the nature of capitalism and its connection with imperialism—the old-fashioned kind but also the more sophisticated kind, wherein corporations rather than armies enter those foreign lands. By the same token, the questions are personal. What kind of children *can* we bring up, however enlightened and decent our schools, however knowing and helpful our child psychiatrists and educational psychologists, and on and on, if in the clutch every boy and girl eventually gets to learn that he or she either controls or is controlled, either works day in, day out for wages others set at their convenience or takes in profits as they accumulate, with no obligation to do anything in particular for anyone, including those whose work in the first place made the whole thing possible? Socialists answer that a transformation of capitalist society is necessary. They say that individualistic economic forces have to be brought under social control, and until that happens slaves working on plantations will give way to cannery workers or migrant farmers employed by agri-businesses; and unorganized men and women crowded into sweat-shops for twelve hours a day and up will give way to a labor force strengthened by the power of unions, at work eight hours a day in bigger, less dangerous factories—but still, the basic nature of the society will persist: a relative handful owns a lot, whereas the large majority of people have a kind of "enough" that never even remotely approximates, either politically or economically, what those few on top and near the top claim as a right.

For Harrington, as for Karl Marx, whom he so very much admires, the point is not to shout and scream at the "bosses" and their ever-ready lackeys. There is a certain grandeur to Marxist historical reasoning, and it comes across strikingly, refreshingly perhaps, in these rancorous times, as the author writes about the history of socialism, which he does in great detail. Human history is seen as the outcome of never-ending struggles for power engaged in by various classes. The cause of these struggles is the "powers of production"—the issue of who gains command over all that man has learned to take from nature and build up into something valuable and productive. As that struggle goes on, social forces develop and become institutionalized, property rights become consolidated, class relationships get arranged and rearranged; and all of that (since Marx knew full well, despite what some critics say, that men do not live by bread alone) is sustained and given sanction by various political and ideological systems, some rather explicitly tied to the "powers and principalities" involved, some vaguer and more philosophical, perhaps in recognition of a changing and uncertain moment in history, when new "interests" are set to take over.

At such moments, definite discontinuities arise in particular societies; social and political structures reflecting a given stage in the relationship between classes become obsolete. A struggle ensues, and new structures appear. The struggles can be slow or dramatically brief, and again, can involve ideas and values as well as votes or arms. In fact the struggles, one is to believe, *are* history; they are what decisively move things along. "Man always makes his own history," Marx said—but he then insisted that man can do so at any particular moment only to a limited extent, that is, in keeping with the material realities then present.

Much of Harrington's book is taken up with a thoughtful and conscientious analysis of all that—how a number of socialists, especially Marx, have regarded the world, with its various and unequal continents, nation-states, and within them, classes. There is no doubt that Harrington has his own point of view, his own belief that certain thinkers were right and others were wrong and sometimes evil. The evil ones transformed Marxist thinking and potentially socialist political efforts into repressive political leviathans of the worst kind, and that outcome clearly haunts the author. That is why he constantly writes of *democratic* socialism. That is why he spends so many pages trying to show that Marx was no cold, aloof, morally neutral observer anxious to spin abstractions that proclaim a love for humanity but also contain ample justification for quite another tack. In particular, he wants us to know that Marx's use of the phrase "dictatorship of the proletariat" had a specific historical context: "The problem is Marx did not mean dictatorship when he said dictatorship. Even in his *Class Struggles in France* which was written during the bitter months in early 1850, the term is used so as to be compatible, even identified, with democracy. 'The constitutional republic,' Marx wrote of the peasants, 'is the dictatorship of their united exploiters; the *social democratic* red republic is the dictatorship of their allies. In each case, it is possible to have a republic, and in the latter instance, a social democratic republic, which is also a dictatorship.'"

Well, I don't know. I rather suspect that anyone, no matter how decent and kind, has his moments of impatience and anger, which in turn prompt some wish for the urgent if not the drastic confrontation that once and for all will change things for the better. In any event, Harrington takes pains to emphasize the moral and activist side of Marx, which better than any intellectual and logical precocity made for a kind of analysis rich in its capacity for irony and ambiguity. If, as he puts it, the "talmudic reading" of Marx that Lenin and others have made such a prominent part of the twentieth century has done the man's ideas a gross injustice, several chapters in this book at least set things straight for the record. But there is more to this book than that. The author is not yet another sectarian polemicist. He is at once a serious scholar, an impassioned social critic, and a man right in the middle of a struggle now being waged in America—between those who want to hold on to what is (and what they have) and those who believe this nation's wealth and power ought to be used and shared by its working people in a thoroughly different way than is now the case. In that sense he is a prophet, not unlike Isaiah in his attitude toward social injustice but, too, not unlike Jeremiah in his willingness to be guarded about human nature—"the stubbornness of the heart" that Old Testament writer refers to. At the end of *Socialism*, we are reminded (in a somewhat startling aside, since so much of the book is devoted to projecting a moderately contented socialist utopia) that "it may even be possible that mankind cannot bear too much happiness."

I suppose with such a remark Harrington weakens his argument—or perhaps reveals some of the spirit or background which years ago caused him to work alongside Dorothy Day in the Catholic Worker movement. He is unlike her in many respects; not for him the kind of strongly emotional and biblical "communitarianism" she and Peter Maurin have advocated, drawing on Christ's life and teachings, with boosts from Tolstoy and Gandhi. More intellectual, more drawn, I suppose it can be said, to the rational and analytic tradition lapsed Jews and Protestants built up in the nineteenth and twentieth centuries, he nevertheless is at home with some of those riddles theologians never stop considering, and not with any intent of "resolution." For him, socialism is over there, way up history's road—to be sought and fought for. Let others decide to stay put where they are or wander from place to place with little worry about tomorrow; Michael Harrington believes he knows what is fair and honorable for his fellow human beings, has spelled it out in more than one book, and no doubt every day of his life will make sure his considerable intelligence and energy go toward achieving not a New Jerusalem but a society so set up that more people than ever before live in reasonable security and dignity, live free of want or the threat of want.

New Republic, June 3, 1972

For Better or for Worse

*I*n the seventeenth century, England went through a political crisis: the monarchy fell and then was restored, though it was never again to be quite so powerful because a rising middle class had secured a measure of freedom for itself. Two great political philosophers, Thomas Hobbes and John Locke, were at hand to comment upon the changes in a nation's assumptions about itself. Though the two did not agree about human nature, or what the social and political order should be, they shared certain values, and they could presume an audience of rational readers, willing to be educated. When Hobbes's *Leviathan* appeared (1651), it was read by the young Locke, and he had to contend with it as he set down his own ideas in essays like *Two Treatises on Government* (1690). In both these books we are asked to imagine a "state of nature," wherein man has not yet become a member of society and lives on his own. Hobbes saw this "natural man" as someone constantly trying to solidify his situation, often at the expense of everyone else, and spoke of the fear that induced men to resort to trickery, deceit, and cunning lest they be conned or killed. Hobbes was a thoughtful, learned, and gentle person, upset by the disorder and threat of chaos around him, he simply presented his "state of nature" as a means of analysis, a step in an argument, to show that men need to be free of their vulnerability, to be protected from their capacity to become almost infinitely exploited. Locke was more convinced of our inherent decency and rationality; in his version of the "state of nature," he emphasized the spirit of equality that obtained. Men basically respected one another, he said, though, like Hobbes, he felt that they were driven by the instinct of "self-preservation." For Hobbes, the fulfillment of that instinct would unleash havoc unless it could be restrained by a strong and universally sanctioned political authority. For Locke, the same instinct caused men to be considerate. Nevertheless, he made note of possible "inconveniences" in the "state of nature": lawbreakers might appear and might be punished without due process—hence the risk that a certain kind of aggressive self-righteousness would be mistaken for justice. To remedy those "inconveniences," which historically have become real and common, Locke advocated a social and political order respectful of each man's integrity, his right to express his ideas, to petition for redress of felt grievances, and to be granted at least a measure of privacy. Freedom means not only the right to do all this but a degree of protection from the officious, the overly expansive and self-important, who want to curb or deny completely the "unalienable rights" that were to become a part of the Declaration of Independence, which was written by men much influenced by Locke.

In the eighteenth century, the scene of political struggle shifted to the Continent, in particular to France, and there was an accompanying increase in speculation about the rights and responsibilities both of citizens and of those who govern them. The Bourbon dynasty would not yield. When the French Revolution came, over a century after England's "Glorious Revolution" of 1688, there were plenty of philosophical "voices" to call upon in support, justifiably or not, even as Hobbes was cited in defense of Stuart absolutism (better that than the lawlessness he feared) and Locke in defense of a strict limitation of royal power. These were voices of the "Enlightenment"—Voltaire's and Montesquieu's, Diderot's and Rousseau's. Critical and unorthodox though such men were, they were respected by the very kings whose mentality and manner of rule are satirized or scorned in *Candide* and *The Spirit of the Laws* and the *Encyclopedia* and *The Social Contract*. Salons celebrated these men, and a few reforms came about but not enough for the needs of the burghers, to say nothing of the working people. The excesses, the awful dangers of the Revolution itself were given thoughtful scrutiny by political philosophers like Edmund Burke and Joseph de Maistre, who, from the comfortable distance of England and Switzerland, looked on in dismay.

This century has had its upheavals, but our philosophers often seem less interested in political theory or what used to be called social ethics than in the nature of "communication" or in analyzing the structure of matter or in developing an "existentialist" viewpoint. They do indeed take political positions, even quite polemical ones, but they do not argue them convincingly. A notable exception is Barrington Moore, whose *Reflections on the Causes of Human Mis-*

ery and Upon Certain Proposals to Eliminate Them, along with
ideas and studies he has already presented, should—but, given the
temper of our times, probably will not—earn him the highest respect and renown. One has to doubt the likelihood of such recognition because his stubbornly honest and analytic mind refuses to consider any conventional wisdom sacred, even that which appeals to
his own political thinking. He doubts and he questions, though his
stand may offend those whose cause he very much favors as a citizen, a voter, a thinker and a dreamer. And he does dream—of a
world without the misery we seem helpless to eliminate, even here
at home, for all our wealth and power. The misery he has in mind is
not the subjective kind; he is concerned not with mental distress but
with the malnutrition and outright starvation that afflict millions of
the world's people. He is concerned with nations whose people are
overwhelmingly illiterate—where children die because doctors are
almost unheard of, where there is rarely sanitation of any kind,
where families huddle in crowded shacks or tenements under intolerable conditions. And he wonders whether all this will ever end,
given the governments that prevail—given, that is, the social and
political order these governments impose, be they in South and
Central America or in Asia and Africa.

Mr. Moore says he has "for some time held that the radical indictment of American society constituted a reasonably accurate description" of it. His classes at Harvard have attracted students who have
become active in the social struggles we have recently witnessed—as
antagonists of the status quo, intent upon changing it. In this book,
he is once more skeptical of doctrine, insistent upon questions that
embarrass friends as well as enemies. He wants his students to feel
just as free, and so he opposes any abridgment of civil liberties,
whatever the excuse for the abridgment. He does not try to rational-
ize all the misery that revolutions have produced in the name of
doing away with injustice. He is not another Edmund Burke, aghast
at the thought of a spreading anarchy, though he writes as intelli-
gently and lucidly and argues as persuasively and eloquently. (The
title of his book is one that Burke—or, indeed, any other seven-
teenth- or eighteenth-century philosopher—might have used.) Nor
is he among the timid gradualists who offer sops to the needy when
pressures build up but in the clutch join ranks with those on top.

What Professor Moore wants, really, is a "democratic and humane socialism," but he considers the obstacles great indeed. On the political right are those who do not want to let go of the money they have or of the laws that protect their money in ways denied other people's money. On the political left are those who refuse to recognize the important social achievements that Western democracies, such as England and the United States, have managed, despite the persistent assaults and, in this country, the more subtle erosion these achievements appear to be suffering at the present time. Eager for the maintenance of "conditions for free intellectual inquiry," he rejects "any implication to the effect that radical movements ought to try to prohibit or prevent the advocacy of the views they are attacking." He is a friend of Marcuse, but he cannot accept his notion of "repressive tolerance"—part of an elaborate argument for radicals' taking and keeping power. The dilemma, as Professor Moore points out, is *"Quis custodiet?"* Exactly who is to make decisions, watch over the course of a nation, hold the keys? A self-appointed politburo? A military junta? A collection of warlords who have stashed away millions in Swiss banks? Or the "vested interests" whom Harry Truman railed against and Dwight Eisenhower called "the military-industrial complex"? Eisenhower's epithet is now a commonplace, yet the military-industrial complex persists, and so does the disparity between the wealthy and the poor. Professor Moore is convinced that a society that hopes to eliminate misery and to guarantee the freedoms of our Bill of Rights must be one in which people like him constantly annoy political activists of all kinds with bothersome essays. So he asks questions:

> The radical can and does reply that pleas for discussion and dialogue are often a smokescreen for delays and evasions, during which time people are dying and suffering. How many napalmed children do American liberals have the right to demand as the price for continuing peaceful dissent through orderly channels? How many twisted lives in the black ghettos? To such questions all possible answers are agonizing. The replies come down to highly uncertain estimates about the future and to counterquestions. How likely is it that the radicals in the present situation may produce even greater suffering and disaster, both in their efforts to gain power and in their efforts to put through their policies? The ultimate test of violence is, after all,

results too. And which radicals? And what policies? What is the appropriate time-span in passing judgments of this kind?

Such questions will not earn applause from the political left. Nor will his charge that the word *fascism* is used too freely by critics of this country, carried away by hysteria and perhaps by spite. Nor will his corollary criticism of those who in the name of activism and radical politics assail us with outbursts that "constitute no more than a form of moral self-indulgence." But defenders of our economic system fare no better. Professor Moore calls us a "predatory democracy," and to some extent he sides with those who decry the manipulative and sometimes coercive role our military might has played all over the world—not without attendant advantage to our economic system. So it is, he points out, that we are allied with dictators and despots while we preach freedom. So it is that our politicians rarely make a frank appraisal of the relationship between America's commercial interests and its military involvements. So it is that the press, certainly less controlled here than in most other countries, largely refrains from analysis of our entanglements with other nations. Yes, we are occasionally told about a government in Greece that spies on and tortures people, a government that denies its citizens even a semblance of democracy; or we hear that Brazil's prisons are full of men and women, among them priests and nuns, who dared criticize the military leadership. We denounce dictators in some countries and embrace them as our allies in others, but the overall pattern is often ignored or else presented in euphemisms. What, precisely, has our "good-neighbor policy" toward Latin America amounted to? What interests prompted Wilson to send troops to Mexico and Johnson to send them to the Dominican Republic? Why did the Central Intelligence Agency conspire to overthrow a government in Guatemala? Professor Moore believes such questions to be part of larger ones, candid answers to which may so threaten important people that the risks of asking them are great indeed.

It can be argued that the critical problem Professor Moore poses for himself and fails to resolve (he is not, after all, writing a platform) has to do with the "little man" he speaks of, by which he really means all of us who vote, and thereby *might* alter the structure of our society. To this author, "the weakness of the demand for change, or its lack of political effect, begins to look like a key aspect of the whole problem of predatory democracy. Certainly it is a puzzling one, about which severe critics of American society disagree sharply among themselves. . . . The lack of effective demand for change may be the key to our whole problem." For some of us, he concludes, it is a matter of indifference or a simple desire to go about our daily lives untroubled by the "inconveniences," or worse, that we think might be generated by social change: we are not evil or mean-spirited; we have but one life to live, and we do not want it threatened—perhaps to no good purpose. After all, we may have to "pay the freight for well-meant efforts at improvement" that do not achieve their aims. Among other citizens, less well-off and so still more wary because more vulnerable, there is, Professor Moore says, a feeling of confusion and outrage. Both psychologically and sociologically, these people are influenced, or even bound, by "the connection between frustrated effort and rage," he notes. "In the present American context, for many little men it is the radical, and especially the romantic and cultural radical, who is the apparent source of frustration." No one will find it easy to take issue with that observation. Professor Moore's unsurprising explanation of the situation is that blue-collar and white-collar workers try to hold on to what they have and that they are envious of people who are better-off. Envy is mixed with rage when these workers are told directly, or by implication (through their critics' choice of language, appearance, manner of living), that they are uninformed, stupid, even dangerous. He notes the "hatred" of the French peasants for urban radicals, the German "white-collar support for the Nazis," the "conservative trends" in our own labor movement. The difficulty may be "that human beings value what they must work for, *not* that they work for what they value," so a factory or office worker goes along with his social and economic situation, however precarious.

But does Professor Moore do justice to America's share of the "little men"? If one is to believe historians like C. Vann Woodward, the populist tradition in this country has been enduring and substantial, if not triumphant. If one is to believe sociologists like Herbert Gans and Andrew Greeley and Richard Sennett and Jonathan Cobb, the motivations and feelings of working-class Americans are as complicated and contradictory as those of our well-educated liberals and radicals. Professor Moore writes about the two latter groups, it seems to me, more sensitively and compassionately—or perhaps it is knowingly—than he does about the others. He has an eye for the foibles of political activists, and for their dangerous blind spots, but also a certain respect for their possibilities as human beings; that eye and that respect are not brought to bear on our labor movement.

This brief and honest book cannot be casually recommended; it is a somber book, intended not to appease our anxieties but to document their sources and what these anxieties may lead to. The continuing capacity of human beings for cruelty to one another—exacting from workers labor at low wages and under unfair, unhealthy conditions; submitting people to peonage; dropping bombs—is a sad and familiar litany, one that makes Thomas Hobbes naively optimistic when he speaks about the "brutish" quality of those who lived in a "state of nature" but speaks with so much hope for those who come later in history. Still, Barrington Moore, patient, intelligent, of kind disposition, is not without hope; as he says, the true pessimist has lost faith in the responsiveness of others and their capacity for growth, and so doesn't even bother writing a book.

If any book can make us think hard about where we are going, this is the one. It is preoccupied with what Hobbes and Locke might have called "woe and weal"—the relationship between our afflictions and the political order that sets so much of the tone and rhythm of our daily behavior. One suspects, though, that Professor Moore wants more from us than hard thinking; he wants us to act in such a way that at least a significant dent is made in the problems whose size and complexity he has made plain to us.

New Yorker, March 3, 1973

"Are you now or
have you ever been . . ."

Although her writing is quiet, reflective, at times touchingly limpid, and always straightforward, Lillian Hellman makes clear in the title of her latest autobiographical memoir, *Scoundrel Time*, that both her mind and heart have struggled for a quarter of a century with an unremitting moral outrage, which this book explains and justifies once and for all. Throughout her life, she has been an outsider of sorts, no one's safe bet. She is a Southerner; her roots are in rural Alabama and the rather special, even exotic cosmopolitanism of New Orleans.

She came to the theater and the movies, to the influential, sometimes nervously insecure, and not always generous or farsighted intellectual world of the Northeast, a strong-minded, fiercely independent woman, a person inclined to be self-observing, even self-critical, and not least, an artist never willing to set aside a highly developed moral sensibility. Her early plays earned her fame and success in a world (Broadway and Hollywood) she had many reasons to question severely, if not hold in contempt. They are plays of subtle psychological observation, not far removed in theme from the playwright's personal knowledge and experience—the workings of the comfortable but inwardly torn, saddened, worried American bourgeoisie.

In the late 1930s and early 1940s, both as a writer and a citizen, she became more explicitly involved with the broader social and political problems that pressed hard, she knew, even upon those very assured and well-off people she gave us in *Watch on the Rhine*. She has never been an ideologue, but neither has she been a fussy and arrogant loner or, certainly, an opportunistic joiner quick to discern where to place her signature in order to gain the approval of a particular clique or age. She saw, early on, the relationship between art and politics; she felt an obligation to characterize and respond to the exploitative cruelties that have passed for everyday events these past decades in the Western capitalist countries. She went to Spain during the Civil War to give her energies to the Loyalist side. She pointed out the dangers and rotten evils of fascism at a time when many of her countrymen were loath to pay heed. A woman brilliantly in touch with Freud's unsparing vision of the mind's deviousness and self-enhancing capacity for illusion, she could not shirk noticing how greedy businessmen and servile, corrupt, or monstrously evil politicians have collaborated to lie, cheat, steal, and ultimately, it turned out, be parties (in one way or another, actively or out of indifference) to the deaths of millions of defenseless human beings.

After World War II, Miss Hellman was as outraged by what she saw happening here as by the continuing horrors of totalitarianism abroad. She refused to join the self-congratulatory chorus of former Communists, now converted to well-paid, confessional red-baiting, or the various cliques of self-described liberals and intellectuals ready in an instant to come up with the most intricate of rationalizations for the "practical," the "necessary." Soon enough our high and mighty evangelists of the Cold War (not a few of them personally quite suspect in one way or another) were after her and others like her—prominent and even revered individuals whose intimidated, groveling, expiative presence, so the McCarthys and J. Parnell Thomases hoped, would not only provide an example but also, and very important, distract the working people of this country from thinking about who owns and gets what out of our economic system.

The inquisitors hauled more and more citizens to Washington for "questioning" in the late 1940s, as Gary Wills tells us in his sharp and uncompromising introduction to this book. The witnesses came willingly, a lot of them—or with fear that quickly gave way to eager ingratiation. Yesuh, yesuh, we'll agree, we'll affirm, we'll tell all—or in the case of some professors or writers, we'll do what we can (a lot, that's for sure) to give a cheap, rotten, phony witchhunt the high gloss of historical necessity and urgency.

Unfortunately for Miss Hellman, she is stubbornly discerning and ethically sensitive. The poor, benighted creature can't stop asking herself what is right. Nor could she stop seeing, in McCarthyism, the distracting—and intimidating—function of political melodrama. She was summoned before a body that, in its exquisite modesty, had declared itself to be the Committee on Un-American Activities of the House of Representatives. She would tell everything she knew—

or else, as the congressmen and their manipulative, calculating aides and lawyers had the power to warn. The result was an honorable but hurtful scene within a larger and disgusting act in which the nation of Jefferson and Lincoln became the property of political Snopses, one of whom would eventually sully the White House itself.

As Miss Hellman makes painfully evident, and the reader must never forget, a lot of important people in her world were falling all over themselves trying to apologize, atone, beg for forgiveness—and for the chance to make a lot more bucks. Nor are a good number of them rushing into print now to examine their motives or express some of the self-doubts Miss Hellman, still eschewing the blandishments of self-righteousness, comes forth with. She was then, maybe still is, a lonely figure—brave precisely because she was afraid and knew the power and cunning of her accusers. She saw them at lunch in the Mayflower, the illustrious J. Edgar Hoover and his sidekick Clyde Tolson; she read about them every day in the newspapers and magazines—the saviors of "the American way." What would she say before them? What would she do? What could have been a quick and rewarding hour or two became something else for her: a moment of self-appraisal, a time of explicit, unhedged moral decisiveness at whatever cost (and, in money and property, the cost was great).

This book tells how her mind worked as she decided to stand up and say no to the prevailing principalities and powers. It is a personal statement and a strong moral document. Kierkegaard would have loved *Scoundrel Time* for its fine, sardonic humor, its unsparing social observation, and not least, the skill of its narration. He had contempt for the smug and phony intellectuals of his day—always anxious to preach to others but ever so protective of themselves. He longed for companions who would summon personal memory, among other modes of expression, to the task of making concrete and specific ethical analyses—as opposed to cleverly worded abstractions that conceal as much as they tell. In Lillian Hellman he has a kindred spirit, and we a voice making itself heard in what still is, alas, a wilderness of bluff, guile, and deceit.

Washington Post, May 9, 1976

Stories and Voices

*I*n the early 1970s, the United States Army Corps of Engineers
set about constructing yet another of its dams to restrain Caesars
Creek, a tributary of the Little Miami River. This project required the sacrifice of the two-century-old Ohio farming village
of New Burlington, which was south of Dayton and just north of
Cincinnati; the town occupied the site of the reservoir that would be
created by the dam's construction. During the sad and final year in
the life of this Midwestern rural community, John Baskin, a young
writer and woodcutter, lived in it, in an abandoned farmhouse, and
came to know its inhabitants. Mr. Baskin, who had recently graduated from Mars Hill College, in North Carolina's western mountain
country, is himself the son of farming people. He has turned the
experience he had in New Burlington into an excellent book—*New
Burlington: The Life and Death of an American Village*—which is
hard to classify. It is certainly not a study by a social scientist; the
author has no interest in conducting interviews, accumulating data,
and coming forth with findings. In fact, in his brief but lively introduction Mr. Baskin refers to the "bleak treatises" of sociologists and
says that he wants no part of them.

Instead, he simply wants to describe a scene that he has witnessed.
He wants to set down the words he has heard—to tell us what the
people of New Burlington have to say about themselves and their
lives. He realizes that these people have managed to gain access to
us only through him—the wanderer, the listener, the visitor—so he
begins the book with an account of the "accidents" of his life that led
to his encounter with the dying town. Soon after he arrived, he
learned from the villagers that before long they would be gone.
Their children and grandchildren would be water-skiing over their
cornfields, some of which were nearly as old as the nation itself.
"Full of complaint," the author says, describing his reaction to the
news he heard, "I thought . . . I would *restore* New Burlington." He
would do so, he hoped, by writing something that breathed life into

the statistics and the abstract reports on the village that the Corps of Engineers had relied upon in making its decision about the dam. He would try to write what he calls at one point the town's "obituary." Before "the world (engineers) crashes in to obliterate the past (the village)," Mr. Baskin tells us, he wanted to take notice, to give us "a book of stories and voices in which the characters ponder some of their time on earth." In this respect, he says, he "perceived New Burlington as a *gift*." The book, too, is a gift: it is an excellent social history, strong on personal statement and deliberately weak on what the author calls "noise" and "messages."

A prologue tells us, on a rather broad temporal scale, about the town's origins:

> New Burlington, Ohio, in the Paleozoic Era was very largely limestone, at the bottom of the sea. Later the ice came, so heavy it depressed the spine of the continent and after the ice, cranberry bogs prepared the ground for the great hardwood forests.

Some fifteen thousand years ago, the Indians found their way to this land. After the arrival of white people, it became known first as the Northwest Territory and then, in 1803, as the State of Ohio. The whites made their way west in increasing numbers. The Indians retired farther west. Settlements like New Burlington grew. A decade or so after the Civil War, Mr. Baskin tells us, the town consisted of "one sawmill, two churches, one school, one hotel, three groceries, one wagon shop, two dry goods stores, two doctors, one carpenter, one cobbler, one undertaker, three blacksmiths, and one chicken thief. Population: 275. Real estate: $16,281."

Nearly a century later, in 1973, just before the moment of extinction, the town had not grown very much. Its single street offered farmers a brief, intimate, tidy stretch of stores and churches. These farmers, along with the people who healed them, ministered to them, and taught their children, were those in whom Mr. Baskin was most interested. Their lives unfold in all their strangeness, banality, drama, and dreariness. One family, the Haydocks, originally came to New Burlington from Yorkshire, England. Their very name connects them to farm life. Sarah Haydock Shidaker, now in her eighties, obviously reminisced with Mr. Baskin a good deal, and from what she told him he has reconstructed old conversations and events:

At the school commencement in 1913, Sarah meets Edwin Shidaker. They have known each other forever but this time they regard each other differently. Edwin drives Sarah home in his buggy. She invites him in but he says no. "My horse is rather fractious and I should get him home," he says.

Throughout the book, in an extraordinary and compelling manner of presentation and evocation, Mr. Baskin has thus woven the past and present together, mixing in old photographs and new photographs, quoting letters written a long time ago, using excerpts from diaries and church records and notebooks, and reproducing fragments of remembered songs, poems, and sayings. The author often uses the present tense to bring the reader closer to the particular person, situation, or kind of existence that is being described. It is obvious that Mr. Baskin collected more than enough material to sustain this novelistic-factual mode of presentation: at various places in the text, Sarah and others are allowed to speak at considerable length without interruption. When the author takes the liberty of acting as commentator or chronicler of events, he does so with a directness, immediacy, and verve that are impressive and touching. He begins a section called "Light" this way:

> In the late Twenties electricity comes to New Burlington. A traveling man comes to do the wiring and boards on a nearby farm where he milks a cow to pay his keep. His work goes slowly because the cow kicks him and breaks his leg. Finally curious neighbors gather outside a lower New Burlington home and watch a porch light switched on. The bare bulb hangs from the porch ceiling on a long cord. When the light goes on the people think they see the darkness shaken as if it were dust settling.

The paragraph immediately following that one indicates how skilled Mr. Baskin is at connecting the general to the specific, the historical to the personal:

> Lights in the village make Sarah happy. Light dispels mystery and she too would have it. An old villager explains to her how it works: "You pull a cord," he says. "On and off, you see." For the Christmas of 1939 electricity lights the Shidaker Yule tree. Sarah buys lights for the tree, the table, the ceiling, a floor

lamp, and a radio. When Edwin turns on the radio a voice is singing.

There are marvelous moments on page after page of the book. Sometimes Sarah and her fellow-townspeople seem informative and dignified—tough, hardworking men and women who have endured. At other times, they show eloquence and wit. "The fall of the year is my favorite time by far," Sarah says at the beginning of a section titled "October." Then she adds a simple "O Yes." A bit farther on, she tells us, "I have always liked the stars. I was born under Libra. Justice, you know, is blind. And erasers are on lead pencils to take care of the wrong we do. The signs have an effect upon our dispositions. If the moon can change tides why not dispositions?" She provides no answer and moves quickly away from metaphysical speculation: "My but I am old. This was once a dimple. Now it's a crack. I have trouble with my feet and my conscience. First one pains me then the other." Then, continuing her almost contrapuntal expression of the straightforward and the slightly rhetorical, she gives this general account of her habits and her thoughts:

> "I do not smoke, drink, or drive an automobile. There's nothing left for me to do but play the piano. Lay not up your treasures on earth where moth and rust corrupt. But if I married an old man I would want him to have $90,000 and a very bad cough. . . . I am the last leaf on the tree and I believe I am outliving everyone else. My love for my people has been very strong. I am root and branch New Burlington."

Near the conclusion of the section about Sarah, Mr. Baskin adds an ironic word or two of his own:

> The old villagers are mostly gone now and Sarah's grandchildren study science in distant universities. A young man lives in the upstairs which she rents out. He is training to be a psychologist. Sarah listens carefully to his definitions. An interstate highway slices in front of the old Shidaker homeplace and she is the last of the family to own any of Preserved Fish's land. New Burlington itself is mostly gone. The rest waits for the waters of the new reservoir.

There are others besides Sarah—from somber Quakers to lively Methodists. They have memories of their own, and they remember their parents and grandparents remembering, and we are thus carried back almost to the earliest days of the Republic. One man, John Harlan Pickin, recalls hearing about the Spanish-American War and about Grover Cleveland's election, when his great-aunt exclaimed, "The country is finished!" (A Democrat had not been elected president in twenty-eight years.) John's mother was a grown woman before she laid eyes on a Catholic, and she knew only one Jew in her lifetime. John offers us particularly vivid descriptions of farm life, which, he tells us, was "hard on everyone":

> "There were horrible stories of people going through manure spreaders, of tractors rearing up and crushing the driver, ragged cuts that led to lockjaw. My aunt felt sorry for the women because they had no one to talk to. They spent their lives looking at the backside of a cow."

We learn that Charles Dickens passed through New Burlington and that it was a stop on the Underground Railroad. We learn that men and women left the town, year after year, to go farther west. They sometimes wrote back home, sometimes lost touch. And they sometimes came back. We learn that drink was a "secret passion" in the village, that it was considered "more shameful than illegitimacy." At Quaker meetings, drinkers were prayed for, long and hard. The man who speaks of these matters—the secret lusts and shames of his neighbors—is one Joshua Scroggy, who, at ninety-two, can still recall the essence of H. L. Mencken's definition of Puritanism: "The suspicion that somewhere someone might be having a good time." There were also what Joshua refers to as "mental problems" in New Burlington—illnesses that used to be regarded as a "curse." And there were suicides. "We had all these things," Joshua says in summary, "all manner of pride and gluttony, and sins real and imagined, but the village life caused a tolerance among us. It had to. Everyone came face to face each day."

Nevertheless, no one in the town comes across as a sage from whom Mr. Baskin seeks "answers." On the contrary, the people of New Burlington for the most part tether their comments about life to the shared, familiar experiences or occasions of everyday life. "Never saw a family tree that didn't need spraying," one old-timer remembers hearing. "A good hot egg is a small miracle," another person declares. Speaking of the Great Depression, Mary Robinson, a woman of seventy-five, recalls, "After the commotion on Wall Street, a farmer down the road came home and said, 'The stock market has crashed!' His little boy heard him and asked, 'Was any cows hurt?' That's all the stock market meant to any of us."

Still, New Burlington did suffer during the Depression—for a long time and badly. Many proud families were reduced to a barter economy. But they never went hungry, as did many who lived in crowded, and thus more vulnerable, cities. "We grew what we ate during the Depression," Mary says, "and husked corn in the flat land for six cents a shock." For all that, the people of New Burlington did not take very kindly to the New Deal or to President Roosevelt; Mr. Baskin gives us a limerick that was current in New Burlington during the Depression:

> There once was a lady of fashion
> Who had a very fine passion.
> To her boy friend she said
> As they jumped into bed,
> "Here's one thing Roosevelt can't ration."

The people of New Burlington watched the seasons come and go with special care and were prepared to take advantage of any generosity that Nature offered. The author is keen and lyrical in a section called "Syrup." He learned from his friends all about the technique of syrup-making, and he also tells us about the patience they brought to this enterprise. The style that Mr. Baskin uses in this section makes one hope for a second book from him in this genre, and a third:

> When the trees are scratches against the surly February sky Charles McIntire goes into the woods where his breath hangs in balloons as if momentarily the balloons might fill with language. He drills small holes in the maples which he recognizes by the dignified bark which looks like marbled slate. And waits for the precarious succession of freezing nights and warm days which makes the sap rise in the irresolute veins of the maple. There is no clue that inwardly the maple seethes in the breaking up of winter. The world seems still and vague. It is as though

color and motion have never existed except in the imagination. For Charles to come here is an act of faith in a dead season. The woods could be etchings.

These men and women may have experienced many hard times, but they were, by and large, stoic, and they maintained a robust sense of humor. The Quakers among them, Mr. Baskin tells us, knew that "human equilibrium is poor and the fall from grace constantly imminent." Severely tested people—even austere people— can manage a smile, or at least develop a certain wry, amused perspective on themselves. Mr. Baskin cites a man named Carl Smith, who at the age of eighty-six acknowledges his luck in having lived a long life and waits patiently, expectantly, for the end: "A long life is partly care, more mystery. Providence watches over fools and children. And I'm no kid." In a grimmer vein of humor, the author tells us about the man who went mad during one of the floods that have periodically devastated or threatened the countryside. He was found splashing in the kitchen sink by the rescuers who entered his house. "You'll all drown," he warned them. "Only I am safe. When the water rises up to me, I'll pull the plug." A time was when there were five-party and ten-party telephone lines. Ten different rings in each house! "Farm houses sounded like fire stations," Della Wilson recalls, and she is only forty-six.

The older people cling tenaciously to their past but stumble during the slow wait of the present; a good number of them are in their eighties—survivors, who did without antibiotics and all sorts of medical technology, and who never dieted or took vitamin pills or had their cholesterol measured or their emotions analyzed. Elizabeth Beam, at eighty-five, acknowledges that she knows "more people underfoot than above." She goes on as best she can, even though her faculties are failing: "With fading eyesight she puts Jell-O in the skillet thinking it is liver." The widow Jemima Boots goes to sleep easily and stays asleep, but she has her secret worries and keeps a cowbell under her pillow, just in case. Her neighbor Ellen Jenkins, also a widow of advanced age, "puts on her best dress when expecting the telephone to ring."

The town of New Burlington is gone now, but in a way it will never be gone. Its landscape, its people, and their traditions and customs, their experiences, victories, and defeats, and their abiding memories have been given new life in this rare moral document, written by a young and imaginative observer. John Baskin now lives on a farm in Wilmington, Ohio, not far from where many of his New Burlington friends, whose ideals and manner of endurance he obviously admires and wants to uphold, settled after their town died. Mr. Baskin's book—which resembles James Agee's *Let Us Now Praise Famous Men* in spirit and in grace of writing as well as in subject matter—demonstrates that he is also not far from what Agee called "human actuality."

Plain People

R ecently, the word *populist* has appeared once more on the American scene. Many modern politicians refer to themselves as populists, and even our new president has connected himself, both in his autobiography and in his spoken statements, with populism—the tradition of political protest, economic analysis, and social criticism that started in the late nineteenth century. As Lawrence Goodwyn makes clear in his book *Democratic Promise: The Populist Moment in America*, it is a tradition often misunderstood and often misrepresented or wrongly appropriated by various essayists, not to mention political activists of one sort or another. Goodwyn is a historian who teaches at Duke University. He is also one of the directors of an ambitious oral-history project, sponsored by the history department at Duke, that is aimed at rescuing from obscurity the memories and impressions of ordinary Southern working people who have been involved in that region's recent episode of painful and important social change, and for years he was a journalist at the *Texas Observer*, a muckraking periodical that has been challenging vested interests for more than two decades.

Today, Professor Goodwyn points out, populism is a vaguely appealing word, partly because it is without clear-cut ideological significance. Clearly it has some connection with "the people," and few of us would ever want to be against them. Those who don't care to be known as liberals, perhaps because they reject some of the assumptions common to many so described, may call themselves populists with the hope that they are thereby expressing a more strenuous dissatisfaction with the prevailing social order. To be sure, the label has also taken on negative connotations. In this century, it has been used by some Southern politicians in the cause of racism and extreme economic conservatism as well as by Midwestern isolationists. Sometimes "the people" become a mob, angry and ill-informed and mean-spirited, and a demagogue is literally a "leader of the people"—a shrewd manipulator of unrest, animosity, and dissatisfaction. But for the most part these days, populism is used in a positive, though unclear, way by those who speak for the small farmer, by political reformers anxious to break up large corporations and strengthen the economic position of the poor and the working-class people of the country, by activists eager to get away from politics as usual and set up what they call alternative institutions, and by conventional politicians—the kind who cite Harry Truman as a true populist, as if to say that a populist has never been more than someone of humble origins who makes good but still has a blunt, unpretentious manner, who favors helping those not so successful, and who proudly says of himself that he is "an ordinary human being."

Although Professor Goodwyn takes pains in the first section of his book to let the reader know that such usages have little to do with the historical movement called Populism, he is not fussy and pedantic when he describes the true sources and philosophical premises of the Populist moment. He simply wants to do justice to a particular effort, serious and honorable, on the part of many thousands to make a significant critique of American capitalism just as it was entering its maturity, in the last years of the nineteenth century. Populism did eventually become the basis of a specific political movement, even of a third party, but in essence it was a general vision of the world, a means by which plain people—mostly farmers and those better-off but in sympathy with them—began to organize their thoughts into a coherent set of social, economic, and political objectives. In the author's words, "populism is the story of how a large number of people, through a gradual process of self-education that grew out of their cooperative efforts, developed a new interpretation of their society and new political institutions to give expression to these interpretations."

The process Professor Goodwyn mentions began in the late 1870s. The Civil War was over, and a ravaged nation had renewed its expansionist growth both territorily and economically. Railroads were probing the frontier. More and more factories were being built in or near the major cities. The United States was not yet a world power, but it was rich in its resources, in its increasing and willing work force, and in its accelerating agricultural capacity. Certain individuals were becoming not merely well-off and influential but enormously wealthy. They were determined to stay that way, to receive special treatment, and to make their presence felt on the national scene. At the same time, the country was plagued by recurrent, seemingly inescapable economic collapses. These disasters raised questions about the very meaning and nature of money: What was it, and who had a right to make it, and with what as a guarantee of its worth—gold, silver, or nothing save the government's promises? These questions, in turn, raised other, larger ones: How was the nation, now intact after a terrible bloodletting, going to be run? More precisely, what would be the attitude of the government—particularly the Treasury Department and the Interior Department—toward commerce and industry, toward agricultural interests, toward the growing number of mine owners, and toward the oil wells and refineries that would soon be a major source of American wealth? Were the president and the congress to maintain a hands-off policy—to let increasingly successful, self-confident, and aggressive businesses have full rein so that they could conspire and combine or squabble and fight among themselves as they pleased? Would Washington become a mediator, an arbitrator? Would it become an ally of the most successful and importunate commercial interests? How would it approach the foreign countries with which American businesses traded and from which they wanted raw materials? And the land, the American land—once the Indians' land—rich with various treasures: how would it be apportioned and developed? For a moment—the "populist moment" that Professor Goodwyn refers to—the nation held its breath and tried to figure out what kind of nation it would be, what kind of assumptions and values would prevail politically and economically.

America of the 1880s and 1890s was made up mostly of farmers. There was a smaller number of factory and shopworkers, and a still smaller, luckier group who belonged to the so-called commercial class. But each group was fragmented by affiliations that prevented clear-cut social, political, or even regional confrontations. The Republican Party contained not only wealthy Northern and Western conservatives but also white- and blue-collar Yankee Protestants and impoverished blacks (those who could and did vote). The Democratic Party contained Southern whites—rich and poor—and Northern immigrants. The Civil War had continued to divide voters along nostalgic and emotional lines that were, we now realize, irrational and often against their own best interests. Men voted "as they shot," thereby denying themselves a chance for redress of legitimate griev-

258 *Politics, People, and Literature*

ances through the ballot. The author speaks of this fragmented and emotional political situation as "a non-ideological milieu." (To a degree, our two major parties still cover a very wide spectrum of opinion, in that both are divided into liberal and conservative wings.) Voters of the post-Civil War period were sentimental and inattentive to the specific positions politicians held with respect to wealth, the rights of industrial workers, and, especially, the needs of farmers—credit, cheap railroad rates, and so on.

The Populists were at the beginning people from the agricultural South and the frontier West—Texas, in particular—who began to take a hard look at who owned what and at who was profiting from the rules, regulations, arrangements, and laws. Under the "crop lien" system in the South, thousands of hardworking farmers were in constant bondage to "the furnishing man," otherwise known as "the advancing man" or—to blacks, who had a way of linguistically stripping things to their bare essentials—"the Man." The South had become, in the words of one historian quoted by Professor Goodwyn, a "giant pawn shop." Interest rates were "frequently well in excess of 100 per cent annually, sometimes over 200 per cent," the author tells us, and, once hooked, the farmer rarely got free. No wonder people went West, left peonage in order to start a new life—even one with new and grave risks—in Texas and beyond. But toward the end of the nineteenth century there was, increasingly, no real escape: "A Tennessean fleeing worn-out land, interest, and the freight rates of the Louisville and Nashville Railroad would arrive in the Cross Timbers of Texas to find that the Texas and Pacific Railroad owned much of the most promising land."

Still they trekked westward, impoverished and bitter and hopeful and determined—the South's white yeomen and not a few black tenant farmers. Every year during the 1870s about a hundred thousand of them went to Texas alone—initially to the warm, wet "pineywoods" section abutting Louisiana, then westward to the open, inviting prairie land. And out there, in east and central Texas, those farmers did more than scratch hard for a living. They began to talk about their fate, their needs, their beliefs. For the first time, they did not feel beholden to creditors or to distracting sectional pieties. In Lampasas County, Palo Pinto County, and Cook County, on the Red River, they formed "alliances"—the basis of the National Farmers Alliance. By the end of the 1880s, more than a quarter of a million American "men of the soil" would be members of the NFA. Rather than pay outrageously high prices for fertilizer and equipment, the farmers joined hands and formed buying committees. Rather than deal individually with buyers who underweighed cotton or overcharged for their services as middlemen, the farmers formed cooperatives and took action that they could not have taken without being organized.

Needless to say, there was opposition. "Town merchants opposed cooperative schemes, as did manufacturers and cotton buyers," Professor Goodwyn tells us. But the movement had its weapons and strengths. Hardy and eloquent NFA organizers wandered from county to county, explaining, arguing, and exhorting. (A number of these organizers and their beliefs, their personal ways, and their travels are presented in this book.) There were, moreover, obvious and tangible financial benefits from the cooperative efforts. Perhaps most important, the rural South and West were still quite removed from the intimidating social and cultural controls—newspapers and established social hierarchies, with their conventions and orthodoxies—that so often persuaded individuals to ignore their own interests, and sometimes even frightened them into positions that worked against those interests. When the farmers of Texas railed against the distant exploiters (the railroads, the banks, the cotton brokers), they were not quickly denounced and isolated as "Socialists." Rather, for hundreds of thousands, they were other kinds of radicals: believing Christians, for instance, who remembered Christ's triumph over "powers and principalities" and his egalitarian Sermon on the Mount.

Populism gradually became more than a shared sensibility or even a series of local cooperative initatives loosely bound into an alliance. By 1892, the word itself had been attached to a full-fledged and vital political movement based on a radical analysis of the fast-growing industrialism of the day. What started as an agrarian revolt spread to the cities. The NFA became affiliated with the Knights of Labor—an early effort of urban working people to fight collectively for better wages. A more explicitly class-conscious ideology gradually appeared in the language of Populist speakers and writers. The wretchedness of the urban proletariat was spelled out. Attention was drawn repeatedly to the corrupt or toadying politicians catering to the small number of fortunate men who owned so much of the nation's wealth. As

W. E. Farmer, a Knights of Labor leader, put it, "We have an over-production of poverty, barefooted women, political thieves and many liars. There is no difference between legalized robbery and highway robbery."

It was a time when children as well as grownups worked from dawn to dusk for a pittance; when factory and mill conditions were, by our standards, unspeakably grim; when the local police—or, if necessary, the state militia or federal troops—almost invariably came down on the side of the employer in labor disputes; when labor unions as we know them were nonexistent; and, as the author keeps emphasizing, when farmers were constantly being manipulated, or cheated outright, by land companies and livestock commission agencies and cotton buyers and owners of wholesale houses. It was, without exaggeration, a time of constant misery and suffering—even starvation. It was also a time of significant "capital-formation"—a cool phrase from economic theory that fails to convey the Dickensian horrors that millions of men, women, and children sustained as a matter of course.

Populists had their own response to such horrors, which was, Professor Goodwyn tells us, a distinctively American one:

> Populists were not capitalist reformers, as we understand that phrase in modern political language; neither were they socialists. Though their mass movement literally grew out of their belief in the power of man as a coöperative being, they also accepted man as a competitive being. They cannot conveniently be compressed into the narrow (theoretically competitive) categories of political description sanctioned in the capitalist creed, nor can they be compressed into the (theoretically cooperative) categories of political description sanctioned in socialist thought.

The movement Professor Goodwyn describes was thus made up of American citizens who cherished the Jeffersonian tradition of political democracy but also, in the spirit of Tom Paine, wanted to achieve true social and economic democracy. Populists feared centralized, concentrated power—that of the corporations, that of the government. Their movement bore no resemblance to this century's state-run, bureaucratized socialism. They were proudly devoted to localism, cooperativism, and not least, democratic principles.

In its brief decade or so of existence, Populism generated a lively and stubbornly idiosyncratic literary and rhetorical tradition in newspapers, magazines, pamphlets, and meetings. Men like Henry Demarest Lloyd and Clarence Darrow were vocal Populist reformers. Journals like the *American Non-conformist*, the *Appeal to Reason*, and the *Progressive Farmer* were forums for the morally fervid and unflinchingly outspoken Populist ideals. All over the country—but especially in the South and the West—people met, listened, talked, argued, changed one another's minds, and agreed enthusiastically. There were prolonged encampments, lectures, and town meetings, in which no one set the rules. Everyone was encouraged to have a say concerning what values children should possess and how the thunderous call to justice of Isaiah and Jeremiah and Amos, or the gentle but unyielding social vision of Jesus, could become an American reality.

Those questions may have been satisfactorily answered in the abstract, but real economic change was quite another matter. Certainly hundreds of thousands of farmers and industrial workers came to know, and to express rather pointedly, what they believed in, and they even managed, through the People's Party, to elect governors, congressmen, and a few senators. With the election of William McKinley in 1896, however, it became apparent that corporate money in enormous quantities, a press owned by the self-serving rich, and the clever manipulations of men like Mark Hanna (a predecessor of many twentieth-century campaign managers) were too much for the poor and the nearly poor, no matter their number. A third party could not make enough inroads, and neither of the two major parties offered much hope. The Populists and their supporters—Tom Watson and Eugene Debs and the nameless, faceless "agrarian rebels" and Knights of Labor—wanted to do more than fight over gold or silver, as McKinley and Bryan did, or arrange for some slight modification of tariffs or a shift in foreign-policy rhetoric: with their parades, rallies, demonstrations, assemblies, and homespun journalism, they looked toward a second American Revolution of sorts. But they soon enough realized the futility of their dream.

The Populist moment was a complicated one, and Professor Goodwyn has done a first-rate job of describing it. His tone is at once detached and sympathetic. He wishes, no doubt, that the Populists had prevailed, but he understands why they didn't. He is very helpful in showing why Populism should not be confused with liberal reformist politics or Theodore Roosevelt's "progressive" policies. And he also makes a clear and very important distinction between Populism and the racism and parochialism that eventually developed in some areas of the country and in some embittered Populist leaders, like Tom Watson, who had at least one election taken from him by corrupt wealth. As our own century has shown, when money and power make justice unobtainable, a resentful narrowness and meanness can set in. If one cannot have the assurance of work and a measure of dignity, one turns to the sinister satisfactions of spite and hate. But Populism is not to be blamed for what happened after its failure.

The proudly radical activists of Populism did succeed in making some helpful changes in America. Industrialists and their political allies and lackeys, who were indeed frightened by the widespread appeal of the Populist indictment of corporate America, began to make adjustments—a gesture toward the conservative guild-unionism of Samuel Gompers, restrained antitrust legislation under the Roosevelt and Wilson Administrations, a gradual end to the more flagrant sweatshop abuses. Then the Depression produced millions of new victims—victims of a system that continued to seem reckless, arbitrary, and anarchic. The New Deal struggled valiantly but with no decisive success. It took a world war to make things economically better, and a Cold War and two "local" wars to keep them better. We could do worse now than to reflect on the Populists and to call upon their candid and eloquent mode of social and economic analysis.

Lawrence Goodwyn has done justice to a much-neglected and clouded segment of our history. He has also given us a potential boost toward collective self-examination at a time when we need just that. His book is scholarly yet accessible to the general reader. Maybe the man who has just moved into the rather large and imposing white mansion in Washington—a man who has called himself a Populist—will cast a glance or two at this book and help move us along toward political reconsideration.

The Humanities and Human Dignity

T he humanities were once regarded as "polite learning": the study of grammar, rhetoric, and especially the classics. We could do worse than encourage such study among our young— so many of whom badly need to know how to write clearly, logically, and coherently as well as to understand what Socrates kept reminding his students: that the truly wise person knows, among other things, how little he or she knows, how much remains to be learned. It is a sad day, our day, in which many school children exhibit a declining adequacy in the use of the English language; exposure to the crudities of certain television programs is constant; and an idiotic and pretentious social science jargon has worked its way into various curricula.

Our lives in twentieth-century America are dominated by the natural sciences. Every time we flick a light switch, get into a car, or receive penicillin, we silently acknowledge the influence of engineers, physicists, and chemists on our everyday assumptions. The so-called social sciences have tried to follow suit, on occasion prematurely, to tell us that they also have begun to master some realms of the universe: psychological and sociological riddles, rather than those posed by organic and inorganic matter or the distant constellations of stars. Still, it has not been altogether a blessing for America's sectarian culture—this technological mastery enabled by the natural sciences, coupled with the increasing conviction of social scientists that our habits and thoughts will soon enough yield to one or another interpretive scheme. Kierkegaard's nineteenth-century grievance—that the increased knowledge of his time enabled people to understand, or think they would soon understand, just about everything except how to live a life—might well be our complaint too. We have at our fingertips the energy of the atom; we have dozens of notions of why people do things as they do; but many of us have forgotten to ask what we really believe in, what we ought to *be* in contrast to *do*.

The natural sciences offer us much-needed answers and solutions. The social sciences, now and then, offer us helpful explanations—along with, occasionally, a good deal of dreary, pompous, overwrought language. The humanities, in the hands of some, can also be reduced to precious, bloated, and murky prose. But the humanities at their best give testimony to the continuing effort to make moral, philosophical, and spiritual sense of this world—to evoke its complexity, its ironies, inconsistencies, contradictions, and ambiguities. The humanities begin for a scientist when he or she starts asking what a particular fact or discovery will mean for those who want to comprehend the obligations, the responsibilities of citizenship, the possibilities and limitations a given society presents. The humanities come into play for a social scientist when he or she starts wondering what some observation or theoretical construct or piece of data tells us about himself or herself—the person who has made a discovery, who lives with and by some larger vision of things.

To make a point, I would like to call upon the voice of an American factory worker I've come to know these past years. The physician in me has tried to contend with the illnesses that have afflicted him and his wife and children. The social scientist in me, a psychiatrist doing so-called fieldwork, has tried to comprehend how a man manages the various stresses imposed by a tough, demanding, exhausting assembly-line job. But there is in this person the stuff of the humanities, and I only hope I am sufficiently responsive to, respectful of, what he has to say: "I feel good on the way to work. I leave the house early. It's the best time of the day. I see the sun come up. I do some thinking. Once I'm on the job, I have no time to think of anything; it's go, go, go—until I punch that card and leave. But on the road to my job I stop and ask myself questions. I mean, you want to have something to aim for; you want to believe in something. My oldest boy, he's starting college this September, the first one in our family to get that far. I told him—I said: Get the best education you can, and it'll help you live better, and you'll get the respect of people; but don't forget to keep your common sense, and don't forget what life is all about.

"Sometimes, I think there's nothing to believe in, except the almighty dollar—and a little influence, that always helps. Sometimes, I see people behaving real rotten to other people, and I remember the wars in my lifetime, and I think of the troubles all over the world, and I think back to my father and how he couldn't find a job when we were kids, and my mother being upset for him, and for us, and I remind myself of what a lousy life it still is for most of the people on this earth—well, I can get real low. But for all the trouble my family has had, and the world has had, I guess I'm lucky, because I don't stay down there in the dumps too long. I stop and say to myself that life may be a big mystery, like they tell you in church, but there's your family to hold on to, and the future your kids will have.

"My little girl, she's eight years old; she asked me the other day if God pays attention to every person, and if He does, where does He get the time, and does He have the patience, or does He get tired? I told her it's not for me to know how God does His job, but I'll bet God thinks each grown-up person should have a job and should look after a few people and try to pitch in—to help people who are in trouble.

"My wife and I have always tried to teach our children to be good and kind. I don't believe in church on Sunday and let the Devil run the show the rest of the week. I don't believe in talking to your children about God and then teaching them to be cutthroat artists. I tell my children to stop themselves every few days and look up at the sky and listen to their conscience and remember what they should believe in: Give out as good as you want to get.

"That was my father's philosophy of life. He didn't have a lot of material things to give, but he had himself—a big person he was; and he was always there to make us think twice before we stayed mean too long, and he was always there to make us realize the world doesn't circle around us. My wife says it's a real stroke of luck to be alive and living in this country and not a lot of other places; and I'll tell you, people ought to stop and say yes, that's right, and yes, I'm here, and I'm going to give of myself, the best I know how—and maybe tomorrow I'll find a way of being a better person. You try to think about this life and what you owe it, and you try to get your kids to think about this life, too, and what they owe it."

His reflectiveness, his effort at detachment and introspection in the midst of the press of everyday life, his struggle for decency and integrity and generosity in the face of inevitable self-centeredness (the sin of pride) with all its attendant psychological mischief, ought to qualify him, as much as anyone else in this land, as a humanist—

a person who draws upon and contributes to the tradition of the humanities. The humanities do not belong to one kind of person; they are part of the lives of ordinary people who have their own ways of struggling for coherence, for a compelling faith, for social vision, for an ethical position, for a sense of historical perspective.

Over a century ago, in Oxford, England, no less, Matthew Arnold urged novelists, poets, and critics to become actively engaged in social, economic, and political affairs—to bring their kind of sensibility to bear upon "the things of this world." He didn't have to send such a message to his contemporaries Charles Dickens or George Eliot; they kept their eyes carefully focused on the world and through their fiction held up a mirror to an entire nation. George Eliot, as a young woman, was constantly letting herself learn from the rural English people she would later write about so knowingly. Here at home, William Faulkner made it his business to spend long hours with his fellow townspeople of Oxford, Mississippi—watching their habits and customs, hearing their stories, learning from them as well as sharing their news and their bourbon. Where does the "real" Oxford end and the "made-up" Yoknapatawpha begin? Of course, Faulkner was an imaginative artist, a man who made brilliant use of his mind's dreams and fantasies. But he came home every day, from what could be called his field trips, a rich man. He had been willing to be taught by his neighbors and as a result had a lot to draw on as he sat at his desk writing.

The humanities demand that we heed the individual—each person worthy of respect, and no person unworthy of careful, patient regard. The humanities are blues and jazz; gospel songs and working songs; string quartets and opera librettos; folk art and abstract impressionist art; the rich literary legacy of nineteenth-century Concord, or of the twentieth-century South; the sayings and memories and rituals of countless millions of working people; the blunt, earthy self-justifications and avowals of desperate but determined migrant mothers; the wry, detached stories handed down on Indian reservations, in Eskimo villages, generation after generation; the cries of struggle and hope of Appalachia's people of the hollows, put into traditional ballads and bluegrass music; the photographs of Lewis Hine and Walker Evans and Russell Lee—ourselves presented to ourselves; the confident, qualified assertions of scholars; the frustrated, embittered social statements of ghetto teachers or children who at all costs want to get a grip on this puzzling, not-always-decent or fair world.

The humanities are Ralph Ellison's essays and the novel *Invisible Man*, so full of a writer's determination that race and poverty, still cruelly significant to a person's destiny, nevertheless are but partial statements—never enough to rob a person of his or her particularity. And the humanities are the essays and novels of Walker Percy, so full of wit and wisdom and shrewd moments of social analysis. The humanities are also the remarks of the New Orleans suburban people, the Louisiana bayou people Percy knows and learns from—whose remarks are indeed worthy of being recorded, transcribed, and added to an oral literature. And, too, the humanities are the musical sounds and the strong, spoken vernacular Ellison has taken pains in his writings to remind us of.

The humanities should strive to do justice to the richness and diversity of cultural life in a nation whose people are not, many of them, afraid to say what is on their minds as well as sing or draw or paint or write what is on their minds. They thereby cast penetrating, knowing, critical judgments on what is happening in the world—judgments that ought to be put on the record and acknowledged as part of America's cultural tradition.

Address at the installation of Joseph Duffey as director of the National Endowment for the Humanities, *Change*, February 1978

Character and Intellect

Before he was shot and especially when he was running for president (in 1968), George Wallace used to give himself much pleasure by poking fun at the smugness and arrogance of intellectuals. Sometimes he'd say that "all of them" are "snobs"; sometimes he'd become a bit discriminating: "a lot of them put on high and mighty airs." I have those quotes on paper—from a talk I had with him in the early part of 1968, before Dr. King and Robert Kennedy had been killed. When the governor was feeling expansive, generous, and unthreatened, he'd back off a bit, play the bemused, reflective Southern stoic: "I don't think college professors are all bad—just the noisy ones who forget what they don't know and grab everyone in sight to tell them what they do know."

He was not himself averse, of course, to grabbing a few listeners to hear his particular words of wisdom. In my experience, following him north on the campaign trail and watching him in action among his fellow Alabamians, he was especially successful with those listeners when he came up with one or another version of this question: "Have you ever heard one of those professors tell you what's right and what's wrong—they've got an opinion on everything—and then seen him get on a bike and fall all over himself or knock down ten people while taking himself for a ride?"

Not all that funny as one reads it in one's old notes or, surely, on this page. Still, many who heard him were not merely being mean or bitter when they applauded vigorously and gave him the familiar, encouraging salutations: "Atta boy, George," or "You said it," or "Amen." Nor will vaguely sociological epithets such as "redneck" or "cracker," or fancy psychological attributions such as "paranoid" quite do justice to the complexity of things—the shrewd observations, say, an unemployed Alabama steelworker could make in retrospect (1981):

You don't notice old George hitting away at college professors any more. Here in Birmingham the University [of Alabama] is our biggest employer. When I started out no one ever thought that would happen. Back then it was coal and it was steel, and I don't even think there was any university here; it was over in Tuscaloosa, and none of them branches. George knows where the votes are: he'll be slapping those professors on the back now, and calling them our best "natural resource"!

I wouldn't mind being a professor myself! My son went to college, and it's done him a lot of good. He has a job. Not like his old man! You ask me, we laugh at professors because they're an easy target. They don't have the money and power that bankers do, or the people who own U.S. Steel and Ford Motor Company, and like that, our corporations here in Birmingham and elsewhere in the country. So, you get your laughs off some guy—like our George used to say— who's all full of big thoughts, but he don't know how to tie his shoes or cross the street without causing a traffic jam; or he talks a big line in his classroom or his books but he's a sonofabitch to his own family or the lady who does the cleaning in his office or the one who answers his phone—and the students who want a second of his time, but he's out in space thinking, or he only associates with people like himself, or those who have something to offer him: a favor, some money, you know. . . .

I must say that those last two words, innocently added, it seemed— a sentence trailing off managed to catch my attention and hold it fast. I looked sharply at the speaker, but he did not at all appear to be looking sharply at me! Nor had he spoken, I concluded, with a touch of irony, never mind with any portentous design. His "you know" was said in a matter-of-fact manner—was, in fact, one of his speaking tics, which ordinarily I edit with no qualms or apprehension. On this occasion, however, my nervousness was all too significantly persistent, even though we did go on and pursued other matters unselfconsciously. I *do* "know," I fear—as do so many of us who try to reconcile the studies we do (the intellectual life we pursue) with the demands (let us hope they are real and pressing!) made by our consciences—the moral life we also live. In that regard, we sometimes try to make splits or divisions or distinctions that are meant to help us (to continue with my Alabama friend's language) *not know*—stop noticing ironic inconsistencies and paradoxical contradictions. Yeats was, of course, more candid with himself, pointedly if not brutally so: "The intellect of man is forced to choose/ Perfection of the life, or of the work,/And if it take the second must refuse/A heavenly mansion, raging in the dark."

Needless to say, there are those who don't feel that the dramatic alternatives posed by Yeats (a secular version of the theological either-or Kierkegaard presented to us) quite do justice to the way this life bears down upon people—and very important, the way some of us respond to the various temptations or possibilities that appear, often out of nowhere, it seems. Surely not a few of us with strong intellectual inclinations, convictions, and attainments have also managed to attend the responsibilities of a home, a family, a membership in a particular community—involvements with friends, colleagues, neighbors. Nor does one want to ignore a contemporary possibility, a consequence of a given culture, its preoccupations if not obsessions: a person who is so attentive to the creature comforts of his or her life, and of course, its emotional aspects, that there is nothing left of any importance—not even, say, "perfection of the work," never mind moral issues to confront or sacrifices to make on behalf of others in distant communities or nations. (Talking about "raging in the dark"—in this case the domain of the self!)

Put differently, Yeats may not have realized what some members of the upper bourgeoisie might have to say about the duality he evokes in the lines quoted above—as in this young man, just about to graduate from one of our country's best-known law schools:

> I wanted to go to graduate school—in English and American Literature. I wrote my thesis in college on Melville. I was all excited. I had great hopes. But there's no future in graduate work—no jobs, no money. I switched to law, like many others. I don't like the law; I've been bored for three years. I'm sure I won't ever really like what I'm doing. I'll just go to a big firm in New York and stick it out. Why? Look, I want to live a certain kind of life, that's what matters to me: I want to enjoy myself; I want to have a good, comfortable home in the country; I want to travel; I want to understand myself—probably go into analy-

sis. I've had two years of therapy, and so has my girlfriend. Let's be blunt: we're from modest backgrounds, she and I, but we've learned all the tastes of the well-to-do Ivy League types! And those tastes cost! I wouldn't be comfortable on the small salaries teachers get, even college professors. I want to be able to live well, and I want my wife and kids to live well, and if I have to be bored at work for that to happen, then it's a small price to pay.

Besides, boredom is something you get bored with—eventually, I mean, you start forgetting to be bored! You remember, as soon as you're bored, that you've just bought a house, or you need a new Brooks Brothers suit, or your wife likes to go to Bonwit Teller's, or your shrink costs a lot and it's money well spent because it'll help your kids be a little less screwed up than you are! So, you start enjoying yourself—just like you have to do when you're studying in college. Well, not really *enjoying* yourself! But I've found education a pain, and yet I'm really glad I've gone through it, and I've enjoyed the success, the getting into the best schools, and I'm sure I'll enjoy my law work in the same way and for the same reasons—the results, what the work means, so far as the kind of life you live.

There is more, much more. At times I have sensed rather more self-assurance and nonchalance and intrepid certainty than the particular speaker may have actually felt. But he is, as he has often reminded me, not alone in his determination to have a certain kind of life—even if the work he does has, on its own merit, no great charm or satisfaction for him. The home he has in mind is, of course, no "heavenly mansion"; and I am sure his psychiatrist will help him, on the quick, if he feels himself "raging in the dark." Yet one wonders about the moral dimension of such a life, and, I suppose, one craves a contemporary poetic analysis of "this side of paradise": that American mix of consumerism, self-advancement, and self-cultivation, which is enabled by intellectual achievement of sorts. F. Scott Fitzgerald, too, one fears, along with Yeats, needs a successor: some of our particular high livers (or more mordantly, budding Gatsbys) belong to another breed.

Indeed, that young lawyer cannot be dismissed as frivolous—or as remarkably, noticeably uncouth. He has, I have to add, taken courses as an undergraduate in philosophy, even in moral reasoning. In law school he studied legal ethics. He has read widely, deeply; he majored in history and graduated summa cum laude with a thesis that examined an aspect of twentieth-century American politics. We have, then, a well-muscled intellect, and as we put it these days, a "stable personality." We even have a somewhat reflective young man, who has done his fair share of reading in Spinoza, Locke, Hume, Santayana, Whitehead. (I mention the philosophers he has mentioned seriously to me—not name-dropped—in the course of our conversations.) We have, too, someone in possession of that almost sacred present-day characteristic: "insight." ("My doctor has really helped me sort all these things out. I've been open with him, and I know where I'm ambivalent and where I'm not. I've thought out what my options are, and I think I know enough about my problems to keep them from dragging me down, or pushing me into a dead-end street.")

As the worn saying goes, someone who appears on the verge of "a long and happy life"! Intellect, he has often reminded me, brought such a fate to his doorstep: those A's in high school, those high test scores, the brilliant work at college, continued at law school. Among his A's were two in "moral reasoning." Moreover, I'm sure his psychiatrist is pleased with what gets called these days "progress." Is he not good, oh so good, at "reality-testing," as we put it? Hasn't he developed a variety of "coping skills"? Certainly he has proved himself "mature," able to handle "stress." His "psycho-sexual development" appears to be in good shape. He appears to have solved without undue difficulty his "identity crisis"; and I suspect that if yet another American tester or American researcher presented him with a number of moral scenarios of sorts—hypothetical situations to which he'd be asked to respond with what he judged to be the ethically "right" attitude or reaction or recommendation—he'd score very well indeed, as he has elsewhere in his triumphant educational career.

In his "American Scholar" address, Ralph Waldo Emerson insisted to his audience that "character is higher than intellect"; and in our time, the novelist Walker Percy has reminded us that one can "get all A's and flunk life." I keep mentioning these two writers and their just-quoted remarks to my students—to myself. I keep hoping that they (and I with them) can manage somehow to bridge the two worlds (it seems) Yeats constructs in those lines summoned here earlier: two worlds supposedly with two different kinds of inhabitants, their destinies quite distinctively separate. I keep wondering whether the law student I just brought in witness might not—with more or better therapy, with a different curriculum, with better, finer, more powerfully engaging and committed teachers—become in future years (well, even right now) a person of broader and deeper moral sensibility. I keep asking myself, as I read Emerson or Kierkegaard, Percy, Dickens, or Dostoevski, how to learn from them in such a way that my intellect grows, the intellects of my students grow—*but also* we become personally more decent and honorable human beings, meaning of higher character than was the case before.

How to do so—to enlarge our store of facts, our "creativity," our originality of perception, of performance—and not end up, as Yeats warned, well on the way to hell? How to redeem our lives—become morally more energetic and forthcoming? One ends with such rhetorical questions—in the hope against hope that the next moment's, the next day's hurdles will provide a chance to live out the start of some answers. But in this regard there is, perhaps, less we can take for granted (including those of us with walls covered by big-deal diplomas) than we may sometimes think.

American Poetry Review, September/October 1983

Life's Big Ironies

N ovelists and poets try hard to appreciate and evoke the ironic strains of this life—the incongruities between appearance and reality always besetting us, if we care to attend closely. Social scientists, taking their cue from the natural scientists who are valued so highly in our Western industrial world, insist upon banishing ironies with all possible dispatch, if such can be done. The point is exploration: if the cobbler's son has no shoes, or the doctor's daughter seems chronically and inexplicably ill, then let's get on with it—find out why, and having done so, change the set of circumstances. Irony thus regarded becomes a kind of fanciful illusion of a decidedly reactionary character. I remember noticing in a certain Georgia city how odd it was, the repeated fires that plagued the homes of firefighters, one of whom I knew well. A friend of mine objected (correctly, I guess) to a certain heightened aestheticism he must have sensed: the delicious symmetry of those incidents. I was not, I hope, sadistically flushed, but I had commented on the peculiarly ironic nature of this particular series of news stories, and my friend wished I'd reserved my energy for his kind of inquiry: the underlying reason for a suspected collection of crimes—a vendetta perhaps, launched by criminals against a group of municipal employees who had insisted on doing their job all too well, thereby endangering some hitherto "protected" property-owning arsonists, anxious to keep collecting money from insurance companies.

Still, an appreciation of irony need not deteriorate into an abstract, self-centered, frivolous, or uncaring posture. Nor need irony become an end in itself, or an obstacle toward further exploration of this life's nature, this world's evils. Often enough, the presence of irony provides a reminder or a signal, if not an important warning. Irony may offer us the best hint we may get of vulnerability or jeopardy. "I'm always fighting violent people," a police officer told me when I was doing one of those research projects my ilk favors, "and I guess one day the enemy will infiltrate my home." He knew, by then, that more than a few of his son's friends had been caught speeding in cars, while tanked up on beer. He also knew the burden and temptation his work placed on his sons, especially: "My daughters seem to be law-abiding; my sons want to test the law, or break it—minor delinquency, so far, and I hope it will all end soon. It's hard having a cop for a father, just like it's hard being a cop—I mean, a clean cop."

He stopped then, to muse—and so did I: a *second* irony, with those last two words! He'd told me weeks earlier stories that chilled me—about crooked cops, and yes, firefighters who helped dishonest, crafty real estate owners collect mounds of money on the fire insurance they'd bought on already broken down tenement houses, which mysteriously caught fire. I remember, at the time, thinking of that old canard—or is there some substantial truth to it?—namely, the noticeable number of psychiatrists whose children seem wayward, or who themselves seem dour and grumpy, or nervously difficult, or plain nuts. In fact, my police officer friend allowed irony to help him collect his senses—and maybe, help someone else do likewise: "I guess you're always most sensitive to the things that matter to you," he observed. Then he broadened his remarks: "If you spend your life fighting crime, you'll be a set-up for one of your kids who wants to fight you! He'll flirt with what's your soft spot! It's like a kid of yours [a doctor's] pretending to be sick, or making himself sick, to catch the old man's attention or shame him. By the same token, when a cop gets cozy with thieves, or a fireman sets a fire—that's turning everything upside down. It's like a lawyer becoming a robber—breaking the law, not upholding it—and it's like a doctor trying to do in a patient, not heal him, maybe for some money from a relative!"

All of the above is not, alas, mere anecdotal reportage. On the grandest scale, in this century, we have witnessed ironies that have (one hopes) given us pause, at the very least. A revolution presumably meant not only to oust a czar but to achieve bread, work, freedom, and justice for the poor and humble of Russia soon enough ended up offering the obscene and vile spectacle of Stalin and his murderous henchmen. Lenin saw, in the last months of his life, a glimmer of a terrible, forthcoming evil; Trotsky died at its hands. Both of these ideologues, like Marx before them, had proclaimed

the necessity, the historical virtue of a "dictatorship of the proletariat," and if that dictatorship has made the czar seem like an exceptionally kind and generous and thoughtful leader—well, so
much for the irony of history's "dialectic." As for the *scientific* basis
of Marxism-Leninism and its well-known and loudly proclaimed
aversion to an "opiate" such as religion, the Lenin Mausoleum and
those placards of Karl Marx paraded here, there, and everywhere are
twentieth-century artifacts of sorts—ironic lessons for us: those who
scorn the beliefs of others do not, thereby, prove themselves without
their own tenacious articles of faith.

As for my own profession, the psychoanalytic speculation that
gave the world *The Future of an Illusion* has not proved adequate as
a warning against idolatry, some of it as mean-spirited and arrogant
and condescending as the Crusades at their worst proved to be. In
the name of clear-headed science, many of us in psychiatry have
become pushy advocates of one or another point of view—and have
not hesitated to insult if not villify those who disagree with us. Our
chief weapon, alas, in these sectarian struggles has been the old ex-
clusionary one of character assassination—a kind of *ad hominem*
(and *ad feminam*) truculence lent enormous power by a general culture obsessed by psychology and all too willing to heed it if not fall in
prayer before its tenets, some of them rank speculation if not assertive propositions (as in so many disciplines) of those on the professional make. No wonder, long ago, Clara Thompson left a meeting of the New York Psychoanalytic Institute with the hymn "Go
Down Moses" on her lips—a terribly sad moment, and a reminder
that we can "repress" not only our sexuality and our aggressive inclinations but our hunger for faith, for membership in a community
of believers.

When I see my kind (after years and years of clinical training and
supervision and personal analysis) torn by angry disagreements and
splits; when I see grown men and women, well educated and supposedly well aware of the reasons for their conflicts, nevertheless
demonstrating nasty, envious, rude behavior towards others, be they
colleagues, students, or fellow citizens, then I realize, yet again, that
"aggression" is not only something postulated by eager theorists but
is part of everyone's life, including theirs—no matter the education,
the accumulation of credentials, the recognition accorded by universities, hospitals, and training institutes. Whether we have, in-

deed, gained all that much by abandoning "the sin of pride" in favor of "the aggressive drive" or "narcissism" is, perhaps, a matter for earnest (and not, one prays, haughty and self-important) discussion. As for the concept of "narcissism," it has recently provided quite a special source of irony for all of us—the example of exponents of one or another notion of "narcissism" engaging in strong and often bitter enough confrontations, yes, narcissistic ones, occasioned by those old familiars of human experience: rivalry, envy, ambition.

Nor have the world's political and military and ideological struggles been without their unhappy, even tragic, ironies. In Vietnam, those who fought European colonialism have shown themselves quite able to subdue their neighbors, quite able to be brutally self-serving, fiercely opportunistic, corruptly insensitive to their own stated historical and social purposes. In Nicaragua, those who fought tyrants have not been without their own tyrannical lapses, as a number of that nation's hurt and vulnerable Indian people have had cause to observe, and too, some of the decent and honorable people who fought long and hard on the Sandinista side. In Africa, too, black despots, cruel and murderous, have replaced, all too often, their white colonialist predecessors. One need not be an apologist for South Africa's government to observe that thousands and thousands of blacks have been murdered by their fellow black oppressors, and not only in the well-known instance of Uganda but in countries such as Rwanda and Burundi, right near South Africa's borders. We who are white and who are concerned with racism anywhere and everywhere are justifiably quick to be alarmed and enraged by news that arrives from Johannesburg or Cape Town but instructively silent, not rarely, when we learn of massacres in, say, Zaire, or yes, drastic infringements on the civil and political rights of the people of such "socialist" countries as Tanzania or Zambia. Sometimes it is not only our silence that proves ironic; we mobilize strange justifications or apologies or excuses—maybe even racist ones: as if black people aren't entitled to the same sympathy, in the face of viciously implacable statism, that the people of, say, Poland or Czechoslovakia have quite justifiably obtained from us.

When Thomas Hardy gave us the phrase "life's little ironies," he had in mind, of course, the continuing distance, in all of us, between intention and actuality—between our stated intentions about how this life should be lived and the manner in which fate and circumstance, chance and accident and incident, end up shaping the particular destiny that is ours. It never occurred to him, one suspects, that he was summoning (God save us!) what some of today's social scientists, in their heavy-handed and dreary fashion, might call "a methodological tool of historical analysis"—irony as a mode of social reflection. Yet, a century that has witnessed so much violence, so much self-righteousness, so much intellectual presumptuousness—while all the while laying claim to more and more progress in the name of science, in the name of technology, in the name of mental exploration and political analysis and sociological investigation—such a century, surely, can begin to give us all some little pause. Did Hardy, after all, know something that some of "our" giants overlooked—Marx and Freud and all sorts of other social and political visionaries: that life's little ironies offer, in their sum, a big lesson for us about ourselves, our limited possibilities, and the ever-present danger that faces us as the creature who has never yet been rid of a capacity for self-deception and polemical nastiness, though also able occasionally (please God) to demonstrate generosity, moral courage, and fair-minded compassion?

American Poetry Review, January/February 1983